HOLISTIC MENTAL HEALTH

Calm, Clear, And In Control For The Rest Of Your Life

LAURA MAZZOTTA

FEATURING: PAM BOHLKEN, MARCELA CHAVES,
VIENNA COSTANZO-D'APRILE, KELLY DAUGHERTY,
CHERI DAVIES, JENNA DIVENUTO, DAISY FARRELL,
STEPH FURO, DR. BONNIE JUUL, TERESA LACORAZZA,
TAMMY LANTZ, BONNIE LUFT, KELLY MYERSON,
ANITA BUZZY PRENTISS, CASSANDRA N. QUICK,
GABE ROBERTS, DR. CHRISTY ROBINSON, MARIAH ROSSEL,
CORINNE SANTIAGO, DARLENE SOCHIN, KATIE STEINLE,
DR. SUMMER SULLIVAN, KATIE WHITE, KRISSI WILLIFORD

EMERGE
HEALING & WELLNESS

Laura Mazzotta

A Special Gift for You, Reader:

Grab your free "Meet Your Core Self" journal to shift from external to internal validation at https://www.theakashictherapist.com/resources

SET THE PAST ASIDE
AND EMBRACE WHO YOU'RE MEANT TO BECOME

"Our past is a story existing only in our minds.
Look, analyze, understand, and forgive.
Then, as quickly as possible, chuck it.
We are not held back by the love we didn't receive in the past, but
by the love we're not extending in the present.
We're often afraid of looking at our shadow because we want
to avoid the shame or embarrassment that comes along with
admitting mistakes.
Our deepest fear is not that we are inadequate.
Our deepest fear is that we are powerful beyond measure.
It is our light, not our darkness, that most frightens us.
We ask ourselves, 'Who am I to be brilliant, gorgeous, talented,
fabulous?'
Actually, who are you not to be?"

- Marianne Williamson

HOLISTIC MENTAL HEALTH INTENTION STATEMENT

May the pages of this book expand your worldview
and self-understanding.

May you experience a-ha moments that blow your mind and shift
your thinking.

May the guidance from these authors activate a sacred remembrance of
what you already know deep within.

May you gaze upon your loved ones with fresh eyes after reading these
words, cultivating deeper intimacy and connections.

May you palpably feel the true essence of who you are so you remember
your magnificence and the spark that's always with you.

May you thrive at the highest level, embodying your deepest truths,
values, and desires. The world is your oyster.

May you experience unapologetic joy and abundance beyond your
wildest dreams.

May you fully embrace your wholeness, appreciating the challenging times
and knowing they're guiding you to the fulfillment of your soul's purpose.

May you celebrate that the hardest lessons always amplify your power.

May you feel the immense impact you have on those around you,
including yourself. The words you speak and the intentions you set will
swiftly come to fruition in your lived reality.

May you always see your own divinity as you continue to navigate this
ever-unfolding path of healing and expansion.

EMERGE
HEALING & WELLNESS

Laura Mazzotta

DEDICATION

This book is dedicated to the humans who've been touched by mental illness or felt their mental health was challenged. Thank you for being brave enough to open this book, read these stories, and explore new ways to step into the highest version of yourself.

To the children of the world who are open to receiving our shared and embodied lessons so they can boldly express their full authenticity. May you know yourself so deeply that you never need physical or mental health symptoms to pursue your grandest dreams.

To the authors of this volume, thank you for sharing your heart-centered stories, brilliant wisdom, and commitment to the service of the collective. Your role is vital for the expansion of holistic wellness. Lives will surely extend because of your bravery.

SPECIAL NOTE TO THE READER

No matter what diagnosis you've been handed:

You get to decide.

You get to choose who you want to be.

You get to write your own story.

You get to take up as much space as you desire.

You get to embrace the wholeness of who you are, even the things you consider negative, which is truly just judgment because nothing in this world is truly positive or negative: Everything just is.

You get to feel free and empowered.

You get to express yourself authentically.

You get to soar beyond your wildest dreams.

You get to claim that version of you you've always desired.

This book is here to break the chains of conditioning that cloud your magnificence.

You are a wildly impactful human and it's time the world sees you for all that you offer.

Turn the page to begin your journey into immense self-discovery.

EMERGE
HEALING & WELLNESS

Laura Mazzotta

DISCLAIMER

This book offers health and wellness information and is designed for educational purposes only. You should not rely on this information as a substitute for, nor does it replace professional medical advice, diagnosis, or treatment. If you have any concerns or questions about your physical or mental/emotional health, you should always consult with a physician or other healthcare professional. Do not disregard, avoid, or delay obtaining medical or health-related advice from your healthcare professional because of something you may have read here. The use of any information provided in this book is solely at your own risk.

Developments in medical research may impact the health, fitness, and nutritional advice that appears here. No assurances can be given that the information contained in this book will always include the most relevant findings or developments with respect to the particular material.

Having said all that, know that the experts here have shared their tools, practices, and knowledge with you with a sincere and generous intent to assist you on your health and wellness journey. Please contact them with any questions you may have about the techniques or information they provided. They will be happy to assist you further!

TABLE OF CONTENTS

INTRODUCTION

If you're reading this book, I guarantee you are multi-passionate, with a flurry of ideas and desires. Most of the people diagnosed with mental health conditions qualify for this constitution and usually end up identifying as ADHD (Attention-Deficit Hyperactivity Disorder), Bipolar Disorder, or Borderline Personality Disorder.

Being multi-passionate is a blessing. It's the cornerstone of massive change-makers like Elon Musk and Bill Gates. When you channel your ideas and energy into something you passionately love, even if it doesn't make sense to others, you'll receive exponential results.

The problem is that mental health diagnoses can make people feel there is something inherently wrong with them, so they focus on the so-called deficiency rather than the passion. What we focus on expands, so if you're focusing on what's wrong, you'll feel and embody that deficiency. This is how people cycle through or get stuck in the mental health system for so long: They continually return to what they lack rather than what they desire and can create.

The other issue with diagnosis is that people often choose someone or something to blame, like their parents, partners, or life experiences, to explain why they operate the way they do. I'm not saying we don't have challenging and traumatic experiences that impact us, but our souls signed up for them so we can extract the necessary lessons for our soul's evolution. It's all purposeful, and our role is to get to know that purpose.

Psychiatrists (doctors who prescribe psychotropic medication) will tell you diagnostics allow them to more accurately identify which medication to prescribe for maximum benefit. Some therapists will tell you diagnosis is helpful to access the standard treatment frameworks that have been proven effective.

I've been a therapist for 20 years, and I'm here to tell you that diagnosis doesn't have to mean shit unless you want it to. Just like I mentioned on the previous page, you get to decide what meaning you give to your symptoms. You get to choose the identity with which you identify. *You are the master of your life experience.*

When you identify with any diagnosis as yours, and this applies to physical or mental illness, you lose yourself in a compartmentalized definition that doesn't take individual factors into account. There is no one-size-fits-all when it comes to helping humans. Every one of us is a snowflake with our own pattern and beauty.

This is exactly the reason *Holistic Mental Health* was born. It's wildly empowering to pool all the resources out there (from experts with reliable results) to determine that perfect mix of practices that suit you, in your own unique way, with your own unique nuances.

There's nothing wrong with any part of you. You simply need to get creative about how to piece together the new and off-the-beaten-path strategies available. This book is an excellent way to begin this process. You get to try 25 practices on for size and tease apart what offers you results and what doesn't. By the end of this book, you'll have your own roadmap and toolbox for how to manage your mental health.

There are truly infinite resources and possibilities within each moment. There's always an easier route available than you can naturally think of. This is why I love working with the Divine because humanity is constantly uncovering new ways to work with infinite energy. We could publish one of these volumes annually and have a whole new set of practices each time.

It's this ever-unfolding process that makes being human fun! Although, we don't look at it that way when we feel like we're struggling with physical or mental health symptoms. I'm here to celebrate all the unique, zany, wildly bizarre ideas and desires you experience! Let's bring them to the forefront instead of hiding behind them in shame.

The first time I really felt into the power of my idiosyncracies was when I entered the Akashic Records and practiced Reiki. I remember when the Akashic Records were first introduced to me by a friend of mine.

"What the hell are you doing now?" I asked her. She was on some kick of entering her Akashic Record, which sounded like another one of those fancy-schmancy spiritual words people make up when they're grasping to find life's answers.

"Try it," she said. "It's really cool."

Cue my eye roll and a deep sigh; while I now had this cute little seed planted in the back of my consciousness. The Akashic Records are a library of information, a Google for the soul. It's like this library high above the clouds, manned by angels and guides, and when you open your record, you have all the information about your soul from its first spark through past, present, and future lives.

Just being in this space is deeply healing and illuminating because of its high vibration. The higher the frequency of energy (how fast molecules are vibrating), the less space there is for illness and dis-ease. You literally tune your body to this frequency when you enter the Akashic Records. This relieves symptoms and opens you up to feeling even higher levels of emotion and experience.

As much as I tried to ignore the call to the Akashic Records, they kept calling my name. They kept knocking on the door with a reminder they were there for me. After about six months of kicking the can down the road, I reluctantly enrolled in an Akashic Records certification program as if to say, *Fine, I'll do it already!*

And the rest is history. Before I even understood much about it, I saw obvious results: My physical symptoms were going away, my anxiety was much lower, I was super clear and confident, and I had immense energy! My husband, who doesn't fully believe in this stuff, said, "I don't know what you're doing but keep doing it because you're so much better." That was the validation my human needed to keep going.

Now, I can boldly say the Akashic Records have changed my life. Connecting with this space has opened my world up to endless possibilities, vitality, confidence, patience, unconditional love, and personal power. To learn more about the Akashic Records, how they operate, and how you can enter your own, visit this link for a video that guides you through: https://youtu.be/svKpe9REKm8

The bottom line is that we're here to do this life together. We all have our unique traits where we soar. I certainly don't want to be doing the things my husband is good at, and he likely doesn't want to do the things where I excel. When we celebrate our unique nuances as gifts, we can work beautifully together and focus on collaborating through our strengths rather than shaming one another for our deficits.

This book is an invitation for you to explore another way. Take notes on how these practices resonate with and work for you. Allow it to be a fun experiment where you narrow down what's meant for you. There's nothing more self-loving than diving into what empowers you most. That's the momentum that creates and sustains lasting change.

CHAPTER 1

WORTHY TO THE CORE

FEEL THE FREEDOM OF EMBODYING YOUR SOUL'S PURPOSE

Laura Mazzotta, LCSW-R, Spiritual Empowerment Coach

A nurse came to my bedside and said, "What took you so long to call 911?"

My reply was, "My fever spiked from 99 to 105 in 30 minutes. I called as soon as I got to 105."

Nurse: "If you had waited 30 minutes longer, I don't know if there is anything we could have done for you."

Me (thinking): *Holy Shit. What. The. Fuck. This is entirely surreal.*

MY STORY

The summer morning of August 3, 2016 began this way, and I was planning to take the kids to camp. I started feeling dizzy and nauseated. It escalated quickly, and I told my husband, "I'm going to need you to drive the kids."

He was rushing around like crazy because he wasn't planning on doing this that morning. He had to take our one-year-old because I felt so sick. I felt bad but knew I couldn't drive. I took my temperature, and it was only 99.1, but my body was fighting something.

I grabbed some fluids and headed upstairs to lay down. During the 30 minutes my husband was gone, my temperature rose to 105. My body was shaking uncontrollably, my head was spinning, and I was literally squirming in my skin.

As soon as my husband walked in the door, I said, "Honey, I think I need to call 911."

His reply: "Really? Can't I just drive you?"

"I don't think I can make it." And I promptly started to throw up.

I've never called 911 for myself. I called for many of my clients (I've been a therapist for 20 years) but was never in a position where someone couldn't drive me to a doctor or hospital.

My husband put our baby girl in her crib and called 911. While he was on the phone, I collapsed to the floor. Seeing how wide his eyes were and how scared he was, was something I never want to see again. He already had two family members in the hospital with life-altering events, one who didn't survive beyond a couple of months. I kept thinking: *He doesn't need this on top of his already existing worry.*

I could hear my daughter, who I was still nursing at the time, screaming and crying from her crib. I couldn't bear the thought of leaving her behind. Being available to her when she was hungry was such an intimate and consistent experience for both of us. My husband kept saying, "She's fine. I'll take care of her."

When the emergency team arrived, they came up to my bedroom and tried to get me to the bathroom. Even with them holding me, I could not tolerate any movement. I kept falling to the ground. They put me on a stretcher and carried me down the steps. I could see my husband watching his wife violently shaking and being carried away by the EMTs when he was already so stressed and emotional about his family.

I just said, "I'm so sorry, honey."

I was crying and scared. He was petrified. He followed the stretcher as they took me to the ambulance. I kept seeing different people around the ambulance and calling their names. No one was there.

Once I was in the ambulance, the EMT kept telling me, "Just breathe, honey. I need you to take long, deep breaths." I did the best I could. She was taking my blood pressure repeatedly and started an IV. I continued to shake, and my arms and legs went numb. She just kept telling me to breathe and was asking the driver which route he was taking and how long it would take to get there.

My head started to spin even faster, and the EMT took my blood pressure again. She then started screaming to the front, "We need to change the route. We need to get there within eight minutes. Turn on the sirens." The sirens howled, and the ambulance sped faster than I've ever felt before. Now I was petrified.

I didn't know what was happening to me. I thought:

I just have a stomach bug! What is happening? Breathe.
Just breathe. Deeply.

Visions of my kids kept dancing through my head.

How long am I going to be at the hospital? Who is going to get the kids from camp? Did my husband get in touch with the babysitter for our youngest? Where is my phone? I need to make sure my husband is okay. The poor guy has to drive to me and then back in time for the kids to get home. Breathe. Just Breathe. Deeply. All the way to your toes. It's okay. It's okay. It's going to be okay. Is it going to be okay? Is something really wrong with me? I'm in the best shape of my life! I just started running! I'm eating like a champ! It's summer, and I'm swimming with my kids! What the actual fuck is happening?

When we arrived at the hospital, I was briskly whisked to a quarantine area to rule out meningitis, among other things. The staff suited up in full-body attire to do preliminary testing. They hooked me up to IV antibiotics and medication to stop the body shaking. It felt like I was convulsing, but I knew I wasn't seizing because I was fully conscious, even though I was super out of it.

A little while later, they opened my door and confirmed that meningitis was no longer a concern. The doctor arrived and asked a long list of questions. I was so short of breath, dizzy, and still violently shaking. I told her, "I. . .need. . .something. . .for. . .the. . .shaking. I. . .I. . .can't. . ." It felt unbearable. I was so uncomfortable. The nurse grabbed medication for me as the doctor and I continued to speak. It took me a while to get the words out.

Now I had to wait. My husband arrived. I was still shaking, but not as violently. He was sitting by my side, and I was trying to explain what the doctor and I discussed between deep, labored breaths. He was asking questions, and I just kept saying, "I'm okay. I'm okay. It's okay. I'm okay. It's okay." I just wanted his hand on my arm. It was comforting to have him by my side.

The doctor came in a little while later. "Everything looks good. You're going to be discharged as soon as the rest of your lab work comes back."

What? Seriously? How the actual fuck am I supposed to go home with this fever, which had come down to about 101 at this point with the meds they were giving me, *shaking and not being able to stand? I can hardly speak!*

Then my bloodwork came in. The doctor promptly came into the room. "I'm admitting you. Your lactic acid level is 3.9, and there are several other labs, including white cell count, that present a concerning picture." She claimed this was likely a tick-borne illness, and I was going to need a few days of IV antibiotics and further testing.

My thoughts:

My babies! No! I can't be away from my babies for that long! I have to nurse! I need a breast pump. Is there a breast pump in maternity that I can use? My poor husband. He has to go home to the kids. He can't be here with me. He needs to go. I will be taken care of.

My husband left to get the kids. "I'll be back after I get the kids settled." After several hours, I was taken up to a room that I was sharing with another patient. No one told me what unit I was going to or what the treatment plan entailed, other than IV antibiotics. The doctor kept forgetting to put the blood work orders in, so they drew my blood about six to eight times within a 12-hour period. I didn't feel well enough to care.

My brother-in-law came to visit me because he was downstairs with his wife, who was also in the hospital! It was a Mazzotta family reunion! He eventually had to leave because I started violently shaking again. Little did I know this was something called the rigors, a very common symptom of sepsis. Unfortunately, I had no idea what was going on until it was printed on my discharge paperwork.

Several specialists came in to see me. Infectious disease said this was definitely not tick-borne, but they were confused because they couldn't find the source of the infection. Overnight, my blood pressure tanked, and they needed to give me more fluids. Apparently, this is another symptom of sepsis, which I'd later find out after doing my own research.

Thankfully, a close friend of mine is a nurse who said I had sepsis from the second I called her to share what was going on. I would cry myself to sleep at night because I missed my kids and being in my home. I felt worse than I'd ever felt in my life. I had no idea what was going on, and the woman next to me was moaning incessantly.

This was not the environment for me. Is it really the environment for anyone? I remember when I gave birth to all three of my kids and appreciated being in the hospital. There were so many people to support and take care of you and your baby as you learned the ropes and navigated a new normal while recovering from the birthing process. It was really a beautiful experience.

Then there was this. *Um, no thanks! I'll give birth again several times over!* But I was grateful for the medical community saving my life, for having a supportive and loving husband, for having my kids well taken care of, and to be alive!

This whole sepsis experience was the beginning of a completely different Laura. From this point forward, I was characterized as having a chronic illness. Unable to find the source of the sepsis, I consulted with top immunological researchers in New York City, who discovered I have CVID (Common Variable Immunodeficiency) and would need IGG (immunoglobulin G, the primary protein fighting infection in our immune system) plasma infusions for the rest of my life. I now infuse plasma once weekly to provide immunity.

I also developed autoimmunity and incurred significant damage to my neurological system from the sepsis. I couldn't walk or drive without severe dizziness for three years. The depths of fear, anger, depression, helplessness, and anxiety during this three-year period post-sepsis were immense.

I managed to work a few hours per week but had to cancel appointments regularly. I started considering leaving my practice because I couldn't provide the consistency my clients were accustomed to. To delay this, I shifted my practice to entirely virtual (about five months before the pandemic). I tried going back to the office a few times but either collapsed (and my husband had to pick me up) or became confused and couldn't continue sessions.

This was when I met with my neurologist regarding cognitive impairment. He told me, "Unfortunately, autonomic neuropathy is degenerative and, with the immunodeficiency behind it, I expect your symptoms to progress."

I didn't believe him. *Wait, miss goody-two-shoes-who-always-people-pleases-and-follows-all-the-rules, is disagreeing with a doctor?*

I grew up conditioned to follow the guidance of authority figures no matter what, and doctors were surely authority figures in my world. So, choosing not to believe my neurologist felt like an act of defiance, but it's also where I started to play by my own tune.

Finding your own tune is not a fast and easy process. However, if you've already started on this path, you'll move much more quickly. Chronic people-pleasers may need several iterations (wink wink).

In this instance, it involved doing my own research on how I could heal outside of the traditional medical system. I saw hundreds of specialists and world-renowned doctors. I could confidently say western medicine could only take me so far.

Upon finding meditation, Reiki, and the Akashic Records, my eyes opened to an entirely different world than the one I was living in. There was infinite possibility here. I learned that energy is always moving, so our reality is always shifting. I learned the energetic impact of our ancestors, past lives, and inner child. I learned the purpose of my soul and the reason for being in this body at this time with these experiences.

Being a therapist for two decades, I felt like a bit of a dumbass that I had never touched the depths of healing with traditional psychotherapy. So, I set out on a new adventure and officially awakened to the absolute brilliance and natural wellness I held within.

I was fine! In fact, I was perfect, just as I was at that moment. I was present. I was focused in ways I hadn't been in my entire life. I had energy and confidence! My physical body was only one aspect of who I was, and it, along with my life experiences, didn't define me. I was part of something so much more.

I'm about to take you through a practice that will undoubtedly get you on the path to feeling this magnificence. All you need is a pen, paper, time to yourself, and maybe even a candle and tea.

THE PRACTICE

Get yourself comfortable. Take a nice, deep breath in. Pause. Allow your exhale to be longer than your inhale. Repeat these breaths two more times, and settle in.

You, my friend, are worthy to the core. You do not need a doctor, loved one, degree, health status, partner, body size, skin color, sexuality, or gender to determine your worth. You get to decide who you are. You get to decide how powerful and full of health and wealth you are.

This decision comes from you. It comes from within. It comes from that voice inside you that knows so clearly who you are and what you're here for. Where does that voice come from? How is it generated? Through your soul and the energetic building blocks that make you who you are.

When you truly feel into this relationship with your soul, others' opinions will not shake the fulfillment of your soul's mission. You won't feel the need to apologize for your uniqueness and off-the-beaten-path, seemingly outlandish perspectives and desires.

So, let's get in touch with your soul! To fully embody your soul's purpose, you need to relax deeply and surrender to its vibration. Feeling into this experience is what makes it sustainable versus just knowing it. To maximize the benefit of this practice, I encourage you to visit www.theakashictherapist.com/resources and listen to the audio version of this meditation.

Take a moment to adjust your physical body so you can sink into the space in which you're sitting. Take another breath in, all the way to the base of your spine. Exhale slowly. Do this breath two more times and close your eyes.

You are deeply well. You are grounded and rooted in your body. Feel the roots extending from the bottom of your feet all the way into the depths of Mother Earth. Allow yourself to extract the nutrients of this root system as you inhale.

Imagine each of your cells lighting up with this energy. Since 80% of the information we hold is sent from the body to the brain, allow this light to travel upward, delivering comforting, nourishing, stabilizing energy to the cells of your brain.

As these illuminate, rays of brightly colored energy extend beyond the top of your head, like you're wearing a radiant crown. Allow this to invite your higher self into this experience. Take note of what your higher self looks like and what it feels like to be in its presence. Bask in this for a moment.

Now take the hand of your higher self and allow it to guide you into the universe. You're floating amongst the stars while remaining grounded and safe in your body. You feel weightless and buoyant, free from your body and the world.

You have perspective here. You can see things so clearly, like how your life events that have unfolded, and are unfolding, are paving a path for your highest good. Appreciate the beauty of the stars and planets and the silence of this moment.

This is your essence. *This* is the frequency of your soul. Loving, patient, spacious, free, and light, with the ability to create anything and everything from this space from which all things are formed.

This dark matter you're floating in is fertile ground, where your soul plants your ideas and next steps. Watch what your higher self is planting right in front of you. Watch the purpose that's already planted here, that your higher self is watering, nourishing, and preparing for your continued journey on Earth.

Know that, whether you have conscious awareness of this purpose, you are energetically witnessing and receiving the codes of it now. You are intimately involved in its expansion.

Take a deep breath to pull these codes into each of your energy centers, mind, and body. Feel as your body expands with the breath, increasing the capacity for actualizing your soul's desires.

Identify where your purpose currently lives within you. Where in your body do you feel it emanating? It may be a physical sensation, an emotion, or just a clear knowing.

Send breath to this area to open even more space to hold this energy. Hold your breath briefly to express your sincere intention to integrate these codes.

Now take the hand of your higher self and float back to the space in which you're sitting. Feel as your higher self rises back into the ether. Connect with the surface on which you're sitting. Wiggle your fingers and toes, stretch your neck, and open your eyes whenever you're ready.

You've just experienced a frequency unknown to most humans on this planet. This is the frequency of unconditional love, permanence, and unwavering clarity. The more you attune yourself to this space, the more it is palpably felt, and worthiness becomes automatic.

And the most beautiful part is, by embodying this vibration, you are inviting others to witness the changes in you, so they are eager for a taste of the same.

Laura Mazzotta, LCSW-R, is a Spiritual Empowerment Coach and Therapist with 20 years of experience. She is an activator of personal power and calls herself the Confidence Queen! Her mission is to guide intuitive women into ditching indecision, chronic symptoms, and burnout by confidently owning their multifaceted gifts and experiencing intimacy, wellness, and freedom. Laura knows the most successful formula for optimal vitality, and limitless business expansion, is potent, core-level healing combined with uniquely soul-aligned empowerment strategies.

With extensive knowledge and skills in modalities such as EFT (tapping), regression therapy, trauma, inner child work, and intuitive development, Laura knows how to guide your journey in a unique, compassionate, and highly efficient way.

During her recovery from a serious illness in 2016, Laura exhausted western medicine approaches and realized her deep passion for holistic methods, becoming an even greater advocate for personal development and transformation. Laura knows true healing occurs much more powerfully when all components (physical, mental, energetic, and spiritual) of a person's issue are addressed. She's here to guide her clients in all steps on that journey and empower them to share their gifts with the world.

You can connect further with Laura through any of the following:

Website: https://www.theakashictherapist.com

Free Facebook group, The Expansion Portal:
https://www.facebook.com/groups/expansionportal

Instagram: https://www.instagram.com/emergehealingandwellness/

YouTube (Includes a Free EFT/Tapping Playlist):
https://www.youtube.com/channel/UCbcQ88JRcZ6blPbWKOzvAxg

Medium (blogs): https://medium.com/@emergehealingandwellness

Pinterest: https://pin.it/1vW3JpV

CHAPTER 2

REAWAKENING YOUR SOUL

TRANSFORMATIONAL JOURNALING FOR GENERATIONAL HEALING

Bonnie Luft, LPC, LMHC,
M.S.Ed, NCC, DBH-C, Reiki Master Teacher

MY STORY

Had I known that in a few moments, my emotional world would begin to crash, leaving smoldering remnants of who I once was, I wouldn't have been standing in the kitchen doing mundane tasks while tending to my kids. I don't know where I would have been, but I like to think I would have been doing something more supportive of myself.

I was blessed with three beautiful children in three years. My perfect rainbow babies were born after three miscarriages. The first—a boy with golden locks and a smile that would melt your heart, followed by two girls, so beautiful and radiant, who made my heart feel complete. At this time, they were three, two, and a newly born. Having them was the joy of my life, but it wasn't without physical and emotional pain. Two pregnancies ended in complications. The first ended in trauma so lasting that the sights, sounds, and smells played in my head daily three years later. I was reminded of my very near-death experience when I brushed by the small scar on my neck from the central line placed to keep me alive or looked into the sweet face of my boy, whom I was moments from never meeting. Thoughts would rush back to me in the strangest of moments—a beep from the stove that sounded like the IV drip, the smell of cleanliness that wafted in the air in the hospital. Any mention of a challenging birth, ICU, or surgery would freeze my body and mind, like my heart was being encased in concrete, leaving me unable to move or feel.

On this particular morning, like so many others, I felt the rush of the day wash over me the moment I opened my eyes. *I have so much to do today that I don't know how I will do it all.* I slowly unwrapped myself from my warm cocoon of blankets and moved to the end of the bed to get up. Sliding my feet into my slippers, I shuffled across the bedroom. The sun was hidden behind the dark gray sky. It was winter again. It always felt like winter. Cold, dark, and dreary like the emotions brewing inside me.

Walking up the creaking stairs always left me with a knot in my stomach. *What will this day bring?* I began to feel myself kick into auto-pilot, running through the enormous never-ending list of things that needed to be done immediately. Knowing the day would begin and wouldn't stop until I crawled into bed some 13 hours later, I slowly and quietly opened the doors, one by one, to see my beautiful babies all bright-eyed and ready to go.

I leaned over, picked up my little ones from their beds, one by one, and rustled through their dressers to grab diapers, clothes, and socks. Each child lay on the bed, wiggling, moving, and trying to escape, as I held onto each one the best I could. Struggling to keep them all in place, I systematically changed their diapers, removed their pajamas, and put them into soft, warm clothes to keep them comfy for the day.

The day began. We made our way to the kitchen as we did each and every day. Leaning into the bassinet, I placed my newborn down. She began to cry loudly, roaring for a feeding that was always coming moments too late. I clicked the buckles as I placed the three-year-old and the two-year-old in their high chairs for their first of many meals of the day. I heard the cries coming from the older two, their cries sounding like screeches from an animal starving for a meal.

I grabbed the pan to fry some eggs. *This is all too much. I can't do it.*

The crying continued and became deafening as I ran around the kitchen cracking eggs into the sizzling pan. My hands worked so quickly but still left me behind. I hurried to make the bottle for the baby. I did this so many times a day, yet it still felt like I couldn't make it fast enough to stop the constant need for feeding. The eggs began to burn on the stove; the smoke and smell filled the room; the sounds of crying kids and water rushing in the sink continued as the feeling of despair began to wash over me. Internally I was screaming for help, a time out, a pause button, a simple two-minute break, but there would be help coming. I turned my attention to the frying pan billowing with smoke. I grabbed the oven mitt, picked up the pan, and threw it into the sink, eggs and all, splashing it with water to calm the burn. As the sound of sizzle filled the room, my attention was diverted once again.

I knew it was coming though it still caught me off guard. I had just a very brief moment to gear up for it. I was ready. I had made all the preparations. I tightly clenched my legs together, positioned my elbow, and let it out. A sneeze! But not just any sneeze. This sneeze was so powerful it would change the entire course of my life. It snuck up on me, and I couldn't hold it in. I couldn't stop it, and I certainly couldn't hold my bladder while it was happening. Anyone else pee in the kitchen? Postpartum moms, you get it, right?

I sneezed and immediately loudly exclaimed, "*I don't have time for this!*"

The smell of the burning eggs still wafted in the air, the babies still cried for food, the enormous weight of parenthood crushed me, and I crumbled to the kitchen floor. It was as if my soul could take no more; it simply gave out. I heard nothing—the sounds of crying fading into the background. My body was so exhausted, overwhelmed, and broken that I couldn't grab hold of myself. As I lay in the fetal position on the floor, I thought: *I can't go on like this; something has to change!* I began to weep.

Tears streaming down my face, my body and emotions weak and worn, I pulled myself up from the floor, leaning on the counter to steady myself, and stood upright. I didn't say a word. I just stood. Silent. Scared. Vulnerable.

In the moments after the sneeze, after crying out my I-am-too-busy-to-sneeze declaration to the Universe while also cursing my mom-bladder, time stood still. I was frozen, unable to know. Unable to be.

I was standing in front of the sink when I began to feel my thoughts return. They flooded in like a river bursting through a dam. I thought a million thoughts at one time: *What is happening here? What am I doing to myself? Is this really life? Am I living or surviving? Should it be like this? This has to stop!*

Then came: *Where do I begin? This has been the way it has been for years with my other two. This is what is expected of me in motherhood, right? Everyone feels this way!*

In those early days, post breakdown, I felt completely lost. I felt like my façade crashed down into a million small shards of glass ripping me open and exposing the truth about me: I was an awful mother. The fog descended over me, blocking my view of the past, present, and future. It was so thick that I couldn't see the lighthouse. There was nothing guiding me on my path. My old self was dying and withering away.

I didn't know where to turn, so I turned inward like I often do when things get hard. My soul was left wondering if it was brought into a cosmic lie about womanhood and motherhood. I wondered if everything I thought I knew about life was simply untrue and never existed as the construct I thought it was. I felt like a shell of a human—a shell of a woman. I began to question every thought, my being, and my existence. I wondered who I was and how my thoughts and beliefs were shaped by social constructs, family conditioning, my ancestors' pain and trauma, and the stories I made up for myself based on those beliefs.

I began to realize motherhood was not what I was promised it would be. It was not sweet, calm, beautiful moments strung together to make up each day, month, and year. That was not the reality of early motherhood. Early motherhood took hold of parts of me I didn't even know existed, and it manipulated those parts into thoughts and words that deepened my doubt. It told me so many lies about myself and resurfaced them until I could no longer deny their existence and truth. It pushed me to emotional extremes until I made an intentional effort to question it. Without recognition, I simply lived in it, the unconscious emotional turmoil, until it became one with my existence.

As I began to listen to the voice inside of me, I knew there was no way I could go back to that place of emptiness, but I also didn't know how to go forward. My foundation was gone, and rebuilding it was going to be a one-woman job. It was time to take action. I felt a longing to learn how to undo all the worldly conditioning set upon my mother and the generations before her. I knew if I was going to heal, I had to heal all the others before me. What arose out of me at that moment was a wounded, scared, but fiercely determined woman who would change the culture and narrative of motherhood. I was going to heal the generational trauma passed to me like a suitcase, never to be unzipped, filled with old memories too painful to unpack.

To disassemble all of my thought patterns, inherited beliefs, and feelings attached to societal expectations, I had to step back and ask myself a few questions. This was the beginning of my journey into generational healing through journaling.

I wondered:

How can I connect with my own heart space?

Who am I?

How do I want to show up?

Beginning to ask me these questions left me with a blank canvas filled with more questions than answers.

I wondered:

Have I ever known who I truly am?

Have I just accepted life as it was laid out for me, picked it up, and carried it forth?

I honestly didn't know. I knew I had to do something. I thought about what I could do in the *very* little time I had at home with the kids.

After all these questions arose from me, I knew I had to get them on paper. I began to journal. I began to freely write my thoughts down on paper. If you knew me pre-sneeze-crisis, you'd know that if anyone had mentioned to me that journaling would help, I would've judged them, convincing myself that they must have liked high school ELA, poetry, and literature, and if so, they couldn't possibly understand me because we had nothing in common!

But I was beginning to learn about myself. Perhaps there were things about me even I didn't know? Maybe I did like to write? I searched journal prompts to get to know myself, and there were so many options to choose from. Some were surfacy, only asking about things I already knew my preference, for example, hot or cold weather, summer or winter, etc. Some were in-depth: Exploring my soul's desires, the stories I was told, those I constructed, and those I deconstructed. But nothing felt quite deep enough to unearth the generational healing that had to be done. I wanted to start at the beginning, my childhood, and explore my child self—get to know her intimately and learn all about her hopes, dreams, and desires, as well as pain and hardships. From there, moving throughout the years and connecting my young self to my current self, I began to assemble the real truth of the pain that needed to heal and the beauty within.

THE PRACTICE

Transformational journaling for generational healing in motherhood should feel like picking up binoculars and focusing on one space at a time to see the depth, beauty, and reality of the experience. To do so honestly, we must remove the filters placed upon our lens.

Exploring childhood is a powerful tool used in journaling for generational healing. Start by placing your hand on your heart space to deeply connect with yourself while reciting the following prompt:

I open my heart to myself. I honor my child within and those who have come before me. I will use this space for healing, exploration, and knowing. All my truths are safe here. I am free to be me. I accept myself as I am.

Once you feel your heart space opening up to giving and receiving, you can begin to explore your past, present, and future.

Open up your journal and respond to the following prompt:

Prompt #1: *When I think of who I am, I think/feel/wonder_____.*

If your response feels hard to pull through, that is okay! That simply means you have yet to connect within. Put your hand back to the heart space and focus on your breath—in and out for the count of six until you feel reconnected. You can do this as many times as you need to. Ask yourself the question again. This time, feel for the answer; don't think about the answer.

Once you've answered, notice if your response felt like it originated in your heart. Cast aside your learned cultural, societal, and familial thoughts by questioning yourself with questions such as: *Does this thought belong to me?* Or, *where did this thought originate?* This self-questioning can be a powerful way to begin to move into your heart space to learn about yourself and the origin of your thoughts, beliefs, and feelings.

Next, ask yourself Prompt #2: *How have I come to believe what I know about myself?*

Do so with the same intention as before—learning more about yourself from your heart. Continue asking yourself: *How does this feel? Is this authentic?* Write your answers out in your journal. Continue on to the next prompts.

Prompt #3: *Who has taught me about myself?*

Prompt #4: *What was I taught that doesn't feel true for me?*

Prompt #5: *What was I taught that does feel true for me?*

Prompt #6: *What do I want to heal?*

Prompt #7: *Why does it need to be healed?*

Prompt #8: *What would healing look like?*

Prompt #9: *How do I heal?*

Prompt #10: *Who do I want to be as a person and as a mom?*

Finally, ask yourself how it feels to enter your heart space and learn about yourself. Beginning the journey of self-discovery can be challenging but is so very rewarding. Stay in wonder with yourself and honor what comes forward.

Deeply reaching within, exploring, acknowledging, accepting, and healing yourself will provide you with the tools to create the life you dream of living. Motherhood does not have to be synonymous with burnout. You can lead a balanced life full of happiness, peace, and harmony.

Bonnie Luft is a psychotherapist, Doctor of Behavioral Health candidate, founder, and CEO of The Therapy Space of CT and Burnout to Balanced™ Motherhood Empowerment Academy.

In her therapeutic practice, Bonnie is passionate about assisting neurodiverse couples, and highly sensitive individuals find balance, peace, and harmony in their everyday parenting lives and relationships.

As an intergenerational trauma healer, Bonnie incorporates her skills as a Reiki Master Teacher and somatic empowerment coach to journey with parents to develop and strengthen their attachment bonds with themselves and their children. Bonnie's mission is to provide parents a safe space to dive deep within themselves and heal the triggers exposed in parenthood.

She believes in the use of holistic, somatic therapies that address the connections between the mind and body, leading to a calm and regulated nervous system.

Bonnie can also be found speaking and writing on such topics as intergenerational healing, creating balance and peace in motherhood, and the challenges and beauty of neurodiverse couples.

Connect with Bonnie

Website: www.bonnieluft.com

LinkedIn: https://www.linkedin.com/in/bonnieluft/

Facebook:
https://www.facebook.com/profile.php?id=100071165013767&sk=about

Instagram: www.instagram.com/bonniemluft

CHAPTER 3

GONE BUT NOT FORGOTTEN

CONNECTING TO YOUR LOVED ONE THROUGH VISUALIZATION

Kelly Daugherty, LCSW-R, GC-C

MY STORY

My sister ran into our neighbor's house with tears streaming down her face. "The hospital called, and they said Mom expired."

Expired? I thought. *She isn't a piece of cheese. This is my mom.*

I was 14. I felt paralyzed and in total shock, like I was stuck in a nightmare. It took several minutes for the emotions to hit me, and then the tears came. This moment ultimately shaped my life and who I am today.

Just two and a half years before, I was standing in the cafeteria at my elementary school Halloween party dressed as a corpse with blue skin and bugs and snakes glued onto my dress and face waiting for my older sister to come pick me up. I saw my sister coming down the hall, rushed over to her, and quickly asked, "How is Mom? Is she going to be okay?" Earlier that day, my mom, Eileen, had a mastectomy. She found a lump in her breast, and it was cancer.

The day after my mom's surgery, my dad sat my sisters and me down to explain that my mom was sick and would be for quite some time. I was 12 years old and just dismissed this conversation. I pretended everything was fine and she would be okay. I never thought she might die from this.

It wasn't until I was at my aunt and uncle's 25th wedding anniversary party that it began to sink in that my mom was really sick. Things were going to change. My mom walked into the party wearing a wig she bought earlier that day with my aunt, who was also dealing with breast cancer. I was furious and thought. *She is going to be okay; why the heck is she wearing that stupid wig that doesn't even look like her regular hairstyle, and she still has all her hair.*

My mom started chemo after Christmas and quickly began to lose her hair. I remember finding a piece of her hair in my meatballs and spaghetti. I didn't say anything because I didn't want to upset her. I watched my mom get weaker and weaker from the chemo. My mom was highly active; she never got her driver's license and walked everywhere. Seeing my mom, a speed walker who was challenging to keep up with, slow down, and accept more rides from friends, was hard to watch. Finally, my mom went into remission, and I thought it was over. Her hair started growing back, and I thought things would return to normal. Unfortunately, that did not happen; cancer spread throughout her body, and chemotherapy started again. I had just started high school, and it was not a smooth transition. I struggled with fitting in with my peers. The new friends I made would come to the house, and I would have to explain, "My mom has cancer and has lost all of her hair, so you may see her without her wig." They stared blankly back at me with no idea what to say, so they said nothing.

I truly felt I was the only teen girl going through this. Towards the end of my freshman year, my mom got lost going into our basement. One of my sisters found her wandering, not knowing where she was. It was quickly determined that cancer had spread to her brain. It was the beginning of the end. My mom changed in so many ways. Her friendly, talkative, generous, caring personality changed, and my mom was now cursing at us (which she never did before) and calling us names. Unfortunately, the memory problems continued to get worse.

They started radiation in addition to the chemo, but that didn't last long. I was still in denial of how sick my mom was and never dreamed that in a few months, she would die. Then, my mom went to the hospital in July and never left. We visited every day and watched her slowly leave us.

My dad sat us down at our kitchen table on July 20th and told us that my mom had a week left to live and we needed to make some decisions. First, we needed to decide if my dad should sign the DNR and what our wishes were for my mom after she died.

I sat numb, confused, and scared. I still hoped for a miracle. We discussed funeral arrangements during this conversation, and I felt guilty because we were giving up on my mom. I still didn't want to believe she would die. I would go to the hospital and think, *If she eats, she'll get better; I will get her to eat so she won't die.* Unfortunately, my magical thinking didn't work, and her body began to shut down. Eight days later, we went to the hospital to visit my mom. She was non-responsive, and her hands and feet were blue. We looked at the nurse. "What's happening? Why are her hands and feet blue?" "The doctor will call you," she said and left the room. After visiting hours were over for that afternoon, we went to the mall and then went to a neighbor's house. Then we got the message from the hospital that she had died.

After the funeral, I went to Tennessee with my uncle's family and spent a few weeks there. When I came home, the reality of the loss began to sink in, and the grief intensified. I was angry, arguing with my father, acting out, and I cried myself to sleep most nights. It was the worst time of my life. That year of my life is quite blurry, I remember bits and pieces, mostly the bad stuff and the stupid things people said to me regarding grief, but I can't remember much about school or anything I learned that year. In addition, I struggled with feeling alone in my grief. I don't remember us talking as a family about my mom's death, except for going to family therapy, which did not always go well. I felt like I was the only 15-year-old who didn't have a mom.

I didn't have the coping skills or the emotional intelligence to deal with these intense feelings. I began to experience physical symptoms of grief with stomachaches. My dad took me to multiple doctors who ran numerous tests, and none of them could find the cause. I was internalizing my grief.

Fortunately, my dad recognized how much I struggled and forced me to go to a grief support group at the local hospice. I was reluctant to go, but my dad told me there would be boys in the group. As a 15-year-old girl who went to an all-girls Catholic high school, I was boy crazy and went, hoping to be around some boys. Of course, no boys were there, but that group changed my life. I met three other girls who experienced the death of their fathers, and I finally felt like I wasn't alone. This group helped me deal with many feelings of anger and frustration and helped me to begin to accept my mom's death.

Renee was the social worker that facilitated that group and helped me through this challenging time in my life. After the group was over, I still wanted more, and Renee invited me to start volunteering with the children's groups. These groups let me help other children in the same situation and helped me deal with my grief. This was when I knew I wanted to be a social worker like Renee and to be able to help grieving individuals. As a social worker for the last 20 years, I have worked at two different hospices as grief counselors, and I continue volunteering at local grief camps. In addition, I have had the opportunity to work with various other mental health programs throughout my career. As much as I learned and enjoyed the different opportunities, my true passion is grief and loss. I'm fortunate to now be in my private practice, focusing on helping clients deal with the death of a loved one through individual and group counseling.

Trying to make sense of why I had to go through this is one of the things I'd struggled with for a long time. While I still miss my mom and would love to have her here with us, I'm grateful I had my mom for the first 14 years of my life. I'm thankful for all she taught me, which I genuinely believe made me the woman I am today. I'm also grateful I could find meaning in such a challenging experience. Finding meaning in grief and moving forward in your life is a unique process for each person. I find meaning in my grief every day by being able to be present for my clients and helping them navigate the uncharted territories of their grief.

One of the goals of my practice is to help individuals and therapists become more grief-informed and how best to support grieving individuals. I've learned many things throughout my grief journey and from my clients over the last 20 years, and these are just a few of them:

- Grief bursts will happen often! Grief bursts are overwhelming feelings of grief that come out of nowhere and may not be triggered by something.

- There is no timetable for grief. You will never get over the loss; you learn to live with it.

- Many people, including therapists and medical professionals, are not grief-informed. Unfortunately, grief courses are not required in most counseling programs. If you seek a therapist to help you process your grief, make sure they are grief informed and have experience with the type of loss you have experienced.

- Many people still follow the stages of grief and loss (denial, anger, depression, bargaining, acceptance) that Elizabeth Kubler Ross developed in 1969 to address the experiences of terminally ill patients. Society has accepted these stages to explain grief, which is not accurate. Grief is a normal and natural process when there is a loss. It's not linear or predictable. This is an outdated model that is misapplied and can make people think they're doing grief wrong.

- Everyone grieves differently. The relationship, its length, the quality of the relationship, and how the person died can all contribute to how a person experiences grief.

- Grief is complicated and can be experienced emotionally, mentally, physically, and spiritually.

- Some of the most common symptoms grieving individuals express are grief brain, difficulty concentrating, issues with memory, sleep disturbances, feeling like they are going crazy, body pains including stomachaches, headaches, tension, and tightness in the jaw, shoulders, back, etc., physical exhaustion, feelings of guilt and many more.

- Lean into your grief; you can't avoid it. Sit with it, feel it and talk about it with others who will listen.

- Grief groups are highly beneficial and can help you feel less alone in your grief.

Although our loved one is physically gone doesn't mean we still can't have a connection with them. Continuing bonds with our deceased loved ones are healthy and normal and allow us to stay connected. It has been found that those who continue to keep a connection to their loved ones cope better with their loss and all of the changes associated with their loss. There are several ways to keep that connection which include journaling, sharing your memories of them, talking aloud to them, doing something they enjoyed doing, paying attention to the signs they may be sending you, participating in rituals to honor them, and visualization. The following practice is a great way to feel that connection. The more you use it, the better it will work, and your connection will strengthen.

THE PRACTICE

Please spend some time answering these questions before proceeding with the next part of the exercise.

What do I need to tell my loved one?

What do I need to ask my loved one?

What do I think my loved one would want to say to me?

We experience grief in our bodies, which can cause tension and tightness. This tool will help you release the pressure felt in your body and help you connect with your loved one.

If you would prefer to listen to this visualization, please visit: www.glgrief.com/resources

Before we start, make sure you have turned off all notifications and are in a place where you will not be interrupted. Now allow yourself to get comfortable, whether lying down or sitting up.

Once you are comfortable, let your eyes close or lower your gaze, whichever feels the most comfortable to you.

Now, take a nice deep breath, filling those lungs from the bottom up. Another nice deep breath now, letting that breath work for you. Notice how refreshing that full, deep breath is. Let this next breath take you deeper inside yourself, and imagine that breath going past your lungs, filling your entire body.

Imagine a beautiful healing white light coming up from the ground, and as you take your next deep breath, imagine pulling that light up to your feet. This light feels so familiar, so natural, and with your next breath, the light moves up further from your feet and into your calves. You are becoming filled like a vessel of this beautiful, healing white light; notice this as best as you can; so warm, so familiar.

With each breath you take, allow this warmth and healing light to grow within you as it reaches your thighs, hips, and belly, flows into your chest and heart area, and you can feel your heart opening like a beautiful flower.

This light moves up into your shoulders, spilling down into your arms, hands, and fingers. And as you start to notice how well it is filling your hands, you notice how warm and heavy they feel. As you continue to breathe, notice they become even heavier and warmer.

The next breath takes you even further as the healing light moves up from your hands, into your arms and shoulders, and into your neck and jaw. The jaw becomes relaxed now, washing away all that old tension you may be holding there.

The light moves up further and fills your eyes; notice whatever colors, shapes, or whatever may be dancing behind your eyelids. See this without judgment or expectations. The healing light fills you up even further into your head, so warm and complete, from your toes up to the top of your head.

So now feel this beautiful healing light throughout your entire body, especially in your heart area. As you focus on your heart area, I would like you to bring one of your hands to your heart. Feel your hand resting on your heart area; notice how you feel your heart beating and how amazing the heart is. You don't even need to think about it; it keeps beating because this is your life force.

As you feel your heart beating, feel the heart-opening, and as it expands, you feel the connection to your loved one who is no longer with us, to your love for them. Perhaps in your heart area is where you feel connected to them and connected to all of your memories with them. Maybe this is where you feel gratitude for them, appreciation for the memories, and gratitude for the lessons you learned from them.

As you feel your heart beating, allow yourself to imagine, recall or remember the memories of your loved one, the happy memories you have of them, the good times, and the funny times. Allow yourself to remember them now. Each breath and heartbeat makes these memories more vivid, brighter, and more robust in your mind. Feel what you feel; notice what you notice. Now go ahead and make those memories clear. See if you can remember your loved one's smile, their smell, the sound of their voice, their laugh.

If you would like, you can choose to connect even better to just one of those memories, maybe to the one that is most meaningful to you. Allow yourself to experience this memory; perhaps you can remember the colors, the smells, the sounds, and what it felt like during this memory. And as you allow yourself to experience this memory, you feel so connected to your loved one. Feeling that connection maybe even brings a smile to your face, feeling the love, that connection you share with them.

Your memories are always within you, within your heart; they are the way to stay connected to your loved one. So, as you remember, feel this memory and the connection you share with them. That connection is always present.

Every time you want to feel that connection and the love you share, bring your hand to your heart center and feel the love, and you will feel that connection.

And as you focus on just your loved one, letting everything else in this memory fade away like a scene in a movie, all the other things, the scene fades away, leaving just you and your loved one and the connection you share.

As you are there with them in this space, sit with them as long as you need, feeling that connection, feel what you need to feel, say what you need to say, and hear what you need to hear from them.

As we are coming to the end of this journey, let those words, feelings, and thoughts echo inside you, allowing them to become a part of you, noticing and feeling that connection living and growing within you. Remember, whenever you want to feel connected, bring your hand to your heart, and you will feel that connection. Once you feel you are ready, only when you are ready, taking all the time you need, allowing yourself to take a nice deep breath in and come back to the room fully feeling connected, loved, and feeling wonderful.

Kelly Daugherty, LCSW-R, is a certified grief counselor with over 20 years of experience in the field of grief and loss. Kelly graduated with her bachelor's and master's in social work from Florida State University. She has worked as a therapist, program manager, and clinical director at mental health agencies and hospices. Kelly currently owns and operates a private practice, Greater Life Grief Counseling, LCSW, in Malta, New York. She has helped thousands of individuals navigate their grief journey by providing individual and group therapy to children, adolescents, and adults experiencing illness and bereavement. In addition, Kelly co-created Healing Strides, combining grief counseling and mindfulness with walk/run-based therapy. Kelly has dedicated her career to helping individuals integrate their grief into their life in a healthy way by developing healthy coping skills and achieving their goals through the utilization of cutting-edge, proven techniques. When Kelly is not working, she enjoys doing art DIY projects and spending time with her husband, Kevin, and their two pups, Boomer and PJ.

Connect with Kelly:

Website: www.glgrief.com

Facebook: www.facebook.com/people/Greater-Life-Grief-Counseling-LCSW/100067294437222/

Instagram: https://www.instagram.com/greaterlifegriefcounseling/

CHAPTER 4

EMBODYING GRATITUDE

HOW TO REDUCE ANXIETY
IN ANY SITUATION

Teresa Lacorazza, M.S.Ed

MY STORY

"So, the results didn't go our way. You have a cancer called Paget's Disease. I'm truly sorry." Those words echoed on the other end of the phone as my feet were soaking in soapy water at the nail salon.

No doctor ever calls after 5:00 p.m., right? Besides, no news is good news.

It was 5:15 p.m., so I had to be safe. It'd been seven days since the biopsy. Those words changed my life forever and started me on a journey of gratitude.

My nightmare started on July 1, 2021—the day Dr. Diehl performed a biopsy on a rash that appeared on my right breast.

Three weeks before the biopsy, Dr. Diehl noticed three flakey spots on my right nipple.

"Hmm, I don't like the way that looks. How long has that been there?" He asked.

"I never noticed it."

"I'm giving you a cream to apply twice a day for two weeks. If it doesn't go away, I'm going to do a biopsy. In *very* rare cases, something like this is cancer."

Cancer! Wait! What?

"Cancer?!" My eyes were the size of half dollars.

"No need to worry. It's uncommon for something like this to be breast cancer. Come back in two weeks, and we'll take a look."

Paget's Disease, the type of breast cancer I had, is very rare. Most of the time, it's something skin-related like eczema.

What the fuck? Cancer?

I returned on July 1, knowing the biopsy was needed.

"I'll do the biopsy, just to be sure." Dr. Diehl stated. "It's usually nothing."

I can't believe this is happening.

My palms were sweaty; my stomach was in knots.

Here we go!

A few minutes later, the biopsy was over; I got dressed, prayed, and wiped the tears!

During the days that followed, I focused on my thoughts. Since 2010 I've been a healing arts practitioner, teaching different tools which rewire the brain to think in more positive, productive ways.

July 2021 was when God said loud and clear, "Put your money where your mouth is; time to practice what you preach!"

The call came; I had cancer.

How? Why? I don't understand. There is no family history of breast cancer.

These questions flooded my mind.

"Can I call you back in a few minutes, please? I'm not home." I asked.

My heart skipped a beat. I immediately became anxious, overwhelmed, and engulfed in fear.

With my hands shaking, I texted my husband, "I have cancer; pick me up." That's what my fingers typed. It was as if they had a mind of their own.

I have breast cancer!

My husband knew at that moment the world we knew was gone. His life, my life, and the kids' lives would never be the same. I had cancer.

Anthony pulled up; I sank into the front seat. He hugged me, and I sobbed. We've been together since college, and he's always been my rock. We drove a few blocks and parked. We thought it would be best to have the conversation with the doctor together in private since my son was at home.

During the call, Dr. Diehl repeated, "The cancer was caught early. You'll have surgery, possibly radiation, and make a full recovery."

"We have a vacation planned, and we leave tomorrow. Should we go? We can certainly cancel," Anthony asked.

Vacation? Seriously? What's wrong with you? I have cancer, dammit!

"Go on vacation; the tests can wait a week. Enjoy yourselves."

He's telling me to go on vacation. He's crazy!

My hands were shaking in Anthony's hands. I cried as we listened.

"Thanks, Dr. Diehl. I'll be in touch when I schedule the tests."

"How do I tell the kids? We leave for Vegas tomorrow. Maybe you take the kids. I'll stay home. I don't want to go; I don't have the head for it." My voice cracked, my head hung, and the tears fell.

"They'll be okay. They're strong. Besides, the doctor said you would be okay; you can go. Make sure you stress that. It'll be good for you. There's nothing you can do at home. It's all up to you. I'm good with whatever you decide." Anthony reassured me as he squeezed my hand and took me home.

When the packing was done, it was time.

I can do this. I won't cry. I can tell them.

I called the boys to the living room. They're 17 and 18. "I have something to tell you." My voice was shaking; my husband nodded as a sign of reassurance, "I have breast cancer," I continued, "But the doctor says I am going to be okay." I fought back the tears. Their faces glazed over. That moment will be etched in my memory forever.

Oh my God, I said it. I said I have cancer.

They both hugged me and kissed me.

"You got this, Mom," Anthony whispered.

"Mom, don't worry, you're going to be okay," James said.

That night I went to bed sad. I cried. I didn't sleep much. The alarm went off at the crack of dawn.

I don't want to go. I have to go. This is the last thing I want to do.

The plane ride was long; I was restless. I prayed. I meditated.

I can't believe this is happening.

My brother-in-law picked us up from the airport. I've known him since he was 12. Joseph hugged me and said, "We gotcha!" He brought us home, and his wife hugged me tight and winked.

Okay, I can do this!

I spent the next several hours on the phone making appointments for more testing. It was overwhelming. I sat at the table, struggling to hold back the tears; I didn't want to make anyone feel uncomfortable. Silently, some tears fell—one, then another, then another. I had cancer. I was scared. I slipped into the bathroom and allowed myself to cry. After some time, I was back in control. I emerged from the bathroom with a smile. I allowed myself to feel peace, even if it was just for a few moments.

We enjoyed our time in Vegas. I had ups and downs, but I allowed myself to feel the feels. I didn't want to go, but so glad we made the trip! It was good for my soul.

We returned home a few days before my tests. Thankfully, I was able to have the MRI and diagnostic mammogram on the same day.

While I waited for the results, I focused on my mindset. I recognized the moments I needed to cry, moments I needed to be alone, and moments I needed to just have someone listen to me. I focused on being grateful for all the amazing things God has given me in my 52 years on this Earth.

When overwhelm did emerge, it was important to do self-checks. What was I feeling? Was I sad, anxious, or mad? Identifying emotions is critical. If I was feeling fearful, I would ask why I was feeling fearful. There were times I felt fear around the actual surgery. There were times I felt fear surrounding the radiation. Once I knew exactly what I was feeling, I knew how to heal that energy.

I used gratitude. I was able to breathe slowly into the emotion, allowing myself to really feel it in my body. It was okay; I was safe. After allowing the feeling to move through my body, I was able to feel gratitude.

I felt grateful that the doctor told me I'd be cured of cancer. I felt grateful my doctor had so much experience and was so kind and gentle. I was grateful I had the most amazing support system. Gratitude is everything during a crisis!

On July 24, my 52nd birthday, Dr. Diehl called with the results of my tests.

"We have good news!" he touted! "The MRI was negative for any other aggressive cancers inside the breast."

"Yes! Thank God!" I exhaled in excitement. My heart rate slowed.

Ninety percent of people with Paget's Disease has a very aggressive cancer inside the breast. I didn't! I was so grateful for that.

The call ended, I cried, and Anthony embraced and kissed me.

"It's all good, babe!"

"I just want to stay home and eat sushi tonight," I told Anthony.

"Are you sure? I will take you wherever you want to go!"

"Yup," I sighed with a smile. We had a drink and ordered sushi!

Over the next several days, many people offered their advice. Everyone said I needed to go for a second opinion. This made me angry. I knew they were coming from a place of love, but I needed to figure this out on my own.

What the fuck! Leave me alone!

My husband spoke with a good friend, a cancer survivor, and she asked if I'd be open to speaking with her. I did. For some reason, I listened to her. Diane forwarded me the names of two different breast specialists at Memorial Sloan Kettering Cancer Center. I researched the doctors and made an appointment with one for the following week.

What will Dr. Capko say? Will I need a double mastectomy? Dr. Diehl said no. What if she feels differently? Maybe I should just stay with him.

All of this made me anxious. I spent a lot of time meditating.

The day arrived. It felt like an eternity, and finally, Dr. Capko entered the exam room.

"Let's take a look!" She said and examined my breast.

"Yup! That's Paget's Disease! It was caught very early, which is good. This is treated with surgery and possibly radiation. You will make a full recovery."

Thank God! I have to ask this question.

I took a deep breath and responded, "If I were your mother or your sister, what would you tell them to do?

There was a pause, then Dr. Capko replied, "Exactly the same thing."

I sighed.

Thank you, God!

I exhaled and then took a deep breath to stop the tears, which didn't work. I cried and laughed all at the same time. I left feeling relieved.

"What did you think of her?" I asked Anthony as we drove home. "I liked her a lot. I like the way she explained everything. I don't know what to do."

Anthony's eyes were focused on the road. He reached for my hand and gave it a little squeeze, "I thought she was great, but it's up to you."

Damn! That didn't really help!

I wanted him to tell me whom I should choose, but the decision was mine.

I thought about it for a few days. I decided that Dr. Capko would perform the partial mastectomy. My surgery was scheduled for August 24, 2021.

Surgery was only a few weeks away. I had to stay calm, so I performed a morning ritual. Every morning before placing my feet on the floor, I thanked God for gifting me another day. I would lay in bed and really feel gratitude in my body; then, I recited affirmations such as, "At this moment, I am grateful for Anthony and the boys. I am grateful I will be healed. I am grateful for the early diagnosis." The list continued. Whatever came to my heart was added to the list!

As the days drew closer to the surgery, I became more anxious. I relied on the tools I've been teaching and using for years. Gratitude, EFT (Emotional Freedom Technique), meditation, and taking one day—or sometimes one moment—at a time helped.

Sometimes I needed to go to my room to cry, take a deep breath, and focus on the feeling of gratitude. I know it sounds impossible, but gratitude will shift your energy immediately.

Surgery day was here. I did my morning gratitude practice, hopped in the car with Anthony, and we headed to the hospital. Anthony held my hand during the ride, and we both were quiet.

I got this! Thank you, God, for Dr. Capko. All is well.

I repeated this over and over until we arrived.

We finally arrived, and I was greeted with a smile and escorted to a space where I would be prepped for surgery. Soon after, I was wheeled to the operating room. The surgery went well. Dr. Capko removed my nipple, areola, and a milk duct that was covered in cysts. It was time to heal.

For the first few days, I couldn't look at the incision that went across my breast. I just wasn't ready. The process was already traumatic, so I made a choice to do it on my own terms, in my own time. A quarter of my breast was gone. No more nipple. No more areola. I just didn't want to look.

On September first, eight days after surgery, we were hit by Hurricane Ida. At about 12:30 a.m., my house began to flood. The water rose quickly.

"Anthony, get up! The basketball hoops are on top of the cars!" I shouted from my son's room.

We had company visiting from California; I heard them downstairs rustling around in ankle-deep water, trying to gather their belongings.

Fuck!

"Carry up what you can!" I screeched.

Everyone did their best to bring all they could to the upper floors. Then we all sat. I was helpless; I wasn't allowed to do anything strenuous. There was nothing left for us to do. I watched as the water kept rising, finally making it to the main floor of the house. It was about 5:30 a.m.

This is a bad dream, right? This can't really be happening.

I went to bed and slept a few hours. The next morning, all our cars were underwater. We couldn't open the door because the water hadn't receded. My house was wrecked.

God, are you kidding me? Is this a joke?

"What the hell are we supposed to do now?" the tears fell.

"We'll figure it out," Anthony stated.

Really? Are you looking at what I'm looking at?

Finally, we were able to go outside and survey the damage. This is not the first flood; our neighbors survived several and were instrumental in the reconstruction.

My brother-in-law flew in from Vegas a few days later to help.

"Holy shit! This is worse than the pictures I saw." Joseph was in shock from all the damage.

The area looked like a war zone—furniture, personal belongings, anything you could imagine lined the streets of my neighborhood. It was heart-wrenching.

Finding gratitude was a challenge, but I did. For starters, we never lost electricity! We were lucky to find an honest contractor and public adjuster to help us through the seven-month ordeal. We also had my brother-in-law helping. The practice of gratitude is simple but not always easy. This story is proof.

In my mind, I kept repeating, *Thank you, God! I am blessed!*

As the days passed, I found more things to add to my gratitude list. I was grateful for our contractor and his workers; I was grateful for residents and restaurants for dropping off meals. I was grateful for friends that came to help tear down walls, empty out the house and garage, and lend us cars. The list goes on and on, but I think the picture is clear.

No matter how rough things seem, there is always room for gratitude. Here is the practice I use. I hope you enjoy it.

THE PRACTICE

1. Close your eyes and relax your jaw.

2. Breathe slowly through your nose and exhale twice as long out of your mouth. Repeat three to four times.

3. Visualize a time in your life when you felt wholeheartedly grateful. I always visualize the moment I first saw my oldest son after giving birth. I went through five cycles of IVF, so believe me, I was grateful.

4. Recreate the memory using all your senses. Where were you? What were you wearing? Who was with you? What did the air feel like on your skin? What did the air smell like? What sounds did you hear? Physically feel gratitude in your body just as if it was happening again.

5. Hold this feeling for at least 20 seconds.

6. Open your eyes. Notice how you feel in your mind and body.

7. Repeat steps 1-6, and if possible, visualize a different memory.

You can do this at any moment!

Hint: before doing this exercise, sit and create a list of all the times in your life you've felt overwhelming gratitude. After making this list, choose the two memories that brought you the most gratitude.

God gave me plenty of lemons over the last year, but I always knew I had a choice. I could choose to be the victim, or I could choose to rise above and focus on the positive things in my life. On many days the struggle was real. It took an abundance of energy not to fall apart and stay in the moment. I truly believe God wants us to live life to the fullest and be grateful for whatever obstacles put on our path. Let's face it, how could we know joy if we never experienced sorrow? How could we experience love if we never experienced heartbreak? How could we experience peace if we never experienced distress? Joy, peace, and love feel better, so why not focus on those emotions? I'd rather be happy instead of angry. I'd rather love than hate. You always have a choice. What are you choosing?

My journey has taught me important lessons, lessons that forced me to live life in the moment. These events furthered my mission to share my story and motivate others to take care of the mind, body, and spirit. Don't procrastinate; make the doctors' appointments. Cancer and dis-ease are scarier than the doctor. And finally, believe that you always have a choice. Remember, don't just live your life. **Love** your life!

Teresa Lacorazza, M.S.Ed, holds a Master's Degree in Education from St. John's University and spent over 12 years teaching in New York City. Teresa is a holistic arts practitioner with over a decade of experience. Her mission is to inspire women and motivate them to identify their self-limiting beliefs, ditch self-sabotaging habits, and retrain the brain to generate new, positive, healthy thought patterns so that well-defined pathways to desired goals are created. With extensive knowledge in modalities such as EFT (Emotional Freedom Technique), meditation, visualization, positive affirmations, NLP, and intuitive development, Teresa knows how to individualize and tailor the healing process for each client that guarantees success.

After raising two children, one being born premature and needing much assistance, relocating several times, and battling breast cancer, Teresa has become passionate about mental health and the mind, body, and spirit connection. She is here to lead women on a journey that will teach them to heal themselves, empower themselves, and love themselves in a loving and compassionate way.

Teresa is a native New Yorker who currently lives in New Jersey with her husband of almost 25 years and their two college-age sons. She loves to visit with friends from Maryland and Tennessee, spend time with family, and entertain.

Connect with Teresa at:

Email: Teresa@HealEmpowerAndLove.com

Facebook: https://www.facebook.com/HEALwithTeresa

Instagram: https://www.instagram.com/teresa_lacorazza/

YouTube: https://bit.ly/39jeIjh

CHAPTER 5

HEAL COMPLEX TRAUMA USING A BODY-BASED APPROACH

GO BEYOND TALK THERAPY TO RESOLVE PTSD

Cassandra Quick, MA, LPC, NCC

MY STORY

Moments of intense emotion or thoughts and a desire to do something to make ourselves feel better, even if it's not healthy, remind us what it's like to be alive. But life can get better, and the unhealthy coping mechanisms can happen less often. That is possible. This is my hope for you.

For the longest time, I wasn't happy. I wasn't healed and wasn't being real with myself in what I truly needed. I can gratefully say, I'm now living a life of authenticity and holistic health. For me, this path needed to include body-based interventions, most importantly trauma therapy and functional medicine. After a decade of healing my mind and body, the journey is still not complete and won't ever be. I still have down or bad days where I want to curl up in a ball under a million weighted blankets and not come out until morning, or maybe the day after. This is part of being human.

I'm on my way to Disney World, inside a full-to-the-brim airplane, flying to Florida with my family for a few days in the happiest place on Earth. This is a place of magic, princesses, princes, and pixie dust. My story, however, is focused on science, self-efficacy, and empowerment.

After all, healing is a journey, not a destination.

And if you haven't already realized, no prince or princess will come to save you. You are your own savior, and there is magic within you through the process of healing. It's a tough road, for sure, but the journey is worth every tear, panic attack, sleepless night, and nightmare. I'll teach you how to start to be curious and listen to your body to begin and deepen connections, insights, and conclusions to strengthen your healing.

Professionally, my focus with clients around 2010 was traditional talk therapy and CBT (Cognitive Behavior Therapy). Don't get me wrong; I'm not here to bash CBT. It's a very effective and empirically supported treatment according to researchers. It works and worked for my clients for years before I became enlightened to other mind-body approaches that worked even better. I had not yet been trained as a mindfulness practitioner or trauma therapist. I began to learn how powerful mindfulness was—and how powerful healing could be—when you pay attention to your body. More experienced colleagues raved about the effectiveness of meditation and mindfulness. They told me stories of using meditation in the 1970s and were the epitome of confident, calm, and inspirational humans. They also had 20 or more years on me as a therapist, so much more wisdom. Not until I started personally learning and practicing these interventions did I truly find the power within and start to share this with clients. This began the next healing phase for me. What I didn't realize at that point was my journey was about to be a painful one.

My self-proclaimed decade of healing truly began when my divorce was final in 2012. I didn't realize the immense impact traumatic experiences from my whole life had on my body, physically and mentally. I was a wreck from the more recent experiences and didn't really know it. Almost subsequently, my primary care doctor diagnosed me with hypothyroidism. I went into a flurry of online research to find out what was going on with my body. The research resulted in a long list of symptoms that could be associated with Hashimoto's Disease, an autoimmune disease associated with the thyroid. Not to be cliché, but I was sick and tired of being sick and tired.

I passionately advocated for additional testing for Hashimoto's with an endocrinologist. I had to argue with the "expert" for additional testing, giving him my long list of symptoms. He later called me with the results stating, "You were right. I was convinced you didn't have Hashimoto's because you don't have a goiter (or inflamed thyroid)." Furthermore, he reported I had normal thyroid levels and stated he wouldn't medicate me or offer any other treatments. This narrow view of symptoms and treatment remains a concern for me even today, with clients struggling with the same issues with "experts." I once again took the power into my own hands and went to see a functional medicine doctor. She helped me truly heal my body. This decision is a pivotal part of my story and a strong example of trusting your instincts, intuition, and listening to your body. How long had I had this disease without knowing it? How was it truly affecting my body and mind? Answer—profoundly.

After receiving this life-changing diagnosis, I decided to try the autoimmune protocol (AIP), per my functional medicine doctor, an elimination diet to examine your body's reaction to certain trigger foods to see if I could start to feel better. At that point, I struggled with migraines, weight gain and loss, trouble sleeping, anxiety, and depression. Seeing the immediate effects of a cleanse of my diet, I saw the benefit of starting to take better care of myself. My migraines resolved to the point that it's now very rare for me to get them, maybe twice a year, if that. I became strictly gluten-free and have been since. I started practicing yoga and pilates more regularly. I went further and hired a functional medicine doctor, who helped me discover food intolerances, adrenal fatigue, and other mineral and vitamin deficiencies.

I took the courageous step to start trauma therapy in my mid-30s, about five years after my divorce. I needed it much sooner, but now I realize I wasn't prepared for what was to come until this very moment in my life. I already had over ten years in the mental health profession, helping others with depression, anxiety, and trauma. Even therapists and trauma therapists can struggle with trauma. We're still human and may not realize certain thoughts, feelings, or behaviors are trauma-related. Denial is a strong defense mechanism and serves a purpose until that part of us is ready to dive deep into the unknown. We just go about our lives, frankly oblivious to our own internal strength and wisdom waiting to be discovered. Through therapy, I realized childhood trauma was the root of my anxiety and poor relationship choices as an adult. I was subconsciously repeating patterns of abuse and trauma in my adult relationships to try and fix what I couldn't for so long. I realized the reason for these patterns with the guidance of my therapist through EMDR (see EMDRIA.org for more information) and brainspotting.

For those with childhood and/or adult trauma, oftentimes, you've felt stuck, overwhelmed, and stagnant, not knowing what to do and where to go to get real help with sustainable results. Not only that, when you find someone like a therapist or doctor who is supposed to help, they really don't. You then think, *well, I tried* and give up. But then, you're back at square one.

I am here to tell you. . .

. . .PTSD or trauma is not a life sentence. It can be resolved and healed.

Your body is telling you something when you have that panic attack, want to retreat into your bed all day or find your mind going blank during stress. I'm living proof that PTSD can be healed if you're ready and willing to put in the work. Not everyone's journey is the same. Each of you will have a unique path with ebbs and flows along the way. Something has led you to this moment.

I challenge you to start exploring what your healing journey looks like when you're ready. Not when your BFF, mother-in-law, or random stranger tells you. Not even when a therapist tells you they recommend it. You can say no. It's your choice. Always. You will be your prince/princess charming and save the day when you are darn good and ready, whether that be today or in a few months or years. Being ready might not mean confidence. It could come with feeling scared and nervous. That's okay. With the right support squad around you, you can get through.

Trauma, especially complex trauma (multiple consecutive traumas with no resolve or compounding symptoms), takes time to heal. This can look like months or years in therapy, depending on the severity of the experiences. I've seen clients come to me after 20-30 years of talk therapy and decades of abuse and finally make significant breakthroughs, often completely healing PTSD or trauma symptoms after working with me. Body-based trauma therapy works.

When you make a choice to start healing, my first recommendation is to develop a plan to seek help with body-based interventions. Body-based approaches in your plan might include:

- Acupuncture
- Breathwork
- Chiropractic care
- Essential oils
- Functional or Integrative medicine
- Massage
- Mindfulness Meditation (specifically trauma-sensitive)
- Tapping or Emotional Freedom Technique
- Movement or exercise: stretching, running, walking, biking, swimming, strength training, etc.
- Reiki or energy work
- Yoga (specifically trauma-sensitive)

As you start to develop a basic plan, start to research finding a darn good trauma therapist trained in body-based trauma therapy, such as:

- EMDR (Eye Movement Desensitization Reprocessing)
- Brainspotting
- Somatic Experiencing
- Sensorimotor Therapy
- Biofeedback

Recommended qualities of a "kick trauma in the butt" kind of therapist:

- One who is not afraid to ask and tackle difficult questions with you. They may ask questions no other therapist has, but with your permission, go to depths you haven't before. We aren't talking surface level here. You might get uncomfortable or scared, but you will know this person has your back along the way. They will be able to tolerate your stories. You will not get a wide-eyed stare when you start to disclose details of your traumas.

- Someone with compassion and understanding. I would recommend someone who has been through tough experiences in their own lives. Most humans have. They don't necessarily have to disclose personal stories all the time, but they should have enough wisdom and life experience to be able to guide you in your journey.

- Now, this is a must: a great sense of humor. You will be discussing and experiencing some intense moments. All of that darkness needs a little light-hearted belly laughter. Maybe even someone a bit sweary. Giving you space to be your true self. To relax and be who you are, not what you think they want to see. Your body will start associating therapy with *Hey, this isn't so scary* and *This is not so bad.*

- Having body-based approaches as part of their arsenal to battle trauma. There are so many research-supported and effective trauma-sensitive approaches. Find a therapist that fits what you are looking for and what you're willing to explore.

Trauma therapy can be intense, but it doesn't have to be void of belly laughter and fun. Yes, I said fun. I'm blessed daily to laugh a lot with my clients. Sometimes to the point of tears. Good happy crocodile tears.

THE PRACTICE

This is when the real magic begins. You've come to this moment to start exploring yourself, your body, and its wisdom. You're making a choice to step into the unknown. Just know you are capable, strong, and resilient. You've been led here to start experiencing healing.

I will guide you through a Trauma-Sensitive Mindful Stretching Exercise. This exercise is intended for all bodies. It's a simple way to start to pay attention to your body in a safe way. Mindfulness is a part of this exercise. If you haven't ever practiced mindfulness, it's okay. Mindfulness is simply paying attention to something in the here and now on purpose. I will be guiding you on how to do this through the exercise. You may notice muscles, bones, tendons, and sensations in your nervous system and skin. You might notice you want to shake out or move other parts of your body in the practice. Even if you are an experienced marathon runner, bodybuilder, or yoga teacher, now is the time to slow down and pay attention. Traumatic experiences teach us to be disconnected, dissociate from emotions and body experiences, and avoid certain sensations, feelings, and thoughts. This practice will teach you to reconnect safely. You're in full control of this practice. You get to decide. You get to make choices. You could even make a choice to be in stillness and just read the exercise today. Whatever you choose, it's meant for this moment.

You can begin this exercise any time during the day, though I do recommend building a sense of predictability and routine by adding this into your schedule. You might want to set a timer on your phone to start practicing daily. This could be incorporated with a pre-or-post-workout regime or before a traditional yoga practice. Feel free to use any supportive tools necessary to make this as comfortable as possible. That might include using blankets, pillows, stretchy bands, yoga blocks, a yoga mat, fan, heater, etc. You might feel pain during this practice. If so, you're welcome to stop doing whatever it is that caused the pain and move to a different position. You'll notice I intentionally use invitational language and offer choices. There is a reason. The trauma didn't give us a choice. You will now be offered this choice every day you use this practice. You oversee how mindful and present you are, how much you stretch, what you choose to test, or how you choose to be in the moment.

After the practice, you could choose to continue stretching other parts of your body, you could choose to be still and quiet and incorporate meditation, or you could move into walking or a more strenuous workout of some kind. You can take the results or insights to a therapy session or your journal for deeper exploration into your subconscious mind. There is wisdom in your body. Be curious about what it's telling you. Beyond this practice, I invite you to start to notice the choices and options before you, where before, there were no or limited options. The benefits of the practice are intended to be generalized beyond the exercise itself.

You can access this exercise in audio and video form along with a visual of the Illuminate Blueprint on Cassandra's website at www.illuminatecounseling.org/blueprint

To begin,

I invite you to come to a position where your feet are on the ground, maybe sitting on a chair or couch. You may want to feel your spine supported by the back of a chair or pillows supporting the arch of your back. Your arms could be resting at the side of your legs or on the top of your thighs. You could start by stretching your hands. Balling your hands into a fist and squeezing gently or more intentionally, whichever you choose. Then you could release, noticing the sensations in your fingers, nails, and skin of the hands as you open the fist into flat palms. You may want to hyperextend the hands to get a deeper stretch.

I invite you to repeat this for a count of three, maybe even in tandem with an in and out breath. Feeling the coolness with the in-breath and warm air of the out-breath.

We could move on to the same sort of movement in your feet. Waking up a different part of the body. Again, you might want to squeeze the toes and hold for a count of three. Noticing the coolness of the in-breath and warm air of the out-breath. Upon taking the last out-breath, you might feel like fully releasing the toes and stretching them, so there is a lot of space between the toes, maybe even an arch in the foot for a count of three.

I invite you to start to move your midsection. You might want to incorporate your arms and legs as well. Oftentimes, we store nervousness, tension, and stress in our stomachs. You might want to start with small movements to more spacious movements. You may want to keep it slow and calm. Whatever you choose at this moment, I invite you to a sitting cat/cow pose. Arching your back like a cat would and "mooving" into a cow pose. That's an intentional bit of cheesy humor. Pun intended. You might want to breathe with the different movements. Again, you could slow this down or speed this up—your choice. I'm inviting you to breathe through a count of four, two cat and two cow poses. Noticing the stretch in your stomach or back muscles. You might even notice your hips want to move along with the stretch. Listen to what your body is telling you, and go with it.

Now, I invite you to incorporate different parts of the body in this stretch. It's a blend of many different muscle groups and body parts, all working together. I call this a whole-body mindful salutation.

This movement is in honor of you—your body and this moment. You may want to start by stretching out your legs, feeling the quads loosen, and then slightly tighten to support you in what you are about to do. Your arms could come loosely to the side of your body. You might, with one unified movement, begin the salutation by stretching the legs out, noticing the stomach muscles tightening to support your legs, and at the same time, lifting the arms to your side into the air. You might want to arch your back and look up to the sky. Whatever you choose to do right now is your choice. You could be looking straight ahead as you lift your arms.

You might want to check in on your breathing. You could start to move through this whole-body mindful salutation by breathing along with the stretch. I invite you to breathe along with me for a count of three. This could be an in-breath as you stretch out and an out-breath as you come back to the center. Noticing again the different muscles coming together to support you in whatever you choose to do at this moment.

Wherever you are now, I invite you to close this practice by placing your hands on your chest in what is called a thymus hold. The thymus is in the center of the chest. You may join me in deep breaths for a count of three. Maybe the deepest breaths you could take all day, and you could sigh in each out-breath, releasing anything that doesn't serve you.

Thank you for joining me in this practice and allowing me to hold space for you in your journey.

Cassandra N. Quick is a holistic psychotherapist, certified life coach, certified mindfulness practitioner, certified trauma-focused cognitive behavior therapist, certified EMDR clinician, emotional freedom technique and trauma-sensitive yoga trained clinician, creator of the Illuminate Blueprint, and founder and board president of the Illuminate Foundation, a Wisconsin based nonprofit serving business owner moms who've experienced trauma.

Helping others with mental health struggles has been her life's work and passion since 1999 as a sophomore at her local community college. Cassandra began her mental health career as an in-home therapist for children and teens with Autism and subsequently children and teens with severe mental health needs. She then joined a group private practice and later served as an outpatient therapist for a local hospital system.

After two decades in the mental health field and with the nudging of the pandemic and an ever-changing mode of delivery of therapy, in 2020, she started her private practice offering specialized trauma treatment via teletherapy. As a holistic psychotherapist, she guides and empowers women to heal after complex trauma by providing a transformational journey through the development of a unique Illuminate Blueprint using EMDR, EFT, trauma-sensitive yoga, and mindfulness.

What has motivated Cassandra to focus on this specialty is enduring childhood and adult traumas and healing through holistic interventions, which are now part of her Illuminate Blueprint. She has felt what it's like to suffer from PTSD and heal those symptoms, giving her a unique and compassionate perspective on serving clients who have been or are currently experiencing trauma.

Cassandra currently lives in Madison, Wisconsin, with her daughter, Makena, along with their dog, Morris, and cat, Chai. Her favorite things are shopping with her daughter, the gym, movie theatre, Thai food, popcorn, snuggling her pets, and travel. Her happy place is the beach.

Connect with Cassandra:

Website: www.illuminatecounseling.org

Email: illuminatecounselingllc@gmail.com

Facebook: https://www.facebook.com/cassandra.quick

CHAPTER 6

TAPOUT-TAPIN

FIND AND FIX MENTAL PATTERNS THAT ARE MAKING YOU SICK

Dr. Bonnie Juul, Expert in Wellness,
Health Restoration, and Healing

MY STORY

I can't breathe.

My back pressed into the corner as more bodies filled the small space. The mix of cologne, perfume, and hairspray hung heavy in the air. My chest tightened, breath quickened. I focused on trying to take deep breaths—the chattering voices faded. Darkness started closing in around my eyes. I needed out.

Oh crap. What's happening? I'm just in a freaking elevator.

The floor jostled under me as it settled on the eighth floor. *We only went down one floor. Are you kidding me?* Blood rushed to my head. *I don't have time for this. Shit.*

The lively crew shuffled out. *Thank you, God.* Only one other person left. I stared up at his broad shoulders, facing away from me. Blond hair. Thinning. My shoulders relaxed. Still a tight chest, but I could do this. The doors started closing. *You've got this.*

The doors stopped mid-close, then started jostling back and forth with a whirring sound. Another blood rush to my head. *Screw it; I'm outta here.* I stepped forward.

The man blocked my exit as he reached for the doors, his tone comforting, "Don't worry. I can fix this." He yanked and pulled until they closed. He stood up even straighter and pressed the first-floor button.

I was frozen in mid-western politeness, barely choking out, "That's great!" *If they got stuck when open, they could certainly get stuck closed,* my mind yelled. I forced my shoulders back and put a calm smile on my face. *Shit.*

The doors opened again on the seventh floor. *You've got to be kidding me.* I exited, heading to the stairwell. It was narrow and dark. "Nope. Not doing that."

I was trapped on the seventh floor. The conference would begin soon, and somehow I'd have to get back up to my room afterward. I observed my body freaking out while taking a clinical note of how irrational it was and applying the emotional and mental work I knew to do. Something new had happened since I had last been in a hotel over a year ago. I had to figure out what it was and fix the darn thing.

Numerous full elevators came and went. I waved them on, a calm smile forced on my face. When the doors closed, I resumed pacing and using the tools I had in my toolbox. They were barely working. Eventually, a fairly empty elevator opened. Someone I knew greeted me. Comforted by her warm smile, I stepped in next to her. "I'm having a panic attack," I whispered. "I got stuck." She gently squeezed my hand until we reached the first floor.

At the conference, I sat in the back and stared blankly at the presenter as I did my inner work. This needed to be handled.

MY REFLECTIONS AND WHAT I DISCOVERED

About a year before this conference, my 90-something-year-old dad went to our small-town hospital for hip surgery. He was in the recovery room, laughing and flirting with the nurses. One was checking his vitals. His voice started slurring. I watched the side of his mouth drop, and a rising horror grew in my chest at the realization that he was having an active stroke. Everyone jumped into action. A medivac was called. It was full-on adrenaline.

I went from being relieved that the surgery went well to being confused, scared, and on high alert. It was in that moment and the following two weeks of constant change in an even larger hospital that my subconscious was taking extensive notes of my thoughts and emotions while relating them to the external environment. New emotional and thought patterns were being imprinted into my nervous system, the strength of my emotions weaving them together into a strong anchor.

Fast forward to staying in the hotel for the conference. My subconscious recognized the hotel as an environment similar to the hospital, bringing forth the related thoughts and emotions. As I sat in the back of the conference room, allowing them to come up and releasing them, EMBeR (Emotional and Mental Balancing and Repatterning) was unfolding.

The emotional and mental imprints were intricately looped and interconnected, keeping the patterns locked in the body, anchored, and ready to play out. I needed results that were simple, powerful, effective, and fast.

Some imprints were significant, and some insignificant. Some in the physical plane, some in the energetic plane, and some overlapping both planes. The subconscious perceived them as traumatic.

- Physical plane, significant: physical abuse, car accident, witnessing health trauma of a loved one (like stroke).

- Energetic plane, significant: verbal assault, controlling, out of control, un-affirming, gaslighting, watching someone die.

- Physical plane, insignificant: tripping over a sidewalk crack unexpectedly, sleeping in a hospital waiting room.

- Energetic plane, insignificant: watching violent movies that show significant physical or energetic traumas, participating in gossip that puts down the subject of the gossip, walking down a hallway while filled with fear.

When the event happened, the *mental and emotional imprints* were reactionary and not logical. The mental imprint created a neurological mental pattern in the brain, as explained by Hebbian theory: "Neurons that fire together, wire together." The emotion felt during the event is then trapped in the energetic field within or around the body and its organs.

The more intense the emotion, the deeper the imprints. It often shows up as a sweeping negative statement as *I hate you,* or a directive like: *I can't trust anyone. You're never going to amount to anything. You deserve this (to suffer). Stay quiet. Don't speak. Eat all you can now. It's not safe.*

When the subconscious recognizes an environment as familiar to the original traumatic event, a similar response or expression of the imprints occurs. The emotional imprint loops with the mental imprint as a protective mechanism to try and make sure that you are ready for the subconsciously perceived dangerous situation you're in. The irony is that when the situation changes and you aren't truly in danger, the imprint still gets activated.

By identifying the mental and the emotional imprints, separately and together, the imprints can be unlocked, released, and changed.

THE PRACTICE

ABOUT BALANCING AND REPATTERNING

The process for emotional and mental balancing and repatterning is to release and replace the imprints. When an imprint is released, a void is created. The void will fill with what was just released unless it's given a new option.

The first step is to handle the mental imprints. When the mental imprint is recognized and released, a new imprint is introduced and reinforced to give the body a different choice.

Mental imprints can be recognized by comments you say to yourself or comments others tell you about yourself that are critical or unsupportive. The imprint is in the body initially to create security and safety, so the body needs to know it's safe to change the imprint. If it doesn't believe it's safe, any introduction of a positive statement will be interpreted by your body as a lie, and your body will cling to the original statement for security and safety.

Recognizing the mental imprint is different than discussing it. Every time you discuss, explore, ponder, replay in your mind, explain, or defend the experience related to the mental imprint, it grooves in deeper. Every time you tell yourself or someone else your story, the imprint grooves in deeper and becomes more ingrained as part of your identity.

When you identify imprints and release them, they lose their place in your neurological system and release their hold on your identity. This creates a void that you can fill with something you want. If you don't fill the void, the path of least resistance allows the neurons to realign themselves and return.

By giving yourself a new statement or a new thought, you weaken the neurons to the old pattern as you strengthen the new ones. If you begin to discuss, explore, ponder, play in your mind, explain and defend the new mental imprint, it grooves in deeper. Every time you tell someone your *new* story, the new neuron connections groove in deeper, offering you an opportunity to create a new experience in your life.

THREE FOUNDATIONAL IDEAS ARE IMPORTANT WHEN WORKING WITH THIS PROCESS

1. You and your body experience two distinct yet intertwined consciousnesses. You are not your body.

2. Your body is always looking out for you. When it trusts you, it's subservient to your will. When it doesn't trust you, it takes control of your actions. Have you ever sworn you wouldn't eat something, and next thing you know, you ate it? That's the subconscious taking over and not trusting you. The trust comes from consistent, loving actions and truth.

3. Your body is like a young child or a puppy. It's eager to please and will do what you want—*when it feels safe and trusts you.* If it doesn't trust you, it will run around and do its own thing. It needs to be fed and nurtured in the way *it* needs. The only way to know what it needs is to listen to it and respectfully respond.

Your body tells you it isn't getting what it needs in the form of aches, pains, anxiety, depression, fear, and other emotions.

You can use the processes in EMBeR to understand, communicate with, honor, and support your body with kindness and love.

THE IMPORTANCE OF KINDNESS AND LOVE IN RELATING TO YOURSELF AND YOUR BODY

Dr. Masaru Emoto did experiments with water and, later, with rice. With the rice experiment, one jar of rice had hate directed at it, one was ignored, and one had love directed at it.

The one that was ignored slowly got moldy and old. The one that experienced hate got worse quickly. The one that was loved continued to look quite good.

In the water experiment, the patterns of the water crystals that had hate directed at them looked disjointed and irregular. The water crystals that had love directed at them had beautiful patterns.

Your body is largely made up of around 50% water. Thoughts and emotions that are of a lower vibration will affect your body negatively. Just like those of a higher vibration will affect your body positively.

Seeking out and investigating these pockets of trauma allows you to release emotions locked in your body in a similar energetic frequency as hate. Some of the pockets may *be* hate. So, can you imagine what that can do to your body if you find the imprinted emotions and mental patterns at the level of hate in your body and release them?

Repatterning your mental imprints is easier when you approach the process with patience, kindness, and love. The body responds to effort, so give yourself credit for your effort. Being unloving towards yourself may be a pattern for you as well, so give yourself credit for your effort. There is flow and relaxation with these that allow for more movement and change. The energy of fighting or force puts up some resistance even as you try to make the change. It may feel counterintuitive at first, so just trust the process.

TAPOUT-TAPIN

Within the EMBeR process, the mental imprints are changed with TapOut-TapIn. To put it simply, you tap out the bad and tap in the good. Often this alone will also shift the emotional imprint.

The beauty of TapOut-TapIn is that it's simple and can be done anywhere at any time, and no one is the wiser. You can use it in the car, in class, or in line at the grocery store.

TAPOUT

1. Pick one statement.

   Observe and identify your thought pattern. It's best if it's raw and ugly.

   Example: Melissa is overweight. To her doctor, she says, "I want to lose a few pounds. I know I'm overweight." But, when she gets real with herself, she knows she's mean, but she hasn't paid too much attention to how she talks to herself. She starts listening to her self-talk. She looks in the mirror and catches herself: "You're a disgusting, fat cow."

2. TapOut three times.

   Tap three times while turning up the volume on the emotion related to your statement.

   Tap the tips of two fingers together gently. I use my thumb and middle finger, but any finger combination will work.

   The TapOut statement is borrowed from the emotional freedom technique: "Even though I. . .I deeply and completely accept myself." Accepting yourself is the act of loving yourself as you are and as you are not. Any inclination to change the TapOut statement is your subconscious trying to control the outcome and prevent change.

   Example: Melissa taps the tips of her thumb and middle finger together: "Even though I am a disgusting fat cow, I deeply and completely accept myself." She repeats this three times.

3. Deep breath.

   A deep breath allows the body to relax and release.

   Relax your shoulders and inhale into your belly. Then exhale forcefully by pulling your belly into your spine with the clear intention of removing the statement. Do this one to three times.

Example: Melissa keeps tapping, takes a deep breath in, and exhales forcefully.

TAPIN

1. Pick one goal statement.

   This statement may be the opposite of the phrase you use for TapOut.

   Example: Melissa chooses the phrase "Be thin." She thought about choosing "Lose weight," but losing weight is a process, not an end goal. The goal of losing weight is to be thin.

2. TapIn the safety release three times.

   "Even though it's not safe for me to (insert goal statement), I deeply and completely accept myself."

   By tapping in this way, you'll release the belief that it's unsafe to achieve your goal. This will allow you to TapIn the new, empowering statement without it being perceived as a lie.

   Example: Melissa taps the tips of her thumb and middle finger together: "Even though it's not safe for me to be thin, I deeply and completely love and accept myself." She repeats this three times.

   > When you have been working on an issue for years, there is often a perceived safety concern that has yet to be addressed in your subconscious.

3. Deep breath.

   Take a deep belly breath in and forcefully exhale. Do this one to three times.

   Relax your shoulders and inhale into your belly. Then exhale forcefully with the clear intention of removing the statement.

   Example: Melissa keeps tapping, takes a deep breath in, and exhales forcefully.

4. TapIn your new statement as safe.

When tapping in a new statement, your body will not manifest something that it perceives as a lie.

If your weight is heavier than you want it to be, then it's important that you do not tap in "I'm thin." Your body will perceive it as a lie. Instead, you can choose one of the following:

"It is safe for me to be thin." Or, "I am becoming thinner and thinner every day."

Example: Melissa taps in, "It's safe for me to be thin." She isn't becoming thinner and thinner every day. Right now, she hasn't even chosen a diet. Once she starts seeing results, she will begin tapping that she is becoming thinner and thinner every day."

To get a visual example of this process, go to www.TapOut-TapIn.com.

EMOTIONAL IMPRINT REPATTERNING

Once the mental imprint has been balanced and repatterned, you can work on related emotional imprints ready to leave. When you do this process on yourself, your body is protective enough to never let you go deeper than what is safe for you to handle.

To get a free report on how to do emotional imprint repatterning, you can visit my resource page or go to www.QuantumEIR.com

MUSCLE TESTING AND EMBER

Muscle testing is a natural biofeedback method that bypasses the analytical mind and taps into the superconscious mind linked to the energetic fields in and around you. If you know how to muscle test, you can confirm each of the statements as the best statement for your being or your body. This is done by making the statement out loud and getting a "Yes" response from the body.

Muscle testing is used to identify and release mental and emotional imprints stuck within different parts of your body. This is useful for chronic health and musculoskeletal issues. When all the right lifestyle changes have been made, these imprints can be resolved or significantly improved in one session with EMBeR.

To learn more about how to muscle test yourself, get immediate access to free instructions at www.MuscleTestingBasics.com

Other resources are available at:
www.DrBonnieJuul.com/ChapterResources

Dr. Bonnie Juul is an expert in wellness, health restoration, and healing. She has advanced training in advanced muscle testing techniques, nutrition, emotional healing, aging, and longevity. She earned her doctor of chiropractic from Parker University in Dallas, Texas.

She has practitioner training and experience in nutrition response testing, emotional freedom technique, the Journey, PsychK, neuro-emotional technique, Reiki, wholistic kinesiology, body energetic technique, and yoga for chakra opening.

Her educational background includes a bachelor of science degree in health and wellness and a bachelor of science in anatomy.

She is the founder of quantum response technique, quantum response testing, and EMBeR, or Emotional and Mental Balancing and Repatterning.

Her vision is to shift the paradigm of health from disease management to one of longevity and vitality with a respect for and understanding of innate wisdom and personal choice.

Her practice is based in St. Louis, Missouri, and Carbondale, Illinois.

Connect with Bonnie:

Website: www.naturalhealthwins.com and www.drbonniejuul.com

Facebook: www.facebook.com/drbonniejuul

LinkedIn: www.linkedin.com/in/drbonniejuul

Instagram: www.instagram.com/drbonniejuul

Podcast: Health Freedomism with Dr. Bonnie Juul

CHAPTER 7

MUSCLE TESTING AND SOMATIC CLEARING

CLARITY FOR PEAK PERFORMANCE

Mariah Rossel, M.Ed., LPC

MY STORY

I had my dream job working in psychedelic psychotherapy. I worked tirelessly for nearly a decade to be doing what I loved with amazing coworkers. And then I dropped everything to move to Bali.

Let me rewind a bit.

I loved watching my clients transform quickly in massive ways.

Then, I took a week off to pray deeply in South Dakota, followed by working only half days for a week as I assisted in Spiral training. The Spiral is an internationally accredited complementary therapy that allows us to quickly find early emotional entanglements and clear them out just as rapidly. I like to say that it's like 20 years of therapy in eight weeks.

"It's really hard to schedule clients for you when you're always gone," our administrative assistant remarked.

But it's this work I'm doing that makes me skilled professionally. I protested in my head.

This is the work that taught me how to hold space for people in altered states.

If it hadn't been for all my spiritual and healing work, I wouldn't have a clue how to approach clients in these deep states.

I wish taking clients through the Spiral was within the scope of practice of my clinical license.

Psychedelic therapy is changing the face of therapy and the world, and I am so grateful to be here.

I was being faced with a deep question about client care. I was being pulled in two different directions. The Spiral wasn't in the scope of practice under my license. And, doing psychedelic therapy required me to work under my license and that of a doctor. The intensity of the therapy and the acuity of their conditions meant that they scheduled as soon as they were ready, and I saw them two to four times a week for three weeks.

I love this work, and I love the spiritual path I'm on, and it feels unfair to my clients to be devoted to both.

Without my continued personal work, I won't be as effective as a therapist.

I feel like I have to choose between my spiritual path and my clients.

While I was in grad school, I met Leah Ardent, who eventually became my business partner soon after we met. So, I was running my own business and doing therapy. After a venue-searching trip to Bali, where we had both fallen in love with the majestic culture, the ever-present jovial sounds of the gamelan, the hot, humid, tropical weather, and the joy of the Balinese people, we said we wanted to move to Bali. However, I wasn't ready to leave the career I had worked nearly a decade to get.

And then the pandemic happened.

In-person therapy was increasingly difficult and risky.

Psychedelic therapy wasn't covered by insurance and is quite expensive, so client numbers ebbed and flowed, which was difficult financially.

There were major Black Lives Matter protests blocks from our house, and we were on curfew.

At the same time, Leah was seriously looking to relocate to Bali just as soon as she could find a way in the middle of the pandemic with the borders closed.

My supervisor always told me that I was going to have to pick, that I had too many strong paths, and I never believed him. Is this the moment?

Am I ready to walk away from everything I have worked for?

After seeing so many trauma therapy clients, I was a bit disheartened in the world. Rarely did my clients come to me because of an accident or as a result of an "act of God." They came to me because someone else hurt them.

So, while I was making huge changes in the lives of my individual clients, the causes of their trauma were not changing. Certainly, as we did the work together, their relationships changed, and the environment where their children were raised changed. However, we still live in a world where people hurt and abuse other people.

Helping people on the healing journey from trauma didn't seem like enough. I knew I needed to help birth a new paradigm where people didn't even have the thought of hurting other people enter their consciousness.

Part of that does still come from trauma therapy. Hurt people do hurt people. We do pass on our patterns. When we've been traumatized, our nervous system seeks safety. What might classically be called dysfunction due to trauma is actually the nervous system responding; however, it knows how to respond to maintain its safety. All intelligence is self-preserving.In this attempt to self-preserve, behaviors and patterns that seem maladaptive in a healthy setting are developed in the name of self-preservation.

Part of that does come from better communication and having healthier relationships. Humans are inherently social creatures, and when we have misaligned relationships, it's indicative of both a lack of skill in communication and a lack of personal awareness.

There are probably a million other things that play a part in how we collectively co-create our reality. We are all-powerful manifestors. We each play a part in birthing the reality we all live in. However, it's important to remember that the reality we create is based on how well we know ourselves, each other, and our attachments to our egos (which have their own self-preservation techniques).

It's through witnessing the world around us that we can easily see our own misalignments because our energetic field will attract exactly what we are. However, what is attracting is our subconscious. By clearing out the emotional entanglements in our subconscious, our world shifts, and things happen with more ease.

Someone is struggling with their mom, and we clear on it. Suddenly, she calls for the first time in eight years.

A client can't figure out how to make six figures. We do the spiral. Within a couple of months, their business is booming.

I wanted to install a new archetype to help me up-level my business, so I cleared on what I admired and abhorred about it, and within a few months, I'm fully embodying that archetype.

I was being triggered by the virgin and the whore paradigm, so I cleared on it to step into my sensual empowerment.

I had pain, so I cleared on the emotions there, and my chronic pain shifted.

I'm angry with someone, and so I clear on it, and my anger is transmuted into love and understanding.

I feel indecisive. I clear on the emotions around it, and suddenly I have clarity and direction.

I wanted a change in my body, so I cleared on it, and my body shape drastically changed.

While each of these shifts feels very personal, they have shifted how I show up in my business and the work I do for my clients, and so this work ripples out instantaneously and shifts the entanglements everyone is having with these same ideas.

When we shift how we see things, this new perspective ripples out, especially if we're using that new perspective in how to run our business or build a movement.

I left psychedelic therapy because I wanted to reach more people and help them shift their consciousness as we collectively birth a new paradigm. I saw that the most effective way to do that was through emotional clearing and group work.

THE PRACTICE

The spiral is an internationally accredited modality that takes people on a journey to clear all entanglements to 22 core emotions to help them increase their consciousness and fully step into purpose.

While the methodology behind the spiral is simple, part of what practitioners receive in training is attunements to specific frequencies. While it's possible to take yourself through the Spiral, I recommend that you're taken through the spiral by a practitioner. After having spiraled hundreds of people and assisted in many practitioner certification trainings, I still prefer to have other people take me through the levels to get to the core of the patterns I cannot see in myself.

The first step to doing the spiral is to learn emotional clearing. This is one of my daily practices and something you can learn to do for yourself to maintain good energetic hygiene.

HOW TO MUSCLE TEST

There are many methods of muscle testing. For the purposes of this course, we will be using our fingers.

Make a loop with your finger and thumb of both hands and connect them.

Keep one hand solid, and the other hand is your working hand where your fingers will either "hold" or "break."

A "hold" will mean that the fingers stay interconnected.

A "break" will mean that the fingers of the working hand will break, and the hands will disconnect.

Photos with examples and a video showing how to muscle test are available on my resources page at https://acutalizationagency.com/holisticmentalhealth

QUESTIONS FOR BEGINNERS

To build your confidence, start with very simple questions to which you already know the answers. Try these questions to start with:

My name is. . .

I live. . .

I like. . .

My children's names are. . .

My parents' names are. . .

The room is [pick a color].

My phone is [pick a color].

I believe [something you believe].

I believe [something that disgusts you]

MUSCLE TESTING FOR YOUR LIFE

Once you get comfortable with muscle testing, now you can apply it to all areas of your life and your decision-making. Remember that muscle testing is simply your body talking to you; we're just taking your ego out of it, so it's easier for you to get the information your unconscious already knows.

When you first start out, pick things that have very low risk. This will develop the communication between your mind and your body. This is also a vital step in developing trust in yourself and in the modality. Remember, the modality is simply offering another way for you to know what your body already knows about you.

Try some of these scenarios to go deeper with your muscle testing:

Pick out two or more outfits that would be appropriate to wear to an event. And, test based on one of these questions:

Which makes me feel most confident?

Which makes me feel sexiest?

Which makes me look most professional?

Which necklace is a more powerful statement?

When you are deciding where to go for dinner, pick a couple of restaurants or cuisines and test one or more of these questions:

Which would make me feel most satisfied?

Which has the upbeat ambiance I am desiring?

Which feels like the most fun?

When you are at the restaurant, pick a few menu items that sound delicious and ask a question to decide on which food to order:

What is my body craving?

What will leave me the most satisfied?

Which will taste the yummiest?

When deciding on a movie to watch, pick a couple of selections that sound interesting and ask:

Which will I find most funny?

Which will lift up my mood?

Which will I enjoy the most?

NOTE: It is easiest to pick one question per scenario. These are just some ideas of questions that may help you decide on the exact aspect you want to decide based upon.

THE POWER OF INTENTION

Intention is a major part of muscle testing. Start with the intention that there will be one thing you'll get a yes to if you're making a decision. You only get to wear one outfit, eat one dinner, and watch one movie at a time. So, one of the things you are deciding on will be better than the others for this specific instance.

Remember to take your ego out of it. There will always be another opportunity to do other things. And, if there isn't, then worrying about what you didn't get to do takes away from the joy of being present for what it is you did get to do.

ANSWERING DEEPER QUESTIONS WITH MUSCLE TESTING

Now that you have the basics of muscle testing down and you trust yourself, it's time to take your work one step deeper into your subconscious. This phase of the work is when we really start looking at ourselves and what is stopping us from living the lives we desire.

ASKING GOOD QUESTIONS

The answer to a question is only as good as the question itself. So, we want to ensure that we ask good questions because we will be given the answers that we ask for.

To get to a good question, start with the end in mind.

What is it that you really want?

Why do you want it?

How will it change your life to have it?

What will it feel like to have it?

What are you conscious about that is standing between you and having it?

If you're not where you want to be, there is something holding you back. Because once you're aligned to what you want, you'll have it. By looking at the space between where we are and where we want to be, we can see what in our unconscious is holding us back and clear it out.

USING AN EMOTIONS CHART

There are many different emotions charts you can use. You can find an emotions chart on my resources page at:

https://actualizationagency.com/holisticmentalhealth

Once you have figured out what it is you want to detangle, say, for instance, fear of success, the next step is to ask yourself a question like, "What emotion is keeping me in my fear of success?" Again, remember that you intended to only have one emotion that would collapse the entire pattern.

To find the emotion in the chart, break it down into chunks. This is one of the reasons I love the five elements chart.

The first test you will do is on the elements. Is the emotion you're looking for in fire, earth, metal, water, wood, central or governing?

Next, test which organ the emotion is in within that element. For instance, if you tested that the emotion was in metal, you test to see if it's in the list of lung or large intestine.

Finally, go down the list of emotions to figure out which emotion is the one that is keeping you stagnant.

GET SOMATIC! FEELING THE FEELINGS

Once you have identified the emotion, it's time to get out of your head and into your body. As we have discussed, the mind is a reflection of what is going on in the body, and the body is a reflection of what is going on in the mind. We know that trauma is stored in the body. So, by clearing a pattern out of the body, we also clear it out of the mind.

Take a moment and feel the feeling that you have tested for. Now, feel how that feeling is blocking you from what the initial query was or how it is keeping you stuck in your undesired feeling.

Really feel into the feeling.

Where is it located?

What color is it?

What temperature is it?

Does it have a texture?

Feel into the feeling, activate it, and amplify it so much that you can't stand it and are ready to clear it out of your system.

NOTE: If the feeling is cold or numb, tread lightly as this can be a sign of repressed trauma. This may be something that is better dealt with using the support of a professional.

CLEARING

"By removing the interference in the body, the body has the innate ability to heal itself." – Marty Johnson, DHM, Owner of Total Health Nutrition Center

Once you have identified the emotion that is entangled and keeping you stuck and felt the feeling, you can clear the energy of the feeling out of the body.

DO NOT TRY TO CLEAR THIS WITH YOUR MIND!

When we try to untangle these energies by thinking about them, we get stuck in the stories that got us stuck in the first place. By feeling the feelings in the body, you can clear them out without getting entangled in the story.

There are many routes to clearing, and there is no better one than another; it's just what works best for you.

My favorite method of clearing is by using the Emotional Stress Release (ESR) points. These points are located on your forehead, about halfway between your eyebrows and your hairline.

There is a photo of this hand position on my resources page at https://acutalizationagency.com/holisticmentalhealth.

Lightly place your fingers on these points. I use my thumb and ring finger, but you could use any two fingers that feel comfortable to you. By using the ESR points, you bring blood flow to the prefrontal cortex of the brain and stimulate relaxation of the thinking mind; this allows you to release the entanglement.

Take a big breath and release.

Feel the entangled energy leave your body in whatever way it wants to spontaneously release. That could be yawning, burping, farting, vomiting, yelling, seeing black smoke come out your mouth, etc.

Let everything be welcome.

Allow any movement or sound that wants to come.

When you feel a shift, the work has begun, and your need to consciously do the work is done.

Release the points on your forehead, breathe into the shift, and allow your energy to flow differently.

Mariah Rossel, M.Ed., is the co-founder of Shamelessly Successful Actualization Agency, where they specialize in messaging, business strategy, and visibility for transformational practitioners. She spent 15 years in wellness coaching, massage therapy, and professional counseling before making the transition to working with high-performing transformational entrepreneurs. She also has 15 years of experience in small business startups and renewable energy. Having started her first business at 18, she brings nearly 20 years of experience in starting and growing businesses both online and in-person. Having taken hundreds of people through the spiral and helped dozens of clients make their first six-figure years, she knows how to help you align your energetic body to your message so you can share your magic with the world and create ripples of change.

Her daily mission is to help fellow entrepreneurs step deeply into their leadership roles and increase their efficacy by doing what they do best and delegating the rest, so their message impacts the most people. She's forthright and has a high-risk tolerance, which has made her journey places few have gone. She loves sharing tales of her travels, journeys into the mystery, and experiences with magick. She believes that by each of us telling our stories, we'll change the world. And that it's through subtle but persistent change that large shifts will occur.

When Mariah chills out, you'll find her singing and dancing in the community, hiking a mountain, SCUBA diving, or sipping coconuts on the beach. And, you may not be able to find her because she lives by the motto of "Have passport, will travel."

Connect with Mariah:

Website: https://www.ActualizationAgency.com or www.ThisisRichcraft.com or www.mariahrossel.com

LinkedIn: https://www.linkedin.com/in/mariahrossel/

Facebook: https://www.facebook.com/mariah.rossel

Instagram: https://www.Instagram.com/mariahrossel/

CHAPTER 8

GETTING BACK ON THE HORSE

HOW TO KNOW WHEN IT'S RIGHT TO STEP AWAY FROM OR LEAN INTO FEAR

Anita Buzzy Prentiss, Photographer, Storyteller, Educator

MY STORY

We were cantering in the arena, and the horse tripped and fell hard and fast to his knees. I rode through trips many times as an experienced equestrian, but this one was different. It happened so fast I was flung into the air before landing on my shoulder and head. I knew immediately this was a big deal, and something was broken. I wasn't sure if I should move, but I slowly came to a kneeling position and felt a bone sticking out in a weird way. My collarbone was broken.

My horse scrambled up, shook the dirt off, and ran away, stirrups flying. He was fine. I was in shock, and the pain was mind-numbing.

I was rushed to the hospital in an ambulance. I had surgery and needed a metal plate with five screws to hold my clavicle together; it was broken in multiple places. Luckily my head was okay. My helmet prevented me from having even worse injuries.

After months of grueling physical therapy, I knew I had to get back on the horse.

I was shaking like a leaf.

My voice trembled.

I knew I needed to get back on, and once I was up there, I knew I needed to get back off.

I knew I needed a break—to leave the thing I love so much.

I didn't need to push through or prove anything to anyone.

I knew I was done for now. I was pushing, trying, and making it work for too long, pretending everything was okay. But I had lost the joy—of riding a horse that wasn't a good match for me. I knew this for a while before the accident. I felt completely out of touch with my reason for riding horses and needed separation and space for understanding. I felt like I couldn't think clearly. Every cell in my body told me to step away, so I had to listen. The memory of my fall and how shaky, weak, confused, and anxious I felt when I tried to ride again was what made my decision. My inner voice was saying, *just step away for a while.*

This time in my life was incredibly sad. I loved horses so much, and they brought an immense amount of joy to my life! I had gotten away from the initial reason I loved being around horses. I was too caught up in riding in horse shows, winning ribbons, switching around to different horses and barns, driving around town training with so many different trainers, competing, and searching for something I wasn't finding. What was it?

I was missing out on the loving connection I felt with my first horse many years ago. Her name was Midnight. I used to love just spending time with her. I would daydream about petting her soft, pretty, black mane, the wonderful smell of being at the barn, the crunch of her hooves as we rode through leafy trails in autumn, walking through a field on a beautiful day, listening to her peacefully munch hay, feeling the love between us as I threw my arms around her neck and hugged her as my heart glowed! I felt like crying as I remembered this distant memory of the simple things and how far I'd come from my initial joy of being around horses. My forced sabbatical was filled with many daydreams that turned into tears. Would I ever feel that kind of love again?

This grief and confusion in my emotions came into my body deeply and turned into chronic migraines, blocked business growth, and depression. I felt like I was painted into a corner and didn't know how to get out. It felt like I had lost my joy and didn't know how to get it back. I was so scared to go back to riding because I was afraid I would get hurt or that I would, once again, get swept up in my competing mentality.

What now? What else makes me happy?

Watching performers at Cirque du Soleil on the silks gave me goosebumps. The combination of daring feats, bravery, freedom, strength, power, and control balanced with gracefulness—like riding a horse! *Could I do that?* But I was scared to death of being upside down or even having both feet off the ground!

Facing this fear with curiosity and playfulness, I knew I needed to get out of my head and into my body in a creative way that didn't involve horses (yet). I started going to an antigravity class on silk hammocks. My fear of heights and being upside down led to initial misery! I got nauseated and dizzy during class and sometimes spent time in the bathroom slapping my face with cold water to help myself feel better, especially after the first time I hung upside down! I felt exhausted for the rest of the day, but something kept bringing me back. There was this nice tingle of excitement and fun after every class—a little dose of danger—but the feeling that I could conquer my fear and get a little stronger every time made me smile. The biggest thing that brought me back was that I felt safe there.

Each class got a little bit easier! Baby steps. The teacher and the people in the class were so supportive and clapped for every tiny improvement I made. Celebration for each small win. There were some parts of class I completely couldn't do, but I would just watch and think *maybe I would do that someday!* The dizziness and nausea went away eventually, and my intuition was telling me: *Maybe this is just what I needed to get stronger and more compassionate with my self-confidence, not pushing, but rather with gentleness, patience, and in small steps.*

Instead of running from my uncomfortableness, I stuck with it. I leaned into it and asked, *what is this trying to teach me?* When I would think about horses, I still felt so scared. I wasn't ready to try again yet. *Would it ever be possible to get back on a horse?* I imagined it in my mind one day, and instead of feeling dread in the pit of my stomach, I started to get those butterflies of excitement again. I knew I could do it when I was ready!

Trusting my body's cues that I wanted to go back to this antigravity class helped me understand that I was doing the right thing—trusting my body cues, working through my fear, and growing stronger. I felt like I was slowly getting back in touch with myself in a deep yet gentle way.

During the pandemic, the studio shut down, so I sadly stopped going to class and decided to get my own silks at home. I got comfortable on my own silks and just had fun with them! I hung around with my daughters laughing and playing together or just laid in the hammock listening to relaxing music. I felt comfy and safe there. When I finally went back to the class, I was able to do all the things I was so afraid to do before! I felt such calm confidence. I left the studio and felt like skipping down the street, feeling like such a super badass!

At the same time, I got myself out of my corner in other areas of my life. I learned that by facing one of my worst fears—hanging upside down—and working through it, making friends with it instead of pushing or forcing it, I increased my confidence and felt empowered. My business grew, my art became more inspired, and I created my first two books! I felt more compassionate, clear, and honest towards myself and in my relationships. I don't think this was just a coincidence; this was a true connection. All of a sudden, I felt so much more in tune, and I could feel this empowerment in all areas of my life.

Because I overcame these fears and turned them into something that felt familiar and safe, I was able to start thinking about horses again. *Could I return and be sincere with my boundaries? Could I find the right horse to ride, take it slow, speak up for myself and make choices that make sense for me so that I don't end up getting hurt again? Maybe I could make a horse friend, enjoy my time with them and not end up pushing and striving and becoming all weird again.*

KNOWING WHEN TO STEP AWAY AND WHEN TO TURN TOWARD A CHALLENGE IS A KEY MOMENT

The answer lies in my body's cues. There is a big difference between the butterflies in my tummy, which I feel when I'm curious to try something that feels dangerous yet fun, scared yet excited and the sense of dread saying, *don't do this—this is bad for you, walk away!* Which feels like a thud in the pit of my stomach.

There are no guarantees in life, but I know I'm ready to start slowly as I climb back in the saddle this time. I know to be patient and compassionate with what feels right to me and not let my ego get in the way. No more striving towards goals that don't mean anything to me, pushing too hard, or trusting trainers to tell me what to do instead of listening to my instincts to guide the way.

I'm looking for a soul-filled situation that brings back the initial joy of simple, early days of communicating with horses and feeling good about the whole experience. To feel safe even while in a challenging situation is a wonderful feeling, and I want to feel that way when I am with horses.

I am a work in progress.

I am ready to get back on the horse.

The very day I started thinking of this possibility, I saw a post from a barn that needed "Experienced riders for their lesson horses," and I felt like my name should have been printed there in capital letters. It was time! I realized at that moment that if I focused on my fear and ignored my joy for another day (and never rode again), I would be heartbroken for the rest of my life.

Knowing what's a little scary and what's just plain wrong for you, when to work through the fear, and when to step away is a huge turning point as an adult when you need to continually choose what's best for you.

I learned that if I feel scared to death but also intrigued and excited about something, that means *do it!* The opposite is if you feel dread. I'm practicing tuning into my body and feeling these cues deeply, and not ignoring them so that I can make good decisions. I see it as a compassionate connection with myself, a lot like parenting a child.

When I was a mom at the playground with my young daughters, if one fell or something went wrong, I would suggest getting up and trying again after a little hug, *or* I'd give them the option of being done if they were really hurt or upset. Whatever felt right at that moment.

There is a fine line between "Do you want to try again?" and "Do you want to be done?" Are you just frustrated, or is this just not right for you? It's okay either way. There's no right or wrong choice. We need to trust what feels right at that moment.

So much of being an adult involves pushing ourselves past the point at which we want to leave a situation. It's unfortunate, but a part of life! Having a job is a big part of why we end up disconnecting from what we really want. We sometimes turn into these drill sergeants yelling at ourselves, "Go! Go! Go! Get your coat on and get out the door, you lazy jerk!" When all we want to do is sit in our comfy chairs and stare at the rain out the window.

This is how we get out of tune with our intuition and end up pushing ourselves too hard and getting in situations that are not good for us. How can we reconnect and be nicer to ourselves? I found the best way to tune in to my deepest intuition was through meditation and journaling. Quieting down, writing it out, and being present and compassionate with ourselves is worth every minute of time and energy. Too busy, stressed out, pushing through sensations, "mean to ourselves" behavior ignores what's really going on, feels horrible, and leads to bad decisions that aren't genuine.

But what if your anxious feelings are just excitement? The body feels both the same way: heart racing, palms sweating, extra alert, a little shaky. You can decide! You get to turn your thoughts around to excitement and not anxiety, and you can use it to your advantage. This positive, excited energy can help you through fear and let you do your best.

ANXIETY AND EXCITEMENT EXIST ON THE SAME SPECTRUM, AND THE ONLY DIFFERENCE IS YOUR BELIEF IN THEM.

You get to choose to align with how you desire to experience the situation you're in, especially if it's keeping you from doing something you really love.

I'm doing the same thing now as I come back to riding after my break. It's scary and hard sometimes, and I choose to let myself have a break if something goes wrong or I feel tired or not ready, but I love it so much, and it's worth all the effort. I'm taking it slow, but I sense deeply that I'm in the right place. Smiling ear to ear, making good decisions, not letting fear boss me around, feeling empowered, joyful, and balanced—the best feelings!

Loving horses and spending time with them was something born in me. Horses have been the catalyst for deep lessons throughout my entire life. I need quality time with them to be at my best. They appear to be big and powerful, but they're actually big scaredy cats, so you have to be brave for them and lead the way—gently. You must be strong yet calm and truly present in their presence; otherwise, you can get hurt. It can be overwhelming or scary, and not everyone can do this.

You have to learn to speak in a way horses understand. Communication doesn't work if you allow the ego to be in charge and treat the horses with too much force. One of my favorite trainers used to say, "You can't outmuscle a horse." But people try! They use all kinds of harsh methods, and it gets so ugly. Those who train in this forceful way end up with horses who are damaged, dangerous, have horrible habits, are resistant, unwilling, and very unhappy.

Being around horses is a humbling experience. You have to be patient, dedicated, subtle, and speak clearly and effectively, most times with body language. To connect with these majestic beings (**or to your highest self**), you need to be patient, dedicated, clear, and celebrate small successes. Getting stuck in the ego, rushing, or using too much force interferes with enjoying the process because we attach too much to the outcome of whatever we're doing.

This strong-yet-graceful clarity carries through to my personal relationships and career and explains how horses bring out the best in me. Taking time away from them and then coming back helped me realize that I need my sacred time with horses to be in tune with the best part of myself.

THE PRACTICE

The following exercise invites you to tune into your body's cues to discover what lights you up and what you desire to walk away from.

Grab a notebook and a pen and dive into the following questions:

- When you were a kid, what were the things that brought you freedom, fun, connection, passion, and energy?

- What was born in you that you *must* do? What is so super important to you that you light up when you talk about it? What does that feel like in your body?

- What connects you to the best version of yourself? What is it you can't stop thinking about? It's pulling you.

It doesn't have to be some grand lifestyle change. It can be as simple as swinging on a swing when you get a chance, throwing a ball for a silly dog, or painting a few rocks some pretty colors at the kitchen table—simple ways to connect to your happy self.

- Is there something that you are afraid of trying? Are you sure it isn't just excitement and not fear? Can you change it around?

Excuses, excuses: List the ten reasons you *can't* do what you're thinking/desiring.

- Observe your list of excuses with curiosity: How can you adjust your attitude about what is holding you back? How can you get creative with your thinking about this situation?

For example, going to the barn takes time away from my family when I could be working more, making dinner, cleaning, or doing other house chores, but the time spent at the barn puts me in a fantastic mood when I come home, and we can still spend time together, but now I'm laughing and smiling, and my family loves when I feel great! I'm much more available to myself and them. This enhances my quality time with my loved ones. Isn't that better than being cranky and miserable and stomping around scowling because I didn't get to do anything fun I wanted that day?

- When was the last time you connected with what you deeply desired? Where were you, and what were you doing? Who were you with?

- What makes you feel fully present and lose track of time completely? What could you do without looking at your phone or a clock for hours? That you could talk about for 30 minutes with enthusiasm?

- Is there a situation you feel you might need to walk away from? What are your body's cues telling you?

- Take one small action step. What is that one small thing you will commit to doing today (or stepping away from)—sign up for the course, make the call, buy the sketchbook, put on the running shoes—towards becoming more of the zingy, lit up, smiling person that you love to be.

Anita Buzzy Prentiss is an intuitive photographer who finds love and beauty in every subject. She has had her own business, Buzzy Photography, since 1996. She enjoys telling the most important stories of people's lives through photos and teaching other photographers how to find their joy through online courses and mentorship with her Buzzy Vibe Tribe.

Connect with Anita:

Website: www.buzzyphoto.com

Facebook: www.facebook.com/buzzyphoto

Instagram: www.instagram.com/photobuzzy

CHAPTER 9

DEMYSTIFYING THERAPY

CULTIVATING A RELATIONSHIP FOR LASTING CHANGE

Cheri Davies, LCSW-R

MY STORY

Anxiety doesn't just live in your brain. It lives in your body. No matter how you try to ignore it, it eventually catches up with you. For as long as I can remember, I had anxiety. It hung around like an annoying younger sibling. I heard it talking in my ear, telling me, *Be afraid; You're not doing that right; What if you make a mistake*—knowing I couldn't make it stop. A constant loop of chatter filled my mind day after day. No one knew what was going on with me. I was a worry wort or being dramatic. Since it was the 70s, no one really understood what anxiety looked like or felt like. It was debilitating being nine and worrying about things none of my friends even thought twice about. At a time when you're trying to find your place socially, I felt like I didn't fit in, and my anxiety fed that irrational thought.

My elementary school had Fire Prevention Week, and, for some reason, in third grade, I knew in my soul that this year would be the one that a fire would burn down my school. Nightmares, feeling sick, and constant worry led up to the big day. Fire trucks and firefighters arrived at the school to teach us how to be safe. Safe is the last thing I felt. I was sure this was the big day that a fire would erupt and burn down my school. Fear had taken hold of me, and no amount of reasoning would work. Since no one I knew talked about anxiety, I suffered silently. But I couldn't hide my physical symptoms. The school nurse called my mom to pick me up because I was "sick." Once I was away from school, I miraculously felt okay again. I knew something was wrong with me, but it would take years to understand what it was.

If being anxious wasn't enough to deal with, my world turned upside down when our house was burglarized the following year. Coming back from my grandparents' house, I pretended to be asleep, so my father would carry me into the house. While I was acting like I was sleeping, a group of teens ran out our back door, down the yard, and disappeared into the woods. At first, the only thing that seemed wrong was our orange tabby cat sitting by the back door. He was staring outside, but the door was open. He was an escape artist, and there is no way he should've been sitting there if we had somehow forgotten to close the door before we left. I didn't think much of it and went to my room. Chaos erupted within minutes. My mother was yelling and crying; my father was rushing around the house. Fear took hold immediately. For a kid that already had anxiety, my safety went out the back door with my mom's jewelry. What the burglars took from me was years of feeling safe in the one place I should've felt safe. These moments changed my outlook on the world and my place within it for years.

Nighttime in my room became the scariest place to be. Closets had monsters, and people were hiding under my bed; someone was coming to kidnap me. Irrational fears became my new normal. Checking the closet, under my bed, and behind my door became a nightly pattern. There was no sleep until all the steps were completed. Sometimes my bedroom door was open, so I could hear an intruder and be able to scream loud enough to alert my parents. The next week I'd get scared they could sneak up on me, so I'd close the door. It was exhausting trying to outrun the constant chatter: *You're not safe.*

When we moved closer to my grandparents the following year, excitement about having a new room in a house without memories gave me hope. My new purple canopy bed was just what I needed to start over. Unfortunately, reality set in quickly, and the new space did little to resolve my anxiety. I suffered in silence, not telling a soul of my fears. I hated being called a worry wort, so why would I speak up? There was no real understanding of mental health issues at the time, so my anxiety quietly overtook my life.

Creating my own coping skills became a way to get through anything that felt uncomfortable, unsafe, or difficult to manage. I became exceptionally good at channeling my anxiety into school and social activities. I ignored my emotional health by focusing on grades, peers, and outside activities. I stayed busy. I immersed myself in dance lessons, drama productions, sports in middle school, and a part-time job in high school. The more active I stayed, the less my anxiety kicked up during the day. Unfortunately, I was back in my room every night, checking for my fourth-grade intruders. This pattern lasted for years. I didn't have the emotional vocabulary to explain to my parents what I was feeling all the time. I didn't understand it myself, so why would I try to tell anyone else?

Living in a constant state of anxiety for my whole childhood took its toll on my physical body. My autonomic nervous system, which produces your fight or flight response, was overworked and exhausted. This part of your system was designed to help keep you safe from real dangers, like someone chasing you. Unfortunately, it cannot distinguish what are perceived dangers, like the imaginary intruders hiding in my room. It felt like I was always in real danger. My amygdala, which is the area of the brain that modulates fear and anxiety, was running the show. In trying to protect myself, my brain became super hyperactive and in a constant state of worry. That little voice in the back of my head that reminded me all the time that I was in danger was like the continuous ticking of a clock—steady and consistent.

But as I discovered, anxiety doesn't just live in your brain. It lives in your body. The two will always be intertwined, so it was no surprise when my body finally said enough is enough. At 22, I was diagnosed with an autoimmune disorder that impacted my physical and mental health. Ignoring both was no longer an option.

An elevated level of stress hormones flooded my body for years, and it was a wake-up call to start taking care of myself. My initial introduction to self-care was purely from a physical standpoint. I started taking medication to address my physical symptoms from the autoimmune disorder. As I began to feel better, I changed my diet and added acupuncture to help reduce my inflammation. After several years, I managed my physical symptoms and felt more hopeful that I could find a way to stop struggling with the anxiety.

By my 30s, I started to really pay attention to what my body was telling me and learned how to manage stress and anxiety differently. I became an expert in how anxiety impacted me, physically and mentally. I changed my mindset and realized I could address my anxiety the same way I did my physical health. Being open to change, finding a new way of coping, and asking for help, started me on a journey towards healing. Having a toddler who needed me to be present also made it imperative that I figure out how to reduce my anxiety. It was a great source of motivation for me. Self-care took on a new meaning. I could do all the things people told me to, like get a massage, meditate, and reduce my stress, but without figuring out how to deal with the trauma from my childhood—I was swimming upstream. And I was only marginally keeping my head above water at this point. Luckily, I started getting my master's degree in social work, and things shifted all at once when I started to understand myself a bit better.

I was fortunate in my graduate program to have a professor who reinforced how important it was for all the students to be in therapy to heal their traumas and experience what future clients may experience. I was open to starting therapy, but it was a daunting process initially. I had so many conflicting feelings about it. *How do you start to find a therapist? How am I supposed to tell a stranger my fears and insecurities when I do not tell my closest friends? Do I really want to be that vulnerable when all I have done my whole life is to try and manage my anxiety? What if I can't change?*

There were so many emotions related to having to seek help from someone. Having other students in my class who had similar feelings was an eye-opener. I wasn't alone in how I felt. Other people experienced anxiety in wildly varying degrees. For the first time, I felt okay being open about how my anxiety presented itself and figuring out how to change my future relationship with it. It was a huge comfort to know I wasn't alone or somehow broken, which is how I felt.

Conversations about mental health are more common now because we understand the importance of how our emotional health impacts our lives in totality. Stories about athletes leaving the Olympics, ending their careers due to their mental health, and gymnasts testifying in court about abuse, have also opened essential conversations about the importance of mental wellness. Being so public about their struggles has normalized mental health treatment for a new generation. Social and emotional programs in school are helping students learn how to express their feelings and ask for help if needed. Television shows are prominently tackling complex topics that address mental health. Although they may be emotional to watch at times, it creates important conversations about the benefit of seeking treatment. All of these are reducing the stigma of getting into therapy. Thank goodness!

THE PRACTICE

Finding a therapist can often feel like an overwhelming task. This practice will help guide you through what to expect and how to make the most of your therapeutic relationship.

FINDING A GOOD MATCH: QUESTIONS BEFORE YOU START YOUR SEARCH

- What is the main reason for seeking therapy? Are you anxious, depressed, going through a significant life event, looking to improve self-esteem, or seeking to heal past trauma?
- What would you like to see improved? Decrease symptoms, release old habits, improve relationships, and learn new coping strategies?
- Does anyone I know have a referral for me that they think might be a good fit? Your friends and family may know someone they think would be a good match for you. Ask anyone you trust that knows you well. You'll be surprised and happy to know that there are many people you know already in therapy.

FINDING A GOOD MATCH: QUESTIONS TO ASK THE THERAPIST

A very good friend of mine, who is also a therapist, describes finding a therapist as trying on a swimsuit. Sometimes you try one on, and it's a great fit. You look and feel amazing, and who does not want that? But other times, you may have to try on two or three before finding one you like. Finding the right therapist for you is the same idea. You'll find what you need by doing some planning, coupled with a bit of luck. Therapy is about starting a relationship with someone. So, you must be able to trust them with your thoughts and feelings. Preparing for the first meeting is a great way to determine what the therapist is like. Asking specific questions can guide your decision about potentially working with that person.

- Does the therapist have a specialty? Find out what areas they are trained in. Ask if they have any training in your specific area of need.

- Is the therapist culturally competent? Do they understand your culture, spiritual beliefs, sexual orientation, and more? Are they open to learning about your cultural beliefs?

- How will the therapist help you plan for your goals? Do they understand what you are looking for in treatment? How will they monitor your goals over time? Will they adjust goals if they need to change over time?

- What types of therapy or modalities do they practice? Many have special areas of training. Some specialties may include EMDR, progressive counting, cognitive behavior therapy, dialectical behavior therapy, grief counseling, Gottman relationship theory, and more.

- What is the therapist's style in session? This is very personal and incredibly important to relationship building. If you're looking for a therapist who is solution-focused but whose style is laid back and conversational, it may not be a good fit. Do you feel they were attentive and open to your concerns in that session? Do you see yourself being able to open up to the therapist? Sometimes it may take a few sessions to determine if you think the therapist is a good fit for you. You may decide after a few sessions that they are not the right person for you, which is absolutely okay. Follow your gut and let the therapist know your feelings. This is highly personal, and it's best to be honest about what works for you. Remember, like a swimsuit; you may not find the right fit the first time. It's okay to keep looking.

LEANING INTO THE PROCESS

In my own experience with therapy, I understand how hard it is sometimes to work through challenging thoughts and emotions. Being vulnerable is not something most of us were taught to be. As a society, we often talk about being strong and brave, but this is rarely in the context of vulnerability. There is magic in being able to be vulnerable with someone else. In the therapeutic setting, it's healing and empowering. So how do you lean into a process that sometimes feels so scary?

- Be honest in sessions: Your therapist can only help you based on what you tell them. They cannot read your mind and magically figure out what you are thinking or feeling. It's okay to express the things that make you feel stuck, afraid, or uncomfortable.

- Ask questions if you're confused or want to know why the therapist is asking you something. This is communication 101. If you do not ask questions, it may create a lack of understanding or miscommunications. Misunderstanding a question's intent or context may lead to hurt feelings or a breakdown in the relationship with your therapist.

- Remind yourself that your therapist is not judging you: They are there to help you through whatever issue has brought you there. They genuinely want to help you get to a place of healing. Talk about your fear of being judged so you can continue to be open in sessions.

- Do your homework: Some therapists, like myself, will often give homework. Change does not happen in one hour a week. It takes time outside of the office to make lasting change. You made that commitment to change by starting therapy. Honor that commitment to yourself by completing your assignments.

- Do not panic when they start challenging you: Therapists have different styles, but more than likely, they will challenge a belief or a thought you may have about a situation at some point. It can feel uncomfortable when someone challenges a belief but take some time to think about why it felt uncomfortable. These can be where the seeds of growth are planted to help you move towards your goal of healing.

- Think of therapy as a river: I use this analogy in my own practice with clients. Therapy can be many things, but more often than not, it flows differently in each session. Sometimes it is steady and calm, then something kicks up a feeling, and the river gets choppy. At times you may have to get out of the canoe you have been paddling to steady yourself on land. Then when you are calmer, you get back in and start paddling. The journey can take you to where you never expected to go. It will often take you to a place of greater understanding and acceptance.

- ·Trust in yourself: This is one of the more challenging parts of leaning into therapy because we have often forgotten how to do this. Connect with your intuition as you begin to heal the parts of yourself that need to heal. Dive into finding what brings you joy and release what does not serve you any longer. You may find that you begin exploring other ways to release emotional blockages. Breathwork, meditation, Reiki, and yoga are all complementary modalities that can provide healing. You are the expert on what you need for self-care. Listen to that voice. Trust your gut.

Just like every part of our daily lives, we want meaningful connections with other people. Therapy is no different. Find someone who guides you through your journey and is a partner in your self-healing. A good therapist will lead you where you want to go; a great one will walk alongside you, guiding you so that you can create meaningful and lasting change.

Cheri Davies, LCSW-R, is a licensed clinical social worker with over 15 years of experience, specializing in the area of anxiety. Cheri graduated from Adelphi University with her master's degree in social work. She has worked as a psychiatric social worker, a school social worker, and a therapist. In 2019, Cheri opened her private practice, Birch Hill Counseling, providing individual and group therapy for children and adults. Cheri wants people dealing with anxiety to know they are not alone and that there are evidence-based techniques that can help. Getting started is the first step toward healing.

Cheri lives in upstate New York with her husband, son, and black lab, Tillman. In her free time, she loves spending time with family and friends, camping in the Adirondacks, doing DIY projects, and dreaming of living lakeside. You can follow Cheri on Instagram at Birch Hill Counseling.

CHAPTER 10

LOVE YOUR FOOD, LOVE YOURSELF

INTUITIVE PRACTICES TO MASTER YOUR MINDSET

Tammy Lantz, RD, LD
Intuitive Eating Counselor, Food, and Body Dietitian Coach

MY STORY

Before I tell you who I am or what is unfolding in my life, let me tell you where I came from. What I share here aren't facts but rather my interpretations. As I share, I invite you to think about yourself: *Who am I? What are my interpretations? How did I arrive to where I am now?* Don't ask from the point of blame, but from the point of curiosity.

Everything in your life has led you to be right here, right now, exactly where you're meant to be.

When you consider your life through a lens of curiosity, there's no room for judgment, only your ability to connect with your truth and personal understanding.

Here is my truth.

By the age of 18, I lived in 18 different homes with either my mom, my mom and dad, my mom and stepdad number one, my mom and stepdad number two, or my dad. I believed my dad to be absent until I was ten years old but have now learned otherwise. This was the interpretation I grew up with and carried with me. I also come from a family that historically "made it by." I was so focused on making things better or having more structure that I forgot to have fun like they originally taught me. Now I realize *they* had it right all along.

From what I recall, I was the first in my family to go to college, except for my dad. He obtained his associate's degree while I was in high school. Throughout my life, I recall others saying things to me like, "You act as if you're better than us," "You're not our *real* sister," "You have what you have in life because of who you married," "I don't know how you do it," or "You are the glue of the family."

They likely don't recall saying those things, and I imagine I received them differently than they intended as a result of my interpretations. I didn't understand this initially, so I allowed these comments to define me, and a massive responsibility weighed on my shoulders. I felt I needed to rise up. I needed to make it through. I lived by the mantra: *I get through things, no matter what comes at me.*

Through this lifelong conditioning process, I learned to be emotionless, to rise up, and become better. I committed my life to not being like those who raised me, unbeknownst to the actual greatness they held. My mother had several marriages and boyfriends. Through my younger lens, I interpreted this *as my mom is always dependent on having a man, even if he was physically or verbally abusive.* I judged her harshly. I thought *I'll never let my children go through what my siblings and I endured.*

I also judged my mom for her larger body. Just typing this makes me sick. We never talked about her experience of living in a larger body. But through societal conditioning, I learned being in a larger body was bad. Again, I declared *I would not be like my mom.* Therefore, when I heard about the dietitian profession, I was relieved. I could finally ensure I would not be like her. I would be better, and I would be smaller, not realizing how freaking fantastic she already was and how the size of someone's body says nothing about them as a person.

My desire to become better resulted in acting like I was rising to a higher perspective, but in reality, I was hiding from my truth.

Hiding equated to constant embarrassment. Embarrassment plagued me and spread like wildfire throughout my life. It kept me from being me. *I am not allowed to be me,* is what I privately declared. *I am embarrassed about where I come from, where I am not already, and almost everything in between.* I learned to be embarrassed, over and over again, but this was my own private experience. I dreamed big but never knew I was allowed to actually believe those dreams because I was constantly focused on shrinking, emotionally and physically. Even if I did achieve those dreams, *I would have to hide the achievement, right? Who was I to think I was anyone?*

Upon realizing how I was hiding, I reflected on if there were any areas of my life I was not embarrassed about. To my astonishment, I discovered I had two areas: true friends I met along the way and having access to food, even when it was through government assistance programs. Food was the one thing we always had, the constant I could depend upon. Food was my anchor of safety.

Here I was holding food as my anchor of safety yet attempting to live up to my mission of being in a smaller body while living a larger life, and not realizing a lick of this while pursuing my degree to become a dietitian. Ironic, isn't it?

Nevertheless, I grew up. I got married and had kids. I went to college. I learned. And I learned children of dietitians have higher rates of eating disorders. I don't know if this is factual, but it drove me. I had to find the perfect balance for my children. I needed to model a healthy body so they could be in a healthy *(smaller)* body, but I also wanted to ensure they wouldn't be too small. I didn't want them to develop an eating disorder, not only because eating disorders are devastating but also because it would be my fault. I didn't want to be embarrassed by this too. Unraveling this realization opened me up to even more layers of guilt and shame. *How ludicrous that I was thinking about how I would feel if my child went through this.*

But this is what happens when our minds are wrapped up in historical chains of diet culture. We carry the weight of the world and attempt to carry the burdens of our children (as if we can). However, we too are unintentionally passing down the burdens we were given unless we intentionally break those chains.

Before realizing this, I was lost. But I kept rising. I hid behind my mission as a mother, and food continued to be my anchor. I felt like I had discovered the perfect solution. I would teach my children that food was just that, food. It was nothing more, nothing less. And I would teach them to listen to their bodies when it came to food, but not about their feelings about their bodies. I strived to teach them not to eat as emotional human beings, as if that was the solution. I felt teaching them this was something I could control. *Somehow, I was better, right?* While helping them to create a positive relationship with food was important, this relentlessness further distanced me from my own needs and the ability to model how much joy can come from food experiences.

I wanted so much to be successful that I found a professional job in pediatric nutrition. Here I could rise up as an expert, but the internal embarrassment didn't stop. It only perpetuated more. And I hid more.

I was also attempting to be who I thought I was supposed to be as a wife and mom while living out my declaration to not be like those who raised me. But I could never reach these unreachable standards I created for myself, and this habit of rising only distanced me from simply being me.

As I strove to rise over and over again, I felt a chipping-away sensation in my body as glimpses of who I am at my core gradually withered away. How was I to talk about these things? *I am not supposed to feel like this, and I'm embarrassed about how I feel.* So, I ignored it. I was supposed to be happy, so I pretended to be. Can you guess how I stuffed these feelings down? If you guessed food (my dearest anchor), you're right. It allowed me to shut off my feelings. Once again, I was protected, but the deeply rooted pathway of embarrassment still ran in the background.

With so many repetitions of embarrassment, I experienced loads of shame and self-blame. I didn't love myself. I didn't love who I was being. I didn't love my life. And I grew to loathe my anchor because, over time, it was no longer keeping me safe; it was making me crazy. I attempted to meet everyone else's food and emotional needs without regard for my needs or my relationship with food. I attempted to be everything everyone else wanted me to be while remaining an emotionless pawn in life. Therefore, when I was alone at night, finally getting *my* time, I stayed awake far past when my body needed rest and allowed myself only three choices. I could stuff down a nice hefty snack, numb out on TV, or stand in front of the mirror picking at my skin. These choices, along with my choice to not rest, furthered the experience of disconnecting emotionally. I now realize those choices helped calm my overstimulated emotional highway, the nervous system, while strengthening the ever-playing narrative of embarrassment and lack of self-acceptance. I'd wake up the next morning with remorse, vowing: *Today I will be different; I will be better.* Do you see the pattern? Do you have any patterns of striving to be better while actually hiding?

By striving to be better, I created a pattern of harshly judging myself, just like I did with others in my life. This continued until I started my journey of becoming an intuitive eater, reconnecting to the emotional shell of my human experience (my body) and gaining insight into how our brains operate. I couldn't learn neuroscience, emotional mastery, and intuitive eating all at once, so I took it one bite at a time; pun intended!

Little did I know when I embarked on this journey of becoming a dietitian just how much nutrition would change me. Years ago, I thought: *I love nutrition because it grows with you.* I thought I could focus on pediatric nutrition while my kids were young, then move into teen/adult nutrition, and eventually end up in geriatric nutrition as I aged. *I'd figure nutrition out perfectly in each stage of life.* However, it did not follow me as I thought. I learned I needed to follow it. I needed to follow my anchor, the gift I was given. I needed to allow it to be my teacher. *Food is thy medicine, but not from its physical properties, from its metaphysical properties.* Food can be one of our most valued teachers in life if we allow it. And I'm grateful for the gifts I was given from those who raised me, including food security.

When I shifted and followed my teacher, I discovered all I have shared here. I also uncovered the path to being fully present through connecting to the highest vibrational frequency available, which is love. This concept was foreign to me, considering I spent so many years being emotionless. Therefore, when I started this journey of rediscovering a love for myself, I thought I needed to rise to the frequency of love. So, I was striving to do all the things to reach love.

But love is always there, waiting in the background. It's not something we have to strive for or rise to. Love rises us when we allow it. I now choose daily to allow love to rise me. I'm not striving to rise; it happens through surrendering and connecting to what has been available to me this whole time.

THE PRACTICE

HOW TO ALLOW FOOD TO BE YOUR TEACHER AND CONNECT YOU TO LOVE FOR YOURSELF

There are three vital ingredients to connecting to love for yourself through what food, food experiences, and food thoughts can teach you. This recipe will support your transition from never-ending shame with food, your body, and life to being awakened to the love and joy awaiting you. The ingredients are:

1. Experience emotional awareness and regulation

2. Develop deep self-compassionate eating and body gentleness

3. Reflect and reprogram your subconscious brain

Each one of these ingredients is helpful, but the utilization of all three unlocks the evolution you long for. You'll discover why every courageous client I've worked with has stopped measuring their daily success by the numbers on the scale and fighting with food. Instead, they've found peace within their mind, body, and soul. The following is a start. For more, get your copy of Your Intuitive Life Journal at www.YourEssentialDietitian.com/Journal.

EXPERIENCE EMOTIONAL AWARENESS AND REGULATION

The first step is to become aware of what emotions you have around food. You may already know this because you have spent a lifetime worrying about your feelings surrounding food, but if not, I invite you to start by calming your mind. This can be done by breathing out longer than you breathe in (for example: breath in for four seconds, hold for seven seconds, and then breathe out for eight seconds). Or utilize one of the other methods I was taught as a child: color, dance, sing, or be silly. Do what works for you.

Then grab a notebook or Your Intuitive Life Journal and begin to search for your emotions surrounding food by scanning your body, not by looking inside your mind. You may notice more negative emotions first. This is normal. Simply recognize which emotions are there and allow them.

Then take a bit of time to write about your emotions and what arises for you. To help, you may utilize these guided journal prompts:

- When I think about how I feel about food, what initially arises for me?

- How long have I been experiencing these emotions surrounding food?

- How does how I feel about food mirror how I feel about my body?

- How does how I feel about food also mirror how I feel in other aspects of my life? (For example: if you feel out of control around food, where else in your life do you feel out of control).

- How would I like to feel about food? If I felt this way about food, how would this change my life?

Allow these prompts and your emotions to serve as guideposts towards what you need to move up the emotional scale and connect with love.

As you practice experiencing and regulating your emotions, avoid asking yourself questions that begin with why. Rather, ask yourself questions with the words *what, where, how, or when*. "Why" is an emotional dis-regulator and will distance you from connecting to love.

DEVELOP DEEP SELF-COMPASSIONATE EATING AND BODY GENTLENESS

The most effective way to do this is to adopt the ten principles of *Intuitive Eating*. This practice of eating is an evidenced-based, weight-inclusive, non-diet, and mind-body health approach designed to encourage a self-compassionate eating framework. It was created by two dietitians, Evelyn Tribole and Elyse Resch. If you're unfamiliar with this practice, I highly recommend the fourth edition of their book, *Intuitive Eating: A Revolutionary Anti-Diet Approach* to use alongside your journey with Your Intuitive Life Journal.

To connect with compassion, consider these journaling prompts and ask your heart center for its wisdom:

- Where have I learned to engage with food the way that I do? How has this impacted my actions/inactions?

- Where can I forgive myself for past choices with food? How can I use this as evidence of my ability to forgive myself in other areas of my life?

- What is the most compassionate thing I could do for myself while enjoying a meal?

- How can I connect to gratitude for what my food experiences gave me, even if those experiences no longer serve me?

- My body has carried me through life and allowed me to experience life; how may I be gentle and loving to it?

REFLECT AND REPROGRAM YOUR SUBCONSCIOUS BRAIN

Your subconscious brain is the part of your mind that makes decisions for you, acts out your behaviors or habits, and holds your beliefs. This all happens on autopilot, without conscious thought. Your subconscious is developed from your environments and experiences at a young age, along with repeated patterns that emerge into adulthood. Likely, your brain has been wired for dieting and body image dissatisfaction without even knowing it's an obstacle. You think you just need to stop eating XYZ food or have more willpower, but this is a broken strategy.

You need to work with your brain, instead of against it, to release any subconscious patterns that no longer serve you. One of the best ways to do this is to adopt reflective practices that enable you to go through an excavation process. This process will allow you to shine a light on the shadows keeping you from moving forward, and then you can release those shadows. As you release, you'll discover the depths of what beautifully and uniquely makes you, you. Self-reflection on your subconscious patterns naturally allows internal communication to shift patterns holding you back and connect deeply to your internal wisdom.

- How old was I when I went on my first diet or started controlling my food? What prompted me to start? How did it serve me at that moment? Does it still serve me? And what does it cost me?

- How often do I think about my body? What comes up when I think about it? Where did I learn to think in this way? How do my thoughts about my body impact how I'm feeling?

- When I take a step back to look at all my eating experiences over days, weeks, months, or even years, what patterns emerge? Where may I now intentionally shift those patterns, now that I'm aware of them?

- Who would I be, what would I do, and how would I feel if I already had peace with my food and love for myself?

Tammy Lantz, RD, is a transformational food and body coach, dietitian, and certified Intuitive Eating counselor with over 20 years of experience. Her mission is to elevate those with female energy through self-discovery and intensive community retreats. You will be empowered to release shame, guilt, and unworthiness with food and yourself. Allowing you to unlock your innate ability to love your food, love yourself, and love your life, Tammy knows the most effective recipe for how to allow food to be your teacher and connect you to love for yourself. With extensive knowledge and skills in intuitive eating, emotional mastery, and neuroscience, Tammy knows how to guide your healing journey in a unique, compassionate, and highly effective way. Tammy became a dietitian to discover the one perfect way everyone, including herself, is supposed to eat. But she realized through her healing that one size does not fit all, and each person holds an innate inner wisdom that can guide them on how to nourish themselves. Implementing this practice opens healing and love to every other part of one's life. She is here to be a guide to this unfolding and provide tangible resources to move you along with ease in your journey.

Tammy was born and raised in Colorado but now lives in Florida with her husband of 24 years, two amazing children, and one adorable bulldog who thinks she is human. She loves warm weather, being close to the beach, and gazing at dolphins. She still treasures the beauty of mountains and connecting with nature's healing.

Connect with Tammy:

Grab a copy of Your Intuitive Life Journal:
www.YourEssentialDietitian.com/Journal

Free Facebook Group Mindful & Intuitive Eating for Women:
https://bit.ly/loveyourfoodloveyourselflovelife

Instagram: https://www.instagram.com/Your_essential_RD/

CHAPTER 11

YOU ARE THE ROLE MODEL

GUIDING OUR CHILDREN TO LIVE A CONFIDENT LIFE

Pam Bohlken, Reiki Master, VSTP, RTTP

MY STORY

I'm startled by the sound of my phone ringing. *It's only 8:00 a.m. Who's calling this early?*

I look at the caller ID and see it's my daughter Mandy. *Oh-oh, what's wrong?*

"Hello? What's up?" There was a brief pause, and then she said, "Tyler overdosed last night."

"Okay, (deep breath) where is he?" *He's in the hospital somewhere. I'm sure of it.*

"No, Mom, you don't understand. He died."

My body instantly hunched over. The sounds that came next were so primal; I have no idea where they came from. My husband came running to me, "What's going on?" I caught my breath long enough to say, "Tyler's dead," and the sobs started all over again.

It's a morning I'll never forget.

Tyler is my grandson. As they say, he's now forever 19. He turned 19 two weeks earlier while he was in rehab. They found half a pill on him that was later analyzed as fentanyl and heroin. He thought he had purchased Percocet. Not that Percocet is good, but it wouldn't have killed him.

There is a huge problem going on within the United States. They're even calling it "chemical warfare." The drugs are coming out of China and Mexico, and they're out to kill Americans. Thousands of teens and young adults are dying from fentanyl poisoning. It's being laced into other drugs, and it's very lethal. I'll step off my soap box now and get to the point. There are people working hard to get the drugs and dealers off the streets. I want to know what we can do so kids don't start taking drugs in the first place. That's my focus.

Losing a grandchild to fentanyl poisoning is impossible to describe. It doesn't feel real, yet he's gone. We know he didn't want to die. Taking just half a pill took his life. Those of us left behind have wondered *what we could have done differently? What could we've done to help him?* In all honesty, I believe we all do the best we can until we learn more, and then we do better. I knew nothing of fentanyl, but I do now.

Tyler knew he was loved, but what was his self-talk like? Did he follow the crowd and do what they did because he didn't know it was okay to follow his own path? Our children need to know they have choices. One of my daughters tells her sons, "Make wise choices," as they're heading out the door. She has no control over the choices they make from that point on, but she plants seeds for them to maybe take a pause and think about the choices they're making during the day.

In the past, I'd let my grandkids have more space during their teen years. *What teenager wants their grandma hanging around?* Well, I know better now, and you can be assured I'll be spending more time with my grandkids, even if it's just sending more text messages than in the past. I can always take the time to say, "I love you."

I'm a Rapid Transformational Therapy (RTT) practitioner using hypnosis. It's been my experience that my RTT clients have had some form of childhood trauma that's been carried through into their adult lives. Most carry forward the side effects of childhood abuse, neglect, or being forced to grow up before their time. Sometimes it's a small event that, to a child, appeared to be much bigger than it really was. They come up with many different versions of their childhood that led to a lack of confidence, self-worth, or low self-esteem. Clients may tell me, "I want to feel safe to express my feelings," "I want to feel close to my family," or "I want the confidence to know I deserve a happy life." I help them release the old beliefs they created as a child and bring forward a more positive mindset, helping them feel safe. I help them shift from "I'm not worthy" or "I'm not good enough" to "I am worthy" and "I am enough, just as I am." They can start to see that being unique is a blessing. There's no one else on this Earth exactly like them, so their job is to be their unique selves.

Wouldn't it be wonderful if we could instill those beliefs into our children from the beginning of their lives? Why do they need to suffer and then fix it as adults?

Our children have many role models, such as teachers, daycare workers, bus drivers, and other children. If you're reading this book, you have an interest in mental health. You can be the biggest role model in your child or grandchild's life, and it really doesn't even have to be someone you're related to. Maybe you have a child living next to you whom you can be a role model for. However, the first step is to make sure we, as adults, are in the right frame of mind ourselves. Have we taken the steps necessary to heal our own past so that we can be in the best frame of mind to help others? If you feel you need professional help, please seek that out. You can be helping your children right along with you helping yourself.

I would love to see children taught that it's okay to show their feelings. They don't have to smile all the time and pretend everything is okay. If they're angry or sad, that's okay. What we would need to show them is how to vent those feelings in a healthy way. We don't want them to bottle up those emotions. That's what brings around the adult issues I talked about earlier, not to mention the health complications later in life. We should give them guidance on healthy ways to express those emotions. They could scream into a pillow or push their feelings into a pillow. The feelings or emotions need to go somewhere. Ask them, "Where do you feel this sadness in your body?" "Do you feel any pain or heaviness in your body when you feel angry?" Just acknowledging it can help to release it. Or they can breathe into that space. Give them your time to let them tell you why they're feeling the way they feel. Give them space if they need it. Then offer a hug. Let them know it's safe to share their feelings and that you care.

When I was young, I remember my mom saying, "Penny, for your thoughts." My response would be, "They aren't worth a penny." I'm sure she was feeling very frustrated as she walked away. She never pushed for more, but I secretly wished she would have.

We can also teach by example. You can instill the beliefs that will carry forward from childhood into their adult lives. These beliefs can be, "My opinion matters." Or it can be, "No one cares what I think." How do you want your child or grandchild to grow up? We are planting seeds. You can help them nurture those seeds. Water those seeds with love and gratitude. Our hope or goal is to see them all grow into well-rounded, self-sufficient adults.

I recently heard about a classroom experiment that some kids did with plants. They had two identical plants, planted in the same dirt, the same type of pot, and they were watered at the same time. One was spoken to with kind words such as, "You are beautiful," and "I love you," while the other one was bullied. "You are ugly," "I hate you." The plant that was bullied withered up and died while the one fed with positive words thrived. If a plant can react this way, imagine what we're doing to our children.

Another study by Masaru Emoto in Japan showed three bowls of rice and water. The first was spoken to with positive words every day for one month, the second with harsh words, and the third was ignored. The results at the end of that month were kind of expected considering the experiment listed above. The first one had a pleasant smell and fermented; the second bowl of rice turned black; however, the third one rotted. Being ignored turned out to be the worst option. Ignoring our children is not an option if we want them to grow up feeling good about themselves. I know I will be working harder at setting down my phone and spending more time talking and playing with them.

One of my favorite things to do with my grandkids over the years has been teaching them to sew and showing them how an embroidery machine works. It's a wonderful bonding time, and they get to bring home a memento from our time together. I've been pegged "Grandma Monkey" by my granddaughter Saylor because of the sock monkey I made for her while I was teaching another granddaughter, Eleanor, and her friend how to make them. That was a fun day.

When Saylor was about two years old, I said to her, "Saylor is strong, Saylor is courageous, Saylor is smart." She looked up at me as if she was soaking it right in. *She believes every word.* The last time she was at my house, she was brushing her hair and looking at herself in the mirror. All I could do was smile and agree when she said, "I am beautiful."

On the other hand, one day, she walked up to me and said, "I want to see the moon." *It's the middle of the day, and she won't be able to see it.* "It's not out there right now, honey," I told her. She got a sad look on her face, turned, and walked away. Later that day, I thought: *I should have taken her out to look for the moon.* Why did I shut down her request—just because I thought I knew better? Being aware, and being present, is what our children need from us. We are all human. We all make mistakes. I'm not going to beat myself up over this, and I don't want you to either. If we try to be present, if we start noticing those little things we could have done differently, it all helps us make better choices the next time. It gives us the opportunity to say I'm sorry and helps our kids see that we may be adults, but we still mess up too, and it's okay. That's what it means to be a role model.

Self-Care is one of the shifts in the world today that I'm so happy about. We were made to feel guilty if we took time for ourselves or we weren't given permission to think of ourselves first. We were raised to take care of everyone else first. Today, the trend is more towards self-care as something required. It's not the luxury we thought it was. We can teach our children that they're worth taking the time to nurture. They're worthy of taking some downtime for themselves. In fact, they need some downtime. Leading by example is the perfect way to start. Maybe it's taking a mental health day from work or spending the day doing what we love. I personally still need to work on this.

Some of the things we can do to help build a child's self-esteem can be as simple as

- Giving them age-appropriate chores. Let them know they are a huge help to you by doing that chore.
- Let them make mistakes so they can learn.
- Don't do everything for them.
- Teach them to cook or do laundry and have fun doing it together.

- Tell them every day that they are loved.
- Remind them they are unique. There is only one of them in the whole world, and they have the job of being themselves.
- Praise what they accomplish without pointing out what they could have done better. If they ask, then yes, help them see how it can be improved.
- Teach them to meditate.
- Show them the beauty that's around them; mindfulness.
- Show them by example how to handle stress.
- Teach them about self-care.
- Let them know they can come to you with anything.
- Help them to help others.
- When they have an idea, see what you can do to help that idea come to life.
- If they say they need a day of rest, give it to them. They work hard too.
- Remind yourself that they're children. They're meant to make mistakes; it's how they grow.
- Give them time to play.
- Have family dinner around the table whenever possible.
- Have a date night with each child individually.
- Let them know you want to know how they feel or what they're thinking. They matter.

I realize we have a long way to go to have a society of less stress and of love thy neighbor as yourself, but it has to start somewhere. You also may be wondering if we're just building up their ego and worried they'll grow up to be egotistical and think they are better than anyone else. Well, that's another part of the lessons, right? Teaching them to help and respect others, to respect life, is one of the greatest lessons we can teach them. Love thy neighbor as thyself indicates we love ourselves first and then treat our neighbors with that same respect.

THE PRACTICE

AGES 3 – 8

I made positive affirmation sticks for one of my granddaughters when she was younger. I just used craft sticks you can buy at any craft department. I wrote things such as, "I had an amazing day," "I am smart," and "I am loved." You can buy stickers or gems to decorate them or draw smiley faces and flowers. Your child can select a stick at the beginning of each day to set the tone for the day and/or one at night, so they are going to bed with a positive thought before falling asleep.

- Create craft sticks with some positive affirmations on them, such as the following:
  - You are very smart
  - You are loved
  - You always try your best
  - You are strong
  - You are going to have a great day
  - The best part of today was. . .

I'm saying "You are" rather than "I am" here since you'd start out reading these to your young child. Once they can read, you can change them to "I am."

- Remind your child of something significant they did that day that could be praised or celebrated. My goal here is to help them see they accomplished something that day. Their actions were noticed. It doesn't have to be a major event. It doesn't have to wait until the end of the day either.
  - They made their bed without being told.
  - They brushed their teeth.
  - They fed the dog or cat without spilling.
  - They lost at playing a game, but they handled the loss with grace.

- ○ They learned a new skill or read a new word.
- ○ They shared their feelings with you.

- Be a positive role model.
- Have dance parties in the living room or kitchen.
- Say I love you.
- Learn about EFT, Emotional Freedom Technique, and teach them how to use it to release stress.

AGES 9 - 14

- Continue to be a positive role model.
- Teach them a new skill. If it's something they are interested in, but you don't have the knowledge, find someone who does.
- Encourage your siblings to be involved in your child's life.
- Listen when your child speaks. Hear what they are saying.
- If your child isn't quick to answer your questions, sit there and wait for as long as it takes for them to respond to you. Eventually, it will start to be easier for them to respond.
- Invite them to help you with a project, even if it's pulling weeds in the garden. Let them know they would be a big help to you.
- Turn off the phones and TV and go for a walk or bike ride together.
- Have a weekly scheduled family game night. Board games are a great way to spend the evening or go outside to play basketball.
- Show them you want to know what they are interested in.
- Ask them questions in a way they can't just answer yeah or no. Start with "What was your favorite part about …?"
- Learn about EFT, Emotional Freedom Technique, and teach them how to use it to release stress.

These are just a few suggestions to get your mind thinking about what would work for the children in your life. The earlier you start, the easier it will be, and we'll all raise healthy, self-confident children. The stronger their base, the more resilient they'll be going out into the world. I do want to address that I realize there are children who have a chemical imbalance or learning disabilities, and there are others who will need professional help. My hope is that the suggestions I've made can be adjusted to work with most children, but please reach out for professional help if needed.

Pam Bohlken is the founder of Healing in Progress, Body, Mind, and Soul. As a Reiki Master, Pam uses both hands-on healing methods and Vibrational Sound Therapy (VST), which brings the soothing sounds and vibration of singing bowls, allowing her clients to release stress from their bodies and relax in order to heal.

Pam is also a practitioner in the Marisa Peer method of Rapid Transformational Therapy (RTT), using hypnosis to help her clients discover deep-seated beliefs that are currently causing emotional or health issues.

Pam regularly performs sound meditations, using her beautiful Himalayan singing bowls to bring the soothing rhythmic tones into individual or group settings.

All sessions are available in-person or virtually.

Pam and some of her grandchildren turned tragedy into positivity following the loss of her grandson to fentanyl poisoning. They created positive mindset cards for both 3-year-olds and up, for pre-teens and teens. They are also working to develop children's books featuring Tyler the Tiger to help them cultivate confidence, acquire coping skills, and live a more authentic life.

Pam lives in rural Wisconsin with her husband, where she can enjoy being in nature. She is an amateur herbalist and loves spending time with her grandchildren, gardening, and sewing. See below to find out more about Pam, future events, offerings, and products you won't want to miss.

For more information on fentanyl poisoning, go to https://the-fac.org/ or https://facingfentanylnow.org

Connect with Pam:

Website: https://www.pambohlken.com/

Website Online Store: https://www.pambohlken.com/online-store

LinkedIn: https://www.linkedin.com/in/pam-bohlken-1537221b5/

Facebook: https://www.facebook.com/Healing-in-Progress-629983640357140

Facebook: https://www.facebook.com/groups/646938666094668

CHAPTER 12

FROM SELF-LOATHING TO SELF-ADORING

HOW TO LOVE YOURSELF ON THE DEEPEST LEVEL

Vienna Costanzo-D'Aprile, LMHC, Reiki Master

"You should go for your PhD!" College professor.

They're just saying that. They don't really mean it.

"You are so gorgeous." Guy, I just met.

Wow, that feels good. I want to be around him all the time because it feels so good being seen and validated like this. Wait, why hasn't he answered my text in two hours? Does he still like me?! Did I do something wrong?!

"You're such a caring person." Friend.

Finally, someone noticed! All I do is care for other people. It's about time I get appreciated.

This used to be me. Do you notice the theme? Low self-esteem, needing external validation from others. Even when I received that validation, I didn't always believe them. Or, the high of being validated soon wore off, and I would continue craving it again and again.

It took me to hit rock bottom to realize that I didn't love myself.

MY STORY

I was raised in the Catholic church.

First, let me start by saying I'm not here to bash Catholicism or religion. If you've had a positive experience with religion, I'd never want to influence you against it. What I'm sharing is how I personally perceived things through my own experiences.

That being said, I'm very grateful for getting to know Christ and for many of the values I was taught in my religion; however, I certainly did not consider loving myself to be important.

Sure, we were told, "Love your neighbor as yourself," but I took on more of the "I am not worthy because I am a sinner" point of view. This was a reflection of my own self-worth. How could I confidently carry out my life's purpose if I was constantly consumed with feelings of guilt and unworthiness?

I never wanted to be greedy, vain, or selfish. Humility and giving to others were the priority. It's not that these values are bad, but I took them to the extreme. I believed I was nothing but a servant, and the *only* thing that mattered was giving to others. I was burnt out. I was such a people pleaser that it was nearly impossible for me to make my own decisions. I had no boundaries. I said yes to everyone that asked something of me, and I spread myself way too thin.

As I continued to get older, I began to notice some things about myself.

I always did well in school, and in elementary school, I received awards every year for my grades. So, while I felt I was pretty confident in myself, I was always externally validated. That first year I didn't receive an award—I was devastated.

Through middle school and high school, I started comparing myself to other girls. I was boy-crazy. If someone, *anyone,* liked me or gave me attention, I jumped at the chance to be their girlfriend before I knew if I even liked him or not. If I had a crush on someone who didn't like me back, I was a wreck. I had friends, but if one of them was mad at me, I could not move on or focus on anything else until things were okay between us.

You could say this is somewhat normal for a teenage girl, but maybe this just means more of us are self-love deprived than we realize.

I was always successful at sports, too, but once I went to college, I sat on the bench for the first time in my life and became depressed. I didn't like myself. I finally realized my self-worth came completely from success and external validation. Interestingly enough, I still had not been to therapy at this point. I didn't feel like talking about my problems. *Plus, why should I deserve to go to therapy? My problems aren't that bad. I just need to suck it up and keep going.*

After college, I moved away from my hometown. Moving to a new area, if new friends couldn't hang out, I felt depressed and called myself a loser. I started dating someone and was in constant fear they would cheat on me or leave me, even though I had no evidence.

All of these were signs I didn't love myself enough.

I carried on, continuing to search for my own fulfillment. I finished graduate school and became a therapist. I was a beginner in the field, being thrown into the gauntlet with a heavy caseload, working with some very challenging clients. Instead of being compassionate towards myself as a beginner, I kept feeling like a failure. Plus, I was burnt out.

In 2016, I hit rock bottom; I contemplated suicide.

One rainy day, I didn't get out of bed. I called in sick to work. I began to formulate a plan on how I could make my own death happen and how to make it seem like it was an accident.

My heart sank.

But you're here for a reason. Your mission in life is to help others. How can you do that if you're no longer here?

*How can I be a good therapist if **I'm** the one contemplating suicide?*

Thankfully, these suicidal thoughts scared the shit out of me.

"I need help, God. Please send me support and guidance."

I suddenly felt the impulse to go outside, so I listened to my intuition.

It was one of those "I don't give a fuck" moments where I just stood there in the rain. I looked up at the sky and thought, *please get me out of this funk.*

It then dawned on me that there was a mental health outpatient clinic within walking distance from where I lived. So, I walked straight there and started feeling gratitude that this was so close by.

My mood suddenly shifted again as I walked into the clinic. I was ashamed to admit to my new therapist that I was a therapist myself. *How dare I feel this way when I should be a master of my own mental health?*

Thankfully my therapist was helpful, supportive, and non-judgmental. I worked through these thoughts and made appropriate changes in my life that helped me. Over time, I began to accept and even love myself for who I was and was happier.

Seeking help was my very first step toward self-love. I felt content for a while.

As I continued to grow as an individual and a therapist, I noticed there were still times I felt lonely, needy, and unworthy. I still fell into comparison traps. I was still affected by what others said about me. I also noticed that if I did something nice for someone and didn't receive appreciation or the same love back, I became resentful. Was I giving just to give? Or was I giving to receive something?

In 2019, I remembered hearing somewhere that if you're lonely, you need to fill yourself up with your own love. I wanted to know how to do that. I started to learn more about Reiki and became attuned to Level I. Giving Reiki to myself daily seemed to give me a boost.

In 2020, when things went virtual, I began signing up for whatever self-love programs I could find. Through therapy, spiritual coaching, transformational programs, dance, movement, meditation, and more, my own self-love started to grow deeper and deeper.

Once my momentum started and I realized how fucking good it felt to be in love with myself, I just kept going. Today, I'm at a point where I can tell myself, "I fucking *love* you," with confidence. I can actually feel my own love for myself so profoundly that it brings tears to my eyes.

I'm not saying I don't still go through moments where I feel insecure, lonely, craving external validation, etc., but now, I just know the way back, and I'm able to arrive there very quickly. I understand the signs that tell me I need to fill myself back up.

Now that I've gotten to this point and understand what being here has done for me, I want to teach others how to do the same. I want people to know that it's possible for anyone, even someone contemplating suicide, to eventually reach this point.

THE PRACTICE

Through my observations of my own self and clients, I developed a *Self-Love Scale* so you can understand where you currently land, as well as tools to help you up-level to the next stage.

Keep in mind that where you are at might fluctuate on the scale from day to day, but once you make it to the higher stages, it's easier to stay there and to recognize if you start to fall back.

The Self-Love Scale

1. Adoration
2. Holistic Appreciation
3. Self-Respect
4. Self-Acceptance
5. Neutral Resilience
6. Self-Dissatisfaction
7. Self-Loathing

Let's go in reverse order, working our way up to the highest level: Adoration. The section below will highlight what each stage looks like and at least one tool to help bring you to a higher level of self-love.

7) SELF-LOATHING

This is when you're completely disconnected from yourself. Most likely, you're actually living to other people's and societal expectations and standards. When you feel like you don't fit in, you dissociate from yourself and even hate yourself.

A person at this stage will likely experience:

- Extremely negative self-talk, in a way that bullies yourself.
- Suicidal ideations: Believing the world would be better off without you in it.
- Self-harm and/or addictive behaviors.
- Risky behaviors because you do not care what happens to you.
- Inability to recognize anything positive or any strengths about yourself.
- Not fulfilling your basic needs.
- Feeling unworthy of pleasure or enjoyment.
- Feeling lonely while also hiding from the world.

If you're in this stage, it's likely you have experienced past trauma and may have a very negative view of the world. Who can blame you if you were hurt in the past? Having a negative view of the world most likely is from your own brain trying to protect you from more harm. However, oftentimes our pain is internalized towards *ourselves* with self-blame and self-hatred.

If you find yourself here. . .

First things first, can you keep yourself safe?

If you're questioning whether or not you can keep yourself safe or have minimal to no reasons for living, you may need to seek emergency services. Take the very first step towards self-love by asking for help. If you are in the United States, you can call or text the **Suicide Prevention Lifeline at 988.** If you're outside of the US, call your local emergency services.

If you're in this stage but can keep yourself safe for now, I still urge you to talk to a therapist. When you're in this stage, it can be very difficult to help yourself out of this alone. If you're already in therapy and nothing is changing, you may want to consider switching to someone new.

Even if you don't want therapy, feel it won't help, or you don't deserve it, I urge you to try it anyway. By opening up this support to yourself, you are already beginning to participate in self-love. Even if your "human" doesn't want this, know that your inner being does. The Universe, God, and your Higher Self love you; they want you to feel the same way about yourself. They want you to be here. You are not alone!

6) SELF-DISSATISFACTION

This is when you're unhappy or disappointed with yourself. You might say you don't like yourself; you may even wish you were someone else. This stage is similar to self-loathing, but here there is a conscious part of you that wants to get better.

A person at this stage will likely experience:

- Negative self-talk and self-judgment of yourself.
- Passive suicidal thoughts without intention.
- Self-harm/addictive behaviors.
- Difficulty recognizing anything positive or any strengths about yourself.
- Often not fulfilling your basic needs.
- Feeling unworthy of pleasure or enjoyment.
- Not enjoying time alone with the self.
- Needing validation from others.

If you find yourself here. . .

First, again seek help from a therapist or other healing modalities if you haven't already done so. Find your support system.

Start paying attention to your self-talk. What are you saying about yourself, to yourself, and others?

Grab a pen and paper.

Identify the voice of your negative self-talk and see if you can separate it from yourself. This voice is not the real you. This voice most likely came from sources outside you, such as parental figures, peers, the media, etc.

Ask yourself, *where or who did this voice, these thoughts, and beliefs about myself come from?*

When you notice negative self-talk thoughts, *write them down.* Notice how it feels to say these thoughts out loud to yourself. Right now, you may even think it feels good to say something bad about yourself. There is no right answer here. Just notice.

Can you neutralize these statements about yourself?

Example:

"I'm such an idiot" ⟶ "I made a mistake."

Or can you eliminate your negative self-talk altogether? It may be helpful to have a go-to phrase such as "I'm not going to speak negatively of myself, even if I'm tempted to."

Remember to be patient with yourself during this process. Try not to judge yourself for your self-talk. That will only make it worse. It takes time to break a habit.

5) NEUTRAL RESILIENCE

This is when you become the casual observer of yourself. This is the space in between, where you don't necessarily feel negative about yourself, but you are not feeling positive yet.

If you find yourself here. . .

You likely will not remain here for long, but you want to level *up* to the next stage of self-acceptance instead of going back down to self-dissatisfaction.

This activity is simple. While you are observing yourself, all you have to do is add, "And that's okay" or, And I can accept that" so that you quickly move up to the next level.

For example:

"I woke up later than usual today. . .and that's okay."

"I feel a little sad today. . .and I can accept that."

If a voice tries to come in and argue with you, try your best to silence that voice. If it makes you feel better, you can add, "I can try again tomorrow."

4) SELF-ACCEPTANCE

This is when you can come to a place of "I am who I am, and that's okay." You may be able to *appreciate* certain parts of yourself and begin to identify your strengths. You start to accept or tolerate your flaws.

If you find yourself here. . .

Become curious and excited about getting to know who you are. What are your likes and dislikes? What brings you joy? What are your values and why? Again, journal your thoughts.

3) SELF-RESPECT

This is when you have a clearer idea of who you are, along with your needs, desires, and how you want to be treated by others. You begin advocating for yourself by setting boundaries to receive the treatment from yourself *and* others that match the vibration you want to embody. You know you deserve to be treated as an equal; you deserve love and respect.

If you find yourself here. . .

Get yourself into alignment with *love and appreciation* to move on to the next stage.

What do you like about yourself? Focus on these attributes and watch them grow. Can you change the word like to *love?*

Abraham-Hicks taught me this. It may be hard to start with yourself, so start to find things you love and appreciate, and see if that momentum brings you to a place where you can start to direct that love towards yourself.

Example: "I love being outside. I am grateful to experience the feeling of the sun on my skin and the cool breeze. I love my dog. He's so playful and cute. I love my hair. I have a good heart."

2) HOLISTIC APPRECIATION

This is where you are aware and proud of your strengths. You can appreciate all parts of you, even your shadows because they all are an integral part of your unique magic. Now you are able to speak positively to yourself, about yourself. However, you may occasionally still be affected by what others think about you. You enjoy time with yourself but still may experience feelings of loneliness.

If you find yourself here. . .

You are in a great spot! This is when I want you to explore the different ways you can actively honor yourself and learn to fill yourself up with your own love so that you can eliminate the neediness to receive it externally.

Explore *The Five Love Languages* (acts of service, physical touch, receiving gifts, quality time, and words of affirmation) created by Gary Chapman. Although this was originally designed for interpersonal relationships, try the love languages on yourself so that you can practice taking the time and effort to love yourself actively.

1) SELF-ADORATION

Congratulations! You've made it to the final stage, which has infinite potential. This is when you're actively honoring yourself and loving yourself unconditionally. You are so grateful to be you and enjoy spending time with yourself. You're filled up with your own love. You have all that you need. You're not constantly looking outside of yourself in order to fill a void. You see yourself as God sees you. You truly give to others from your overflow, not because you expect something in return.

It's not that you don't have desires, but instead of those desires being something to "get a fix," your desires are in alignment with the highest good, inspired action, your growth and enlightenment, and provide lasting joy and fulfillment.

If you find yourself here. . .

There's no stopping you now! Love is infinite, so this is where you get to be creative and love yourself in all the different ways you can imagine. When you continue to love yourself more and more, you will increase your capacity for love in general. Enjoy being here, and keep sharing your love and your awesome self with the world! By being you and being in *love* with you, you are 100% having a positive effect on those around you!

Vienna Costanzo-D'Aprile is a New York state-licensed mental health counselor, Reiki Master/Teacher, and spiritual life coach. Vienna's mission in life is to help others fully love and embody their authentic selves so they can carry out their life's purpose and contribute to the highest good of the world. Vienna uses her education, experience, and intuition to offer holistic therapy techniques in both individual and group settings. She believes true healing occurs through a deep connection with the self, others, and a Higher power.

Vienna's own spirituality and self-love development has helped her through the most challenging times in her life, and it invigorates her to be able to incorporate this in her work with her clients. While she still enjoys using therapeutic interventions, internal family systems, dialectical behavioral therapy, and Jungian techniques, she has moved past conventional therapy by bringing in spiritual practices such as manifestation techniques, Reiki, and regression therapy techniques in her sessions.

Vienna was born and raised in Long Island and now lives in the Hudson Valley in New York with her wonderful, supportive husband and the silliest, sweetest golden retriever named Obie.

There is even more information and resources about self-love on Vienna's website! You can find her at www.thespiritualtherapist.net or on Instagram @the.spiritualtherapist.

CHAPTER 13

FROM THE INSIDE OUT

A SACRED RITUAL FOR EATING TO HEAL

Jenna DiVenuto, M.S., Akashic Reiki Master

MY STORY

"You need to eat," my father insisted. I stared down at my full plate. It wasn't that the food was unappetizing—my mother made delicious meals for my siblings and I. It was because I was desperate for some type of control.

Growing up, my father was the typical strict Italian. I loved and still love my father (and my mother, too—she and I saw eye-to-eye much easier). Being the first born meant I took a lot of hits in the parenting department. I had to break my parents in. I had the toughest rules and curfews so my siblings could get the looser versions after I suffered through missing events like the Sweet 16s. It was a rule that I couldn't attend them until I was 17. I digress.

"No food, no gym," he reiterated. *Shit, I need the gym,* I thought. So I mindlessly inhaled my food and put my sneakers on. Since being diagnosed with an eating disorder at age 15, I could no longer go to the gym unsupervised. I wanted my life back. I wanted to be able to decide to go to the gym without coordinating with a parent. I did what I had to do to regain control, not necessarily because I wanted to. The top of this list? Eating.

It's no wonder my eating disorder came back with a vengeance at the age of 22. I realized that a lot of my initial eating disorder onset had to do with inner child trauma, as I learned through my therapist. For those that may not know, the inner child is our true selves, which may or may not have acquired damage during childhood. I felt like I was a bad child after having all of these rules imposed on me. This was far from the truth, but I didn't know any better.

This inner child trauma was triggered when my parents began their divorce, which was toxic and agonizing, to say the least. To cope in my 20s, I did what I did the first time around: I increased my calories, stopped doing cardio, added more snacks, and turned to weights for muscle gain. I truly enjoyed a lot of these components. I loved building muscle. I loved feeling strong. But everything else? That was just being done to check off the box. I was getting better, so who cares, right?

And this time around, I sprinkled in some spirituality. My therapist became an Akashic Reiki master, and it was in beautiful alignment that she shared some of her energy work with me. For the first time, I felt something—deep. From the inside out. Meditation? Cool. Crystals? Loved them. The energy? Palpable. I wanted in. I wanted this feeling all of the time. I dove in head first.

Looking back, this was my spiritual awakening just starting to brew. Within six months, I was an Akashic practitioner, using the Akashic Records for divine guidance and healing. I went from having one crystal to 50 crystals. I craved the feeling of a crystal in my hand and meditation in my ears. I was energetically up-leveling, and I was doing it fast. The idea of healing not only myself, but my family, along with me, absolutely set my soul on fire. Healing friends and strangers too? Let the blaze burn. I had a lot of work to do.

Eventually, I was so in love with energy work that I became attuned to Reiki, powering through and completing Reiki 1 all the way up to Reiki Master teacher. For those unfamiliar with these energy lines, the Akashic line of energy is masculine and offers very direct healing and guidance. The Reiki line of energy is feminine and offers gentle healing wherever it is needed. Using the Akashic line of energy and Akashic Records in combination with the Reiki line energy allowed me to align with my soul's mission, and I knew it instantly. My cells buzzed. My chakras vibrated. *This is it,* I thought. *My soul is totally healing.*

Throughout all of this, I was rehabilitating my eating disorder. But I was so focused on my spiritual growth that I was eating reflexively and mindlessly. Sure, I was gaining weight and eating regularly. But I felt nothing surrounding it. I heard in many meditations the importance of the divine union of mind, body, and soul to reach my highest potential (or highest self), but I knew my physical body was taking a back seat. *It will catch up,* I always reasoned. But would it? I was in denial.

Fast forward a few years later, I'm 25 years old. I'm still healing. And as I'm writing this beautiful chapter, I find out that amidst my parent's freshly-initiated divorce, my father has been diagnosed with glioblastoma. His prognosis was exceptionally poor. My inner child took a hit again. Thank goodness I was so much more spiritual at this point in my life; it was, and still is, the practice that unwaveringly helped me navigate difficult life events like this one.

I want to take a minute to explain one of my core beliefs, a belief I share with many energy workers. Everything is energy, and it has levels of manifestations. If you do not address energy at a mental level (such as a thought), it will manifest on an emotional level (such as sadness/anxiety in reaction to that thought). If you do not address energy at an emotional level, it will manifest on a physical level (such as a physical illness). I truly believe that due to the path my father chose to follow in his life energetically, his diagnosis was self-inflicted. It all made sense to me. And that's when it clicked.

If you know me, you know I'm sensitive. This became my greatest gift. I don't have a mean bone in my body. I want to help and heal everyone every minute of the day. But what about myself? I was healing my soul, I was healing my mind, but I wasn't healing my body. I was bypassing my own self-care. My eating disorder was essentially a physical manifestation of me not dealing with my energy at a mental or emotional level; I put everyone else as a priority ahead of myself. I wanted to make sure everyone was okay. Because of this continuous though not conscious neglect, the eating disorder kept coming back. It made sense. I needed to heal this energy at its root, at the mental level. I started this healing with how I thought about my body in general and ways to consciously nourish my body, and it all shifted from there.

THE PRACTICE

As I experienced my spiritual awakening, I found that what I thought to be my biggest curse became my biggest blessing: food. Once I initiated this self-made ritual with anything I consumed, my overall healing absolutely skyrocketed. I was immersed in learning every chakra and the foods to consume to heal each one. When my chakras were fed, they were balanced, and I was constantly grounded while simultaneously receiving divine guidance. I went on a spiritual retreat where it was me and my healing face to face; I decided to make every meal sacred. Before I teach you how to implement this magical ritual, I want to explain the basics of our chakras.

Chakras are energy centers, and each human has seven of them. These chakras run from the base of our spine to the crown of our heads. The names of our chakras are the root, sacral, solar plexus, heart, throat, third eye, and crown. Each chakra corresponds with a location, color, and emotion.

It's important to become familiar with the location of each chakra to start paying attention to where physical sensations are arising in our bodies. Regarding locations, our root chakra is located at the base of our spine; our sacral chakra is located below our belly button; our solar plexus chakra is located above our belly button; our heart chakra is located at our heart; our throat chakra is located at our throat; our third eye is located in between our eyebrows, and our crown chakra is located at the crown of our heads.

When we bring colors in, our root chakra is red, our sacral chakra is orange, our solar plexus chakra is yellow, our heart chakra is green, our throat chakra is blue, our third eye chakra is purple, and our crown chakra is white.

Finally, each chakra corresponds with basic emotions. Like the location of our chakras, knowing the basic feelings each chakra is in charge of will help us tune in to what chakra to heal. Our root chakra houses our survival/feeling safe, our sacral chakra reflects our creativity/passion as well as holds inner child trauma, our solar plexus chakra embodies our self-confidence/ self-empowerment, our heart chakra houses our love and adoration for life/ others, our throat chakra allows us to speak our truth, our third eye chakra highlights our intuition and our crown chakra funnels in divine guidance.

Any of these chakras can become over or under-active; foods help rebalance and heal them. You can do this by eating foods that are the color of that chakra; eggplant is great for the third eye, while spinach is great for the heart. How do you know when to eat what? You pay attention to the physical sensations you feel at the location or the emotions arising.

It was on my spiritual retreat as I picked fresh kale from the garden, eating directly off Mother Earth, when this ritual was intuitively downloaded to me. I was in such alignment with my Highest Self dancing around like a little earth fairy that the knowledge flooded in clearer than it had ever had: every food I would put in my body, from that moment forward, would heal me—from the inside out.

I floated inside and quickly constructed a snack. It consisted of raw red, orange, yellow, and green peppers, blue tortilla chips, a plum, and hummus. If you're keeping track, I indirectly hit every chakra. To add to the magic, I made a cup of straight-up cacao with Ripple milk to bust my third eye wide open. I decided to eat outside to thank Mother Earth for her food and connect deeply with her. In the grass, I placed all of this goodness in front of me. My hands immediately went into prayer at my third eye and instinctively spread over my meal. As the sacred ritual began to unfold through my body, I realized I was crying. My physical body was so thankful and thanked me in a way that I would pay attention. It all poured out of me.

While the order in which you consume your meal isn't exceptionally important, I intuitively started with my root chakra. I would recommend starting with the food that corresponds with your lowest chakra that you're healing in that meal.

As I took the first bite of my red pepper, divine words flooded in: *I am safe.* I was in awe. My angels were sending me affirmations to say as I mindfully consumed Mother Earth's gifts. In my state of alignment, the affirmations came to correspond with every chakra. These were the affirmations that came through for me: root chakra: *I am safe;* sacral chakra: *I am playful;* solar plexus chakra: *I am powerfully powerful;* heart chakra: *I am loving and love beyond limits;* throat chakra: *I speak my light to heal myself and others;* third eye chakra: *I am wildly intuitive,* and crown chakra: *I am angelically activated.* Feel free to refer back to and utilize these affirmations, but I encourage you to surrender and listen deeply to your body. Your body sends the whispers of what you need at every moment of every day—we just need to be still and hold space to hear it.

I finished my meal and felt weak at the knees. I let my knees hit the ground. I bowed and pressed my forehead into the grass. And what happened there, I'm *positive,* was because of my chakra eating ritual. I felt any last energy that no longer served me seeping out of my forehead and into Mother Earth. By honoring her in my chakra eating ritual, she was honoring me in return. She took my stagnant energy and replaced it with purified, white light energy. I watched an energetic seed plant in me from Mother Earth, right over my heart chakra. I don't even know how long I was in this position, and honestly, I didn't care. When I picked my head up from Mother Earth's support, I saw my life in a different way. I was changed. I healed to a level I had never reached before. And I was just getting started.

I *need* you to experience this magic. I know you will never go back. Here's how to do it:

1. Before you eat, tune into your body by dropping into it. I like to do the 5-5-5 breaths (inhale, hold, and exhale for five seconds each) to settle my energy. I follow my breath's journey through my lips, down into my lungs, deep into my belly, and back out into the universe after it's replenished me. If my mind wanders, I gently guide it back to this. After I've done the 5-5-5 breath five times, I pay attention to any physical sensations or emotions that arise and where they physically arise in my body. Sometimes I feel nothing, and that's okay.

2. Depending on what came up for you in Step 1, you can chakra eat to assuage it. For example, if you drop in and pick up a headache and tingling in your right leg, I would grab some purple concord grapes and strawberries.

3. Arrange your food mindfully for whatever you wish. The grass outside is totally warranted, and I recommend it. Show gratitude to

Mother Earth, thanking her for her gifts that construct what we are about to consume.

4. With your meal in front of you, place your hands over your heart chakra, accumulating love and healing for yourself. Now, if you are a Reiki Master as I am, feel free to Reiki your food and implant any symbols. If you aren't Reiki attuned, I want you to pull energy from your heart chakra, hold it in your hand and sprinkle this healing, loving energy to infuse your meal with it.

5. As you begin to eat, you may either begin with the lowest chakra you are feeding in this meal and work your way up or let your body intuitively guide you.

6. Either out loud or in your mind's eye, start repeating the mantra that corresponds to the chakra you are healing.

7. I remember the saying, "Eat your liquids and drink your foods," as a way to eat mindfully; chew everything you eat 22 times, and hold liquids in your mouth for seven seconds before swallowing.

8. At the end of the meal, bow your head and bring your hands back over your heart chakra in the prayer position. Offer thanks to Mother Earth and the Universe for collaborating with you to heal from the inside out.

As you practice and come home to your body, you can even get fancy and start combining affirmations. For example, if you're eating a blue potato chip (throat chakra) dipped in guacamole (heart chakra), you can say, "I am loving and lovingly speak my truth." And that's it. That's all you need to heal to the deepest level.

I'll leave you with a bet. Try it for seven days. That's it. And after seven days, I know you will feel the immense love and healing you're accumulating in your body every time you eat. Dig deep, love yourself eternally, and heal endlessly. From the inside out.

Jenna is an Akashic Reiki Master teacher fulfilling her soul mission to heal all those who cross her path. She is 25 years old and the oldest of her two loving siblings. In addition, she works as a speech-language pathologist at a children's hospital with the goal of intertwining both callings. With extensive personal experience with healing relationships surrounding food, the inner child, the ego, and the ancestral line, Jenna has a way of not only deeply healing the individual but healing those that became before and after, as shifts made within the individual extend beyond them. She loves implementing crystals into her sessions to bring in Mother Earth energy, kicking healing into overdrive. She shares her authentic journey and divinely guided expertise with refreshing transparency. Get ready for the ride of your life because working with her will instantly bring stagnant energy to the surface to be released and bring you into alignment with your highest self, creating your best life.

When Jenna chills out, you'll find her doing self-Reiki while basking in the sun, cradling her crystals, grounding and exploring in nature, playing at the beach, and drinking her nightly Tamarind Paste tea. She highly recommends this third-eye-opening goodness.

Connect with Jenna:

Instagram: https://www.instagram.com/theliftedlightbeam/

Facebook: https://www.facebook.com/jenna.divenuto

Email: jennadivenuto@gmail.com

CHAPTER 14

THE HIDDEN POWER WITHIN YOUR ANXIETY

MASTER YOUR ENERGY FIELD AND THRIVE

Daisy Farrell, Psychic Medium, Reiki Master

MY STORY

I decided I would die by the time I was 23 and accepted it fully as my fate.

There I was again, sitting in my car, unsure where to go. I ran from work early yet again, completely overwhelmed with anxiety and panic. Nowhere but home felt safe. I didn't understand what was happening to me. I had been through unimaginable trauma, several years of solid sobriety, and tons of therapy. On the outside, I should've been a picture-perfect example of mental health. But I felt completely unhinged, like I was spiraling out of control in a way I had never experienced.

How did I end up here? My whole life, I've been hypersensitive to the world around me. I always perceived things differently from my peers, and it caused me lots of social struggles. It always felt I was missing something others had figured out. I felt everything deeply, including the struggles of those around me. This led to hospitalization and an early diagnosis of depression when I was only 13, along with a prescription for antidepressants. I spent years deep within addiction and pain. I was constantly in abusive relationships, always looking to escape my reality and treating my body like a disposable piece of trash.

Thankfully I found the beautiful program of AA (alcoholics anonymous). I turned my life around and did the work. It was a beautiful and magical experience. I finally understood myself and cultivated self-love. I felt stable and started building healthy relationships. What I didn't realize was there was a whole other piece to this puzzle under the surface.

It wasn't until two years sober that I began to experience some weird stuff. I experienced premonition dreams as a child and always had very vivid dreams but never thought anything of it. I also experienced paranormal things throughout my life. I saw a full-bodied apparition in my bedroom while in college, heard unexplainable sounds such as crying and voices, and I've seen several different types of orbs of light fly right in front of me. But again, I didn't think it was for any reason.

Growing up, I was always fascinated with the paranormal world, and I was obsessed with ghost hunting. There are psychics on both sides of my family, so I was always open and interested in that world but never thought I had any ability.

I just came through one of the hardest years of my life and lost three people in less than a year. I began having insanely vivid visitation dreams and more premonitions. But they were different from anything I'd experienced before.

The people in my dreams were attempting to give messages to other people. At the same time, I experienced odd paranormal activity in my apartment, and my anxiety began to skyrocket. My lights turned on and off on their own, things disappeared, and I heard strange sounds. I also became physically sick and experienced many days at work where I felt strange symptoms that magically disappeared the next day. I was also playing with oracle cards and kept pulling a mediumship card every single time.

I didn't understand what was happening. I was so confused and overwhelmed. I was always a hard worker, and suddenly I dreaded going to work. I was always late and ended up leaving early almost daily. The minute I stepped into my job, I felt exhausted, overwhelmed, paranoid, extremely out of it, and as if the whole world would explode. I thought I'd be hospitalized again. I was so full of fear. I ran to my therapist, desperate for relief. She said, "I really think you have something powerful going on here. Go to a medium and see what they think."

I went to a medium, and the first thing he said to me was, "Daisy, it's a fucking party in here." I remember having the most unbelievable sensation of pressure in my head and of an overwhelming presence in the room with us. He was able to validate and clarify everything for me and brought through all of the people in spirit supporting me. He explained, "The veil is extremely thin for you; it's effortless for you to connect, and you are definitely a medium. Spirit has signed you up for this path." I remember leaving the session stunned but also unsure of what to do next. I thought, *How could this be possible? Is this really what I want to do with my life? How can I trust if it's for real?* I still felt completely overwhelmed but curious, so I reached out to another medium for guidance. She was kind enough to call me on the phone. She said, "Imagine a white bubble of light protecting you. You definitely have something going on. I recommend taking a beginners class with me to see where it goes." I still wasn't convinced I was a medium because I had never experienced connecting with a past loved one while I was awake. But I had to try it.

We went through various exercises to tap into our psychic abilities. Every time it unfolded very naturally for me. Halfway through the class, we finally connected to spirit for the first time. My teacher walked us through a meditation to connect and then asked me, "Who do you have?" I explained, "I feel crazy! I feel like I can't move from the neck down. I also see a man that is very well dressed and surrounded by books. He is also showing me a vintage-style coffee table. "A man in my class suddenly said, "I know who you have. That's my friend. He was a paraplegic, a teacher, had tons of books, always dressed well, and collected vintage furniture." I was completely stunned and couldn't believe what was happening.

From that day on, things were never the same. I continued to do practices in that class and started to do practice readings on people outside of class. My abilities rapidly expanded from that point on. I realized I was born this way, and it was a natural ability for me. I simply needed a person to show me how to do it the first time.

This also explained other things from my past I simply chalked up to being an alcoholic. For the longest time, I was fully satisfied with that answer and felt like, *well, that makes sense.* But now, knowing what I know and looking back, it explains so much more on a deeper level.

No wonder I constantly felt the need to numb myself. I was experiencing my pain, but I was also feeling the people around me and people in spirit. I also think this explains why I was bullied in school. I just saw the world differently, and many children did not understand me. It's because I was connected to something greater, and I thought that was normal. It was honestly a huge relief to finally understand this, and it made me love myself even more. However, there was still a lot for me to learn and experience.

Now that I understood, it was reassuring. However, I still felt the same, if not worse. I became even more aware of the shift in energies, the presence I felt around me, and the energy of others. When I went to work, I was bombarded with spirits and often hid in a corner to allow them to talk to me. I wrote everything down, which temporarily helped me to get it out of my system. But it still wasn't a cure.

I reached out to multiple different psychics and mediums and had several different mentors. All of them offered different advice. They talked about doing protection rituals, using different methods to tell spirit when I wanted them to leave me alone, and recommended designating a time each day to allow spirit to channel through me. For the most part, none of it helped.

The biggest healer of my anxiety was time. Not just time in general, but time doing lots of hard work. I needed time to understand how spirit worked with me and what it felt like when certain energies were coming into my field. I also had to understand what worked best for me.

Unfortunately, there's a lot of misunderstanding out there and a lot of fear around the spirit world. Several teachers told me I needed to protect myself, and for a time, I did a grounding and protecting exercise every morning before I left the house. I do think it helped, but it was more of a mental trick. I now never use protection rituals because I'm no longer afraid and know better.

The other misconception is that we're at the mercy of what spirit wants. That if we're in a public place, they can bombard us without our permission. This is entirely untrue. I always like to remind my students that we are the ones in control of what comes into our energy. Quite often, when you're new to your abilities, you'll want to be on all the time because it's exciting. But this is often not the best tactic, as it can lead us to overwhelm and fatigue. It will also not serve you when you're trying to do this as a profession. In the beginning, I hated being in public places and became quite agoraphobic. But over time, I learned I simply didn't have to pay attention. Now when I go out, spirit can get my attention at times if I feel like it, but for the most part, I'm not bothered by it unless I want to be.

One huge relief from the anxiety was listening to the call from spirit to be a channel for messages. Once I started doing mediumship readings regularly, I felt much better because I allowed this excess energy to flow through me versus being built up and overwhelming.

I also want to make clear that the expression of your abilities can look any way you desire. It doesn't mean you have to be a professional psychic medium. In fact, I don't encourage you to do that if it doesn't feel right because that'll do more harm than good. We are all unique, and the world needs our uniqueness. There is incredible beauty, strength, and power when people can channel these abilities in everyday work or their encounters with regular people. So don't think there is only one option if you relate to this story.

My goal is for you to be able to deepen your understanding of where these cues are coming from. Because they have power, even if it doesn't feel that way right now, it typically requires us to dive into the fear and overwhelm at first to come out the other side. But I'll tell you right now, it is endlessly worth it.

When I started this path, there were several times when I felt I'd need to be hospitalized, that I was completely crazy, and that my life was over. But being on the other side of it now, I'm eternally grateful I was put through this and so grateful I was given the gift of truly understanding myself and how I operate. And best of all, being able to help the world with these abilities and my experience.

The following tools are for anyone who has experienced anxiety or mental illness and for anyone who has felt overly sensitive. This doesn't always mean you're going to end up a medium like me, but I can guarantee you that most people with these difficulties have intuitive abilities of some kind. By unfolding and understanding these abilities, you can tap into your superpowers and not only heal what ails you but empower yourself and enhance your life. You never know where these abilities could take you and how they can change the course of your life, so dive in with an open mind and let me know how it goes.

THE PRACTICE

This practice is a structure for you to follow to ground yourself, get a better understanding of what your anxiety is telling you, and how to separate energy that isn't yours. This is a crucial tool for anyone experiencing an influx of energy and will certainly help you feel saner.

The first and most simple thing you can do is meditate for ten minutes every morning before you do anything else. You can use a meditation app if you like, especially if you find sitting still difficult. If you struggle with meditating, start with five minutes. You can also move your body before meditation to sink in more deeply.

When you sit in this meditation, tune in to how your energy feels. Get as detailed as you possibly can. Try to use all your senses. To take it a step further, you could use your journal to describe how you're feeling after meditating. I also encourage you to make this practice special in a way that feels good to you. This could include lighting a candle or incense, reading a daily meditation book, writing a gratitude list, holding crystals, or even pulling an oracle card. The possibilities are endless.

Once you do this meditation, go on with your day. At the end of your day, I want you to do a check-in. If you feel like it, you can do a whole other ten-minute meditation at night or simply take a few minutes to sit with yourself quietly. Tune into how you feel differently from that morning, and again, to take it a step further, you can write this down. This is the key because this is where you're going to tune into how your energy has shifted since being around other people, places, and energies and what may not be your energy.

Do this for a couple of weeks and see if you notice any patterns. For example, see if you feel the same way at the end of the day after seeing the same person. Noticing any coincidences like that. From there, you can continue to build on that information. If you're experiencing panic attacks or waves of emotion throughout your day, use those as an opportunity to learn. The next time an emotional wave appears and it doesn't seem to have an understandable trigger, go somewhere where you can be alone for ten minutes and sit with yourself in this emotion. Take a few deep breaths and simply ask: *Is this mine?*

See what comes up. Don't question it. If the answer is no, ask: *Whose is this?* And see what you get. Once you identify whose energy it is, I want you to do a brief body scan and ask your body where this energy is being held. Once you identify the location, place your hands over that area and repeat this in your head: *Thank you so much for giving me this information. I have understood the message, and I no longer need it.* And imagine that energy going into your hands, down your body, through the bottom of your feet, and into the earth. You can repeat this as many times as you need, and you could also put your spin on it in any way you like. The idea is that we're acknowledging the message we have been given, we're showing gratitude for it, and then we're explaining to spirit that we no longer need to hold it in our bodies.

Over time, these practices can develop. A few other tools I recommend adding are grounding crystals, such as black obsidian, jet stone, black tourmaline, smoky quartz, and dravite. I also recommend taking a 20-minute Epsom salt bath or foot soak at least once a week. When you do that, imagine the salt absorbing the energies that aren't yours.

The next step would be to decode what your abilities are trying to show you. Start with basics here and focus on understanding how your body and intuition work and communicate. Documentation is super important throughout this process because it's through patterns that we begin to understand how our intuition works. One thing you can do is sit down in meditation with a pen and paper, say, "I am open," and write down whatever you get. Don't worry about what it means or if it makes sense. You can try doing this weekly and begin to compare your notes. This is a helpful tool when you feel like you haven't fully unloaded excess energies. To get deeper into understanding how your intuition works visit my free resources page here: www.daisyfarrell.com/resources

Overall, the most important part of these tools is consistency. The more you practice, the more in tune with the energy you become and the more in control you will feel.

One last piece of advice is to have an open relationship with spiritual energy and open dialogue with it. Spirit wants to work with you, not against you. Quite often, they're trying to show you something, but they may not know it's upsetting you. All they care about is getting their message across, but you need to tell them what works for you, and they will honor that every time. If you're experiencing physical symptoms you feel are not yours, you can say, "Thank you for giving me this information, but from now on, please show me this in a different way." This is also true for empathic abilities. You are in control. You have full power to thrive with these abilities. Take it a day at a time and trust the process. You have no idea how much magic is on the other side.

Daisy Farrell is a psychic medium, Reiki Master Teacher, and artist based in the Hudson Valley, New York. She is passionate about helping others explore their psychic abilities and working with their shadow to empower and ignite their most authentic life. She loves using multiple modalities of spiritual work to give her clients a unique, multifaceted healing experience and encourage them to blaze their own magical path. She loves dispelling the confusion around the spiritual world and helping others remove the fear that comes with the unknown.

Through her experience of addiction and mental health struggles, she was able to discover not only her abilities as a medium but also the incredible world of alternative healing. She loves being able to bridge mental health and addiction with the spiritual world to help show her clients a brand new perspective on their struggles and allow them to understand themselves in a way they never thought possible. She loves to constantly challenge herself to find new ways of working with spirit, deepening her skill set as a healer and sharing these methods with others.

Daisy loves spending time with her husband, exploring the outdoors, cooking and baking, creating art, hoarding crystals, and not taking life too seriously.

Connect with Daisy:

Website: www.daisyfarrell.com

Instagram: https://www.instagram.com/innerkeyalchemy

Facebook: https://www.facebook.com/groups/182932440413209

https://www.facebook.com/innerkeyalchemy

CHAPTER 15

HEALING THROUGH WRITING

USING THE CRAFT TO ACHIEVE EMOTIONAL FREEDOM

Corinne Santiago, MFA

"I can shake off everything as I write; my sorrows disappear, my courage is reborn."

~ Anne Frank

MY STORY

It started with a boy. I'd be kidding myself if I didn't admit to feeling a little embarrassed writing that, but since I was only in fifth grade, I'll try to cut myself some slack, and I hope you will too. Remember, if there's one thing you can be sure of, it's that there's no room for judgment of yourself or others as you read this book.

A crush that begins in third grade and clings to you for two years is basically an eternity by elementary school standards. The then eight-year-old Corinne may not have had the courage, but ten-year-old Corinne was light years more confident, practically a woman already. As February approached, the stars aligned in my head, and I felt like if there was ever going to be a perfect time to make my truth known, it was going to be then.

It's now or never! You can do it!

The affection was going to burst out of me, but that go-getter, confident attitude was only taking me so far; there was no way I was gutsy enough to just walk up to him and make a verbal confession of love.

There had to be another way.

Write him a letter.

Brilliant.

I sat in my bedroom with a fresh sheet of notebook paper and a red pen for added dramatic effect. My childhood soul poured out through that ink, my hand dotting every "I" with a heart as I recollected every minor encounter we'd had over the last two years, even though I'm sure he'd forgotten them as I cherished them. I told him how much I liked him, how I had the biggest crush on him since I met him in third grade, and I ended with a simple question: *Will you be my Valentine?*

I slid the note into his desk the next day before sitting down at my own, face flushed and knees bouncing with nerves. I didn't dare watch him in case we were to make eye contact as he reached inside his desk and felt the loose page floating around in there. I felt both like a badass for taking charge and terrified that I had made an awful mistake.

To my dismay, the latter turned out to be true.

The object of my affection went on to read the letter aloud to his entire lunch table, the laughter carrying throughout the whole cafeteria. My face turned the color of the ink I so carefully curated, now being brandished to the room as it was recited. Every inch of my skin was on fire.

"I wish I was invisible," I said under my breath.

I was tortured for the rest of the day, escaping to the bathroom as often as I could with tears streaming down my face. My naïveté had not allowed me to even consider this outcome as an option. I thought he would either say yes and we'd walk off into the sunset holding hands, or he'd tell me he didn't like me back, that would be the end of it, and I'd move on, slowly but surely getting over my crush. Putting what I considered to be an act of love and bravery on display as though it were part of a freak show never even crossed my mind.

The bus ride home was a continuation of the disaster. People were literally pointing and jeering, leaning over the seat in front of me to get a better look as I made myself as small as I possibly could, curling up with my head against the window, watching the houses go by, praying for my stop to come sooner.

"I can't believe you did that," they laughed, "He was so embarrassed."

He was embarrassed?!

I ran down my driveway and burst through the back door, crashing into my mother's arms.

"He laughed at me," I bawled, wiping tears and snot all over her shirt. "He read the letter out loud to everybody, and they all laughed at me!"

In my fit of devastation, my sobbing continued into the evening. I assumed the fetal position in my bed, scolding myself for having done something so stupid and wondering what I was ever going to do to recover from this. Not only had I done detrimental damage to my social life, but my heart had taken its first official blow. Then, not totally understanding why, I took out another fresh piece of notebook paper. This time, I used a black pen that better matched my emotions because whether I'm smitten or scorned, I can't help but be dramatic.

I wrote my first poem—not counting those acrostic poems we all wrote in grammar school using the letters of our name. I took everything I felt, all the hurt, shame, anger, and betrayal, and put it on the page. I literally unloaded. Each word was a piece of baggage from my unrequited crush, every sentence a chunk of the burden that was my classmates tearing me down. With one stanza at a time, I built myself back up.

"I'm going to kill the kid that made her feel this way," my dad told my mom when he read it.

I didn't realize until much later in life that for both instances in which that younger version of me had big feelings, she used writing to release them. My overwhelming grade school devotion needed an outlet, and so did my misery.

My letter gave me a voice when I was too scared to use it otherwise, and, more importantly, my poem gave me the strength I needed to bounce back from the rejection and subsequent bullying. My eyes began to roll instead of filling up with tears, and after another week or two, the letter heard 'round the school became old news. My writing had given me an anchor to hold onto when the doubt and hurt started to creep up again.

You were able to let it out, I told myself. *Read it again. Look what you were able to make.*

That poem, containing all of my childhood attempts at soul searching, went on to be published in my elementary school's literary magazine. I suddenly had an empowering feeling of accomplishment that somehow outweighed the wound. It was something tangible I could hold onto—a healthy outlet I'd used to muddle through all those overwhelming feelings that consumed me that afternoon.

I will forever be grateful to that boy for leading me to the tool I would go back to for the rest of my life, through every feeling and experience, spanning from catastrophic to sublime.

When my best friend died in a car accident three days before my 18th birthday, my grief turned into countless poems, letters, essays, and stories, about him, for him, and to him.

When I fell in love for the first time in college, some of my most beautiful poems spilled from my soul—I wrote even better ones during the second (not to mention healthier) time around.

Regardless of whether or not I could find the words with my voice, I was always able to find them through my pen or my keyboard.

Finding a creative outlet that brought me joy and ignited my passion in my youth allowed me to have a foundation upon which to build my emotional growth as I matured, learned, fell, soared, and lived. While some people make music, paint, or build, I write.

Perhaps you're trying to find what works for you; perhaps you're trying to work a little something extra into your self-care routine. Regardless of why you came to this book, I encourage you to write. Write in any way that feels best for you because the only thing that matters is that you're letting yourself come through organically in the stories you tell. You are worthy of telling them exactly as you are.

THE PRACTICE

The number one rule of practicing this craft, and quite possibly the only rule, is to remain honest. As long as your writing is honest, you'll be working through your experiences in a healthy way. Even if you choose to write a fiction piece, there is truth to be told, even in the most fantastical story. I naïvely used to think fiction was just making things up and telling lies in a creative way, but several brilliant professors and wise authors taught me otherwise.

Maya Angelou described it best: "I don't know about lying for novelists. I look at some of the great novelists, and I think the reason they are great is that they're telling the truth. The fact is they're using made-up names, made-up people, made-up places, and made-up times, but they're telling the truth about the human being—what we are capable of, what makes us lose, laugh, weep, fall down, and gnash our teeth and wring our hands and kill each other and love each other."

Turn your bully into the grotesque monster you see them as; write a fairytale that describes the relationship you're yearning for. Not only will this validate what you're going through, but you'll be scratching that itch, seizing the opportunity to get creative instead of hopeless. Your writing doesn't have to be for anyone's eyes but yours. By all means, if you wish to share, publish, or take it to another level, do what feels right, but every finished piece can serve a purpose even if nobody else ever reads it. Whether it be a poem, an essay, a short story, a rough stream of thought, or a locked diary full of your daily musings, be honest with yourself so you can be honest on the page. It's the only way you can feel that beautiful release of everything going on internally.

Decide *Why* You're Writing

Take the time you need to ask yourself what you're feeling and why you're feeling it. If it's anger, what brought it on? If it's grief, whom or what are you lamenting? Give a name to those emotions and triggers—big or small—and absolutely do not judge yourself for having them. No matter what form they take, those feelings are valid, and the fact that you're sitting down at your computer or with a pen and paper proves you're doing your part to move through them. Maybe the only reason you'll be able to come up with is, "To try and feel better," and that's perfectly fine. Be as gentle or tough on yourself as your soul needs you to be but strive for as much self-awareness as you can muster. Defining these feelings will make it easier to take the next step.

Decide *What* You're Writing

Any and every form of writing can be therapeutic. I have used the personal essay to unpack my traumas, telling my story as truthfully as I can; personal essays help to organize racing thoughts attached to distress.

Perhaps you've felt silenced by someone, earthside or passed on, and there are a million things you wish you had said. Write them a letter. Take it from me; even a less than ideal outcome can wind up being rewarding in the long run. In the past, I've taken letters I've written and ripped them into confetti, tossed them in the fire while setting the intention to let go, or just hidden them in the depths of my computer in a folder I purposefully title something funny so that my future self can crack a smile when she stumbles upon it again.

A stream of thought can turn into a gorgeous poem as you keep going.

Journaling daily, weekly, or even just monthly can help create a space for you to release what has been building up in your mind.

Any kind of writing can benefit you, so long as every word is deliberate.

Ready? *Start* writing!

I know what you're thinking.

But Corinne, it's not that easy!

Believe me, I know. The blank page is simultaneously beautiful and torturous to me, but as Stephen King said, "The scariest moment is always just before you start. After that, things can only get better."

As my students embark on their first drafts, the best advice I give them is to *word vomit*.

If you're going through something, chances are your mind is not blank. The most helpful thing you can do for yourself is to just get it out. Let it flow out of you naturally, in all the grammatically incorrect, disjointed, nonsensical ways it forms in your head. Just get it out of your mind and onto the page where it belongs. If you have plans for your piece post-word vomit, there will be plenty of time later to tidy it up and move things around. To begin, however, don't censor yourself. Let it flow, and you'll have no choice but to embrace it. These feelings and these words shouldn't have a home in your heart or your head, but you have the power to put them where they should live.

If your mind is blank, it always helps to start with a grounding exercise. This is where an informal journal might come into play. Rely on your senses by writing down all the things you can see, hear, taste, touch, and smell. Let those observations carry you into the next thing you'll write about. Maybe you'll realize you smell the grass from the neighbor's freshly cut lawn, which will take you back to when you were younger, playing in your own yard with your childhood friends. Or maybe your eyes will land on the framed picture of your mother, and that'll start an avalanche of things you have to say. Doing this exercise alone will help to bring you back down to earth, back to your physical body, ready to do whatever's next to take care of yourself. Don't get overwhelmed when those gears inevitably start turning; they're supposed to!

Stand firmly in the voice you create with your writing, even if it's shaking or reads like a whisper. What matters is that it came from you.

Writing doesn't have to be all gloom and doom. While it has proven to be my most cherished coping mechanism, capable of holding me in safety through my suffering, my happiest moments have also resulted in some pieces I'm immensely proud of. It's true, I feel my personal essays about betrayal and grief are testaments to my strength and badassery, but the poems I've written about the love of my life fill me with warmth and satisfaction as well. It all comes back to our golden writing rule: honesty. Whether you're working through a painful situation, inspired by a miracle, trying to calm your racing thoughts, or just feeling hopelessly romantic, you must mean what you write and write what you mean. It will never fail to align your body, mind, and soul.

When finished, you'll have something solid to hold, read, or destroy, depending on the purpose you went into your writing practice with. Or maybe you'll never be finished. That's okay too. Keep going back as often as you need to. Keep adding, subtracting, playing, and feeling. It's all allowed.

Any emotion can be felt more deeply and wholly through the written word. You can put your thoughts in order, calm your anger, relieve your pain, and breathe a sigh of relief as you leave it all on the page.

As James Baldwin so eloquently put it, "One writes out of one thing only—one's own experience. Everything depends on how relentlessly one forces from this experience the last drop, sweet or bitter, it can possibly give. This is the only real concern of the artist, to recreate out of the disorder of life that order which is art."

Let your words be the remedy, the celebration, the truth, the evidence of everything you are, and all the experiences that helped make you that way.

Corinne Santiago has a bachelor's degree in journalism from SUNY Purchase and a Master of Fine Arts degree in creative nonfiction writing from Sarah Lawrence College. She has served as an adjunct professor of college writing at her undergraduate alma mater since 2019. She has been published on various blogs and websites and freelances whenever she gets the chance. Her poem, "Ode to my Thighs," won the John B. Santoianni Award for Excellence in Poetry from the Academy of American Poets in 2018.

Having discovered her love and passion for writing at a young age, she now encourages her students (and anyone who will listen, for that matter) to see the potential for growth and release in the writing they create. Being her most unapologetically authentic self, both on and off the page, and helping others do the same, is one of the most important things to her.

When she's not writing or reading, Corinne is probably bingeing a show with her partner in their CT home, spending time with her parents, siblings, and nephews, or adding to her collection of dog videos on social media. Corinne also finds joy and stress relief in coloring and jigsaw puzzles, even when her adorable four-legged son eats a piece, and she doesn't find out until she's finished. She is determined to fall more deeply in love with herself and her life each and every day.

Connect with Corinne:

Portfolio: https://bycorinnesantiago.journoportfolio.com/

LinkedIn: https://www.linkedin.com/in/corinnesantiago/

Facebook: https://www.facebook.com/corinne.santiago

Instagram: https://www.instagram.com/bycorinnesantiago/

CHAPTER 16

HOLOGRAPHIC MANIPULATION THERAPY

THE WHOLE APPROACH TO REVERSING ADVERSE CHILDHOOD TRAUMA

Dr. Gabe Roberts, DC, DM

MY STORY

Your key to achieving permeant and dramatic healing in your body always begins with your mind.

My journey of over a decade led my primary focus to understanding the mind because the answer to healing is not in another energy treatment, pill, supplement, parasite cleanse, or liver detox herb.

My experience comes from working with chronically ill people who suffer from numerous conditions, including autoimmune diseases, physiological illnesses, and cancer. I have worked in functional medicine, having a diplomat in nutrition, dozens of certifications in energy medicine, acupuncture, quantum integration, as well as a variety of different techniques focusing on stimulating the body's natural healing systems. My focus today is on applying the arts and science of psychosomatic medicine.

My experience also comes from living through my own traumatic experiences, including being born into a world of substance abuse, physical abuse, and emotional neglect, which created tremendous pain and distress that followed me for years, despite my best efforts to mask the pain. These included years of drug use myself, being associated with the worst-of-the-worst crowd, criminal activities, and eventually, as an attempt at getting a clean slate, joining the Marine Corps and completing several oversea combat tours.

The day I was born, my father was drunk and passed out unconscious on the floor when my mother went into labor. My uncle had to literally kick him on the ground yelling at him, "Wake up, your wife is going into labor!"

Knowing what I know now about how the earliest experience shapes the brain, including in the womb, it's no wonder why I spent so much of my early life in fight or flight mode. My brain centers were formed while I lived in threatening conditions.

Looking back, I only remember days of living in fear. My stepfather was always intoxicated, extremely violent, and carried some of his own biases and traumas he was acting out—a trait passed down in nearly every family. As a child who experienced fear, physical beatings from him, and a mother who was emotionally absent, it was no wonder by the time I had any chance, I engaged in substance abuse, including smoking marijuana, drinking alcohol, and harder street drugs, all as a way of numbing the pain. Any type of engagement in using drugs, whether it's alcohol, narcotics, marijuana, or even prescriptions, is usually tied in one way or another as an attempt to dull pain. It's important to understand that emotional and physical pain is felt in the same identical areas of the brain. So, emotional rejection stimulates the same area in neurology as stepping on a nail.

By the time I was a teenager, I was so into drugs I barely graduated high school and even spent time in jail for illegal drug use. This, of course, was all unintentional, but I was unconsciously seeking out what was most familiar to my psyche, or the earliest and most powerful memories. I was looking for a way, without knowing it, to maintain the emotional states from which I was born into and keep myself emersed only in what felt "normal."

When I was 20 years old, I hit rock bottom and decided to abandon everything in an attempt to become something else. Never knowing my father growing up and only having an emotionally absent, drunken stepfather as the only male figure I was ever around, I intuitively knew I wanted to be around someone with true leadership qualities. I wanted someone who was above all new, so I decided to join the Marines and leave the part of the country I grew up in. Of course, this allowed me to meet leaders and influential people who helped me become more than I was, but the pain was always still there.

Years later, I became a doctor, looking to find out what to do about this underlying, deep, relentless pain that was hidden and not on the radar of any academic studies. No one in my educational curriculum ever mentioned the subconscious, other than as a part that regulates the heart and digestion and other autonomic functions. This only came to me when I began studying the effects of repressed emotions, traumatic impact's effect on the body, and focusing on a psychosomatic approach, which is what completely dissolved a lifetime of pain for me.

Psyche, meaning the soul, is also another name for your subconscious mind and soma, meaning the physical body and all the primordial substance that your body is comprised of. This is the basic definition that begins the meaning of psychosomatic. I once believed all diseases began in the gut, but this is not true. All diseases begin in the mind.

If you have chaotic thoughts or conflict in your subconscious, which is typically from traumatic overwhelm during childhood years, the body will manifest this, and the impact of acupuncture, nutritional supplements, and regular exercise will not necessarily resolve this conflict. Conflict in the mind is the causative factor in a majority of diseases, self-sabotaging behaviors, and addictions, as it was in my life. Smoking marijuana was the activity I most engaged in to escape the pain boiling down below. Even the famous Rolling Stones guitarist, Keith Richards, said something that concurs with this from his years of being a heroin addict: "All the contortions we put ourselves through, just not to be ourselves for a few hours." This is indicative of drug use (including all other distractive behaviors) and is in all attempts to get away from pain.

This means you can unintentionally be addicted to drugs and eventually develop diseases by having conflicts in the deepest pockets of your mind that are beyond your conscious understanding or awareness.

Today, my professional focus is to help alleviate, assist, and treat by successfully reversing a host of physiological illnesses, mystery symptoms, chronic pain, autoimmune conditions, addictive behaviors, and more, which all have repressed emotions at their root cause. The focus of our approach is primarily on memories—traumatic, overwhelming encoded moments captured in the millisecond of overwhelm and stored when our nervous system snaps a picture through the five senses, which immediately stores this moment of overwhelm in any of our body's neurons throughout our nervous system. This was the source and the mechanism of the pain I carried through most of my life, and with holographic manipulation therapy, it's now completely gone.

It's important to understand that when it comes to the factors that compromise your health and happiness, or the physical well-being of your body, the problem is very simple. It's not the past haunting us. It's how the body and mind store the past. That is the real issue.

Although this is not well known by most professionals in the healing arts, one of the biggest factors compromising our health is that we have the remarkable ability to freeze the flow of consciousness when we're overwhelmed with an experience. Our neurology can instantaneously "pause" the flow of consciousness at the peak of neurological arousal, momentarily holding the breath, snap a photograph of everything our senses are picking up, and store the entire quantum perception in any of our neurons. This encoded memory becomes the nagging back pain or neck pain that doesn't completely disappear after a massage or a chiropractic adjustment. As a chiropractor, I know from clinical experience that most people's ongoing pain is not from segmental displacements in our vertebral column—it's stored memories.

Dr. John Sarno was fully aware of this type of phenomenon occurring in his patients. As I began focusing on repressed emotions, traumatic memories, and releasing the moment of overwhelm in my patients, I too witnessed chronic pain disappear and never return. Stored memory is that powerful. It becomes the lump in the throat, the weight on the shoulders, the vice on the head, nausea that arises when the person is very nervous, and the aches in the jaw when any frustrations are triggered.

The way that these memories are stored and how the past is encoded in your neurology is what creates a series of health challenges in people in numerous ways.

First, your memories are recorded as holographic imprints, which are three-dimensional and composed of millions of fragments of light particles. Each individual light particle is holographic or holonomic (behaves like a hologram), and each light particle contains the entire memory and every detail of exactly what happened. If you encounter anything similar to what was encoded, a fragment of the memory is triggered, and suddenly the entire memory returns to our neurological awareness.

Ever known someone who is stuck in a fight or flight type of condition? It's because their subconscious mind does not know the threat or overwhelming circumstance is over yet, even if their conscious mind is fully aware it has passed.

Secondly, we're trance machines, constantly going in and out of a hypnosis-like state, day in and day out. Think about this for a moment. Driving a car down the road, waiting in line at a supermarket, and walking down the sidewalk on a nice day are all examples of simple things we do on a regular basis without being aware of how often or how many times we gaze off, leaving the present moment and revisiting past memories. Our mind drifts into previous memories anywhere from 15 to 50 times per hour, and this is just a normal part of how our mind works. If those memories coming up into our awareness have an imprint of anything threatening, like a scene on the TV, an argument we had with a loved one, being late to work, or anything else that is perceived as a threat by the nervous system, our Hypothalamus Pituitary Adrenal axis, and adrenal system immediately responds by activating the fight or flight system.

This combination of reliving previous memories, with the nervous system reacting as if the memories are still presently going on in real-time, is the most significant contributor to why people are often plagued with chronic pain, autoimmune conditions, and worse, even if they're living healthy lives on the surface.

The third factor in understanding is that according to research performed by Mihaly Csikszentmihalyi, your unconscious mind forms 99.994% of your overall awareness, and your conscious mind is 0.006%.

This means the thoughts you're aware of and the thoughts you're thinking about right now make up less than a thousandth of your overall awareness, and this tiny part is what most of us are convinced is in charge.

The conscious mind is largely dominated by deeper centers of the brain that regulate feelings and impulse control, so it's these deeper systems that are responsible for controlling your life. By the time you have a conscious thought, that data has already been run through countless lenses, your identity or self-image (formed at ages 0-6 years old), several apertures, and two other fundamental sections of your brain before finally becoming something you're aware of. In other words, your thoughts and conscious awareness have been watered down and skewed, in large part, by early experiences from childhood.

Imagine you're walking outside on a dirt road and suddenly see something that makes you jump in fear. Your nervous system, within nanoseconds, believes there is a snake on the ground, causing your heart to suddenly jump and your muscles to react, and you instantly leap back to only realize that what you saw is just a rope on the ground that resembles a snake.

Now ask yourself, what happened?

The information that came into your eyes was instantly interpreted by your unconscious brain centers that have first dibs on all information. Before you even had a rational thought or idea of what was going on, your body reacted, and you physically jumped back, only to realize, *Oh, it's just a rope.* Your conscious mind was the last part of you to realize this, and by then, the other, more powerful parts of your mind had already initiated a response, long before you had a conscious thought of what was happening. This is how it happens with every incident you come across in life, whether you're aware of it or not.

Now that you're aware of how your mind is orientated, it's important to understand that we will only conform to what those earliest brain center commands are. How this applies to health and wellness is that if you have an identity that doesn't match health, or it believes that "I don't deserve to feel good" or "I am worthless" or "I don't matter," you're only going to achieve a level of health that conforms to this command. Your identity, or self-image, is one of the most powerful lenses of how you see yourself, and this is anchored into these deep centers of the brain that has first dibs on the information. Every patient we've ever met had an identity that did not reflect one deserving of health. Remember, this is all going on below the surface of conscious awareness. Every cell in the person's body is eavesdropping on this kind of message, even if they are taking the best supplements and eating whole, organic food.

You cannot override the signal of a poor self-image by attempting to live a healthy lifestyle. A woman who came to us with chronic Lyme condition for over eight years had every symptom disappear and never return when we helped her transform her identity from "I deserve to suffer" to "I deserve vibrant health and happiness." Why? Her self-image matched "health," and her body was no longer vulnerable to the cyclic illness brought on by the bacterial infection.

If you're going to have real changes in your health, physical well-being, or income and influence the deepest, most powerful parts of your nervous system to heal your physical body, you must get the deepest centers involved. This is where the technology of Holographic Manipulation Therapy (HMT) comes in.

HMT is a client-focused process that facilitates the complete removal of the traumatic encoded memory and therefore proves to the 99.994% subconscious mind that the event is over. It's not hypnosis but is more accurately described as getting you out of a hypnotic trance, which is what a traumatic event does to your mind.

It can pinpoint the earliest moment of trauma, including ones from in the womb, childhood, or ancestral memories, and disarm the holographic conflicts and memory imprints, allowing the body to fully facilitate the healing and repair mechanisms inhibited when the nervous system is in a constant state of alarm—a consequence that happens with adverse childhood experiences.

HMT provides a bridging point, allowing a language for us to dialogue with the 99.994% (which doesn't use any type of words) and allows us to turn the deepest pockets of conflict or chaos into harmony. It allows these changes to take place in the highly unconscious brain centers (that have first dibs on the information, as we discussed earlier), so our neurology has a signal of peace, harmony, connection, and love—even if we were raised in traumatic conditions. Using HMT on my earliest memories allowed me to fully heal from all pain, the PTSD, and the unconscious distress that followed me for nearly 40 years. Those things disappeared after everything else I attempted provided minimal results.

There's nothing I've ever studied or experienced that compares to the level of trauma clearing HMT provides. It does this by locating the very first and most powerful overwhelming memory, usually from between the ages of zero-to-six years old, cancels out the frequencies of the entire holographic memory, and honors the mechanism of the memory itself so the nervous system fully allows the releasing of the memory.

What does that mean?

Let's say, for example, that with the specific memory, there's a lesson or an encoded message the subconscious mind wants you to hold onto from that experience. If you clear the memory without extracting this message ("safety lesson"), the neurology will resist letting the memory clear, and it will come back. Another scenario that happens is that while trying to clear the traumatic memory, a part of the unconscious does not want the memory cleared, or it wants to hold onto something from that memory; If you try to clear the memory, it wants to hold onto, the neurology will resist the changes, and the memory will return, complete with all the unwanted symptoms. These are reasons why many people do change work, as I have myself, and they will get some level of change, but before long, the memory and the symptoms return. This is what makes HMT different and places it as the golden standard for reversing the negative impact of traumatic memories and adverse childhood experiences.

THE PRACTICE

A simple yet powerful practice to streamline your nervous system to orientate on a subject you desire, such as creating health, happiness, or any other desire you have, is to work with an emotional, motivational checklist. This is something you want for yourself and understand, and it is okay to be selfish with this.

I want to share with you the Emotional Motivation Checklist. Everyone has these. Think of something you want and be selfish about it. What is something you want—a desired monthly income or healing of a health condition? Use this for whatever it is you want. As you look at this, I want you to think about it; close your eyes and really think about that for a moment. What is it that you really, really want?

Now when you look at what you want in your mind, ask yourself this question: What is important about that? Jot down the answer that comes right to you. On a different line, write your next response of what is important about that? Then on a third line, write the answer to what is important about that, each time digging deeper and using different answers. Write down what comes up first, don't edit it or overthink it.

Here's the power in this: When you ask your neurology any question, it's going to give you an answer. It'll pop up within three seconds and whatever first pops up is the answer you write down. What's important about that? Suddenly, things just start coming up in your mind. Quickly jot them down. Immediately, more answers come to your mind. This format forces your unconscious mind to pipeline into deeper and deeper answers that will change your physical state when you say them out loud.

Understand, it's important to say what you want out loud, then repeat all the answers five times out loud as to why it's important to you to get this. This is a great start to change your emotional state and thus begin your nervous system moving you in the direction of these desires, both consciously and unconsciously. When you are ready for the next steps, please visit https://thesubconscioushealer.com to start clearing your nervous system of past traumas.

Dr. Gabe Roberts is the co-founder of Holographic Manipulation Therapy and is a specialist in psychosomatic illnesses, including autoimmune conditions, chronic pain, chronic fatigue, digestive illnesses, neurological conditions, depression, and a host of mystery conditions that have at their root cause repressed emotions. He has extensive experience working with patients from around the world, helping them resolve their body's health challenges by reconciling conflicts in their unconscious minds.

Dr. Roberts is a Holographic Manipulation therapist, clinical hypnotherapist, NLP practitioner, self-sabotage coach, and Quantum Integration practitioner who has a doctorate in metaphysics. He holds a Doctorate in Chiropractic and is certified in functional medicine.

Connect with Dr. Gabe:

Website: https://thesubconscioushealer.com/

CHAPTER 17

END THE CYCLE OF CARETAKER BURNOUT

TAKING THE SHAME OUT OF PRIORITIZING YOUR OWN HEALTH

Darlene Sochin, MS, RMT

MY STORY

The brilliance of this beam of light was unmistakable, and I dared not blink my eyes or want to look alarmed. Bewildered and breathless that my new office was apparently a portal to the Divine, my client sat across from me, pouring her heart out.

The light behind her grew bigger and brighter as she sobbed, uncorking months of bottled-up emotions now escaping and cascading down her face.

"I am so sorry. I'm not usually so emotional. It's just been so stressful this last year as a therapist during such awful times. I've never felt so tired and depleted. I want to cut back my hours, but there are just so many people in crisis."

She continued.

"I thought learning Reiki for myself would support my own health. My clients are struggling, and my heart goes out to all of them, so I keep giving and giving, and I now have very little if anything for myself at the end of the day, even on my weekends. I feel like I'm just a curled-up fetus on the couch with barely enough energy to feed myself, shower, or change the channel on the remote. I thought movies could distract me but just trying to watch and follow the images move around, and hear voices coming at me felt like an assault on my defenseless fetus body.

I can't keep going like this, but I love what I do, at least up until last year. My angels, I don't normally talk about them with anyone because people I know would think I'm nuts, but my angels keep telling me I need support. I didn't know what they were talking about. I kept ignoring them. But I could tell I wasn't well when I woke up one morning feeling totally paralyzed and then realized I had five clients who were waiting for me that day. Or maybe I first thought of all of them and then froze. All I know is whenever I look in the mirror; I keep seeing words as clear as day scroll across my forehead like a banner that spells out, *"How can I help them if I can't even find the energy or mental capacity to get out of bed to brush my own teeth?!"*

As she spoke, the light I saw when she first sat down took shape. Now, clearly standing behind and enveloping her was a beautiful angel. The angel was wrapping my client in a big embrace, and I could see her body physically relaxing, her sobs subsided, and then she took a huge, deep sigh and sat back in the chair.

It wasn't alarming to me at all seeing her angel behind her comforting her during such a pivotal and difficult moment in her life. When I was struck with the scariest moment of *my* life, that was exactly who showed up for me, too. Instead of one angel though, three came to me as I was curled up, also sporting a fetal position, under a desk in the middle of the night. I was terrified and in shock. A cancer diagnosis can do that to an exhausted and sensitive person.

My angels comforted me and offered their counsel, too. It was my first experience with such an extraordinary encounter, so I didn't hesitate to listen!

It was funny that both my client and I were led to the same answer.

You will find strength and healing with Reiki.

Unlike me, however, my client heard of Reiki before her angel suggested it. When I was instructed the next day to go to the bookstore by what I then knew only as an inner knowing, I was dazed, yet without a doubt, certain this eastern system of hands-on energy healing was going to be my saving grace, too.

Sixteen years later, and positively aware I'd never have to experience that health crisis again, I knew why this client, guided and accompanied by her angel, was sent to me. I made a pact with my angels and other team members that day in the bookstore as I read every book on the shelf about Reiki. I could never again underestimate the importance of prioritizing my health in an effort to save, protect, appease, or try to pacify another human.

Even before the doctor called and I heard those words over the phone,

"It's as I suspected. It *is* cancer," I already knew.

Before I started down this new alternative, holistic, and beautiful path as an energy healer and spiritual teacher, I was intuitively aware of how the disease in my body manifested. And even though my client, and several more that year, were not all diagnosed with cancer, we were all dutifully playing the role of the *sacrificial lamb,* surrendering our time, love, compassion, and sympathy to the world, allowing others' health and wellbeing to come before our own. They were all therapists, teachers, nurses, or healers in some capacity and loved so much and so deeply. What we all had in common was this ingrained belief in the myth of sacrifice versus selfishness. We were living as *the healer who chose for the greater good,* feeling obligated to choose the solution that benefited someone else over what was our own highest and best solution. We were guilty of habitually putting everyone else's *masks on them,* so by the end of the day, there was no strength to put on our own.

As a caretaker and healer, you open your heart to share your love and compassion. You open your heart and feel so deeply. During the day, you're an open well from which your clients sip. At night you're the well from which your friends and loved ones drink.

In the moments in between, you tend to do daily tasks. You take notes, run errands, sit in traffic, and start hearing those voices in your head playing *over and over again.*

What did I say?

What didn't I say?

Will they have a good night's sleep or call in the morning to schedule an extra appointment for the week because I fucking said something that upset them?

I wonder if she'll try that exercise on her own that I walked her through in the office.

Will he have the same courage next week as he did in the office and call his mom on her birthday?

Is reducing her sessions as we agreed really what will benefit her most? Is she ready?

Every day.

Never mind just considering the clients and meeting *their* needs. You then spend time reviewing your own life continuously in your mind. It never stops. It's always running, and what would you give for some peace and quiet?

Am I doing the right thing? Am I really meant to be here to have this much responsibility for other people's emotions and mental health?

I have an education but do I have the personal resilience it's gonna take for the long haul?

When can I take respite time while my clients and friends need me? Just one "No, I'm out of town" could be the one I'd regret forever.

Good Lord, pray over all of us, and why am I feeling so exhausted? Will I ever not be so tired?

Now, home from the office, the day continues into the evening, making dinner, organizing the house, and attending to the needs of those you love to make sure they are happy and satisfied. You have just enough strength to do the dishes, return client and business emails, and call the loved ones that don't live in the house, making sure they're doing okay and trying to convince them you're doing fine.

Climbing into bed, setting the morning alarm so you can do it all over again tomorrow, you realize you're exhausted, out of breath, and thirsty. You're too tired to drink from your own well when it should be your turn to quench *your* thirst and refill *your* cup.

You drift off to sleep recognizing another day was completed without you attending to your own health and satisfaction. You start a cycle of feeling bad about how you're treating yourself because you talk about this all day long with clients. Then lying in bed, the berating thoughts begin:

I ignored myself again today. There wasn't time for that damn morning smoothie I promised I'd start making with all those damn supplements I bought last week because I don't give myself enough time to eat lunch. All the fruit and vegetables I bought just shriveled up and grew mold in the refrigerator. How many times am I going to say I'll do something and only half do it?

Aw, and that writing class I finally stopped procrastinating over and registered for, it started, I think last week. It'll already be too far along to catch up with homework.

Sally and Pam are probably so done with me not returning their emails to go for that hike.

You finally fall asleep thinking about all the dinner invitations and text messages that go unanswered, too tired to respond.

This is my life. And that is how the day ends.

It turns out that the well you share with everyone else is seemingly not infinite when it comes to nourishing, talking nicely too, and replenishing yourself. You wake up more thirsty and tired than ever.

The heart space you leave open is beginning to feel heavy and more difficult to keep open. The consistent flow of compassion and understanding for those in front of you, whether at the office or home, feels constricted. Giving your all is leaving you tired and unable to give love or compassion to yourself.

Where did this cycle start? How is it that someone who chose to be a caretaker, a healer, a space holder for those who hurt and need support can feel empty, too tired to enjoy her family, and be depleted and void of self-love?

I'd like to take an opportunity here to pause and return to the conversation about being the sacrificial lamb. In my role as an energy healer and Reiki teacher, I took some time to interview my own clients, as most of them are therapists, caretakers, and healthcare professionals. There was an undeniable theme that presented itself within the answers my clients provided.

Most healers just naturally put others' needs before their own, usually without even realizing they are doing so. My following questions then came forward.

Do healers truly want to sacrifice themselves and give until they have nothing left?

Do caretakers truly believe it's okay to feel exhausted and burnt out at the beginning and end of the day as long as their clients and loved ones are taken care of and satisfied?

Personally, I don't feel that this is the case. As healers, we find joy and fulfillment in caring for and supporting others. Therefore, it does not seem plausible that one can feel joy and fulfillment *simultaneously as* being so exhausted and burnt out that it's a struggle to wake up every morning and then try to serve those we're here to champion for and assist.

As the imbalance grows between giving and sacrificing and then trying to find the energy to take care of oneself, the healer's health, life force energy, and ability to care for her or his own needs will most likely deteriorate. This constant giving and sacrificing is not sustainable. That is why there seems to be an unconscious and possible underlying reason why those who dedicate their time and work to helping others often feel inclined to make sacrifices regarding their health and wellbeing.

Culturally and traditionally, we're taught that caretakers and healers commit to taking care of others by:

- Always being available and feeling responsible for others at all times.
- Always listening with great tenderness and compassion.
- Offering our hearts and souls for the wellbeing and best interests of those we serve and care for.
- Accepting that the work may involve some sacrificing of one's own time and needs.

You may have learned techniques to put boundaries in place and sometimes even practice them. However, every circumstance where you "just let this one slide" and succumb to someone's request for your attention, time, and energy, starts to drain your own health and energy well. As you continue to give away your personal, precious life force, that is when the exhaustion creeps in. It can happen slowly if you're unaware of your own warning signs that it's time to take a break.

If you have found you're already at the point of total exhaustion and burnout, it may take longer to recuperate. But no matter where you are on that exhaustion and burnout scale, there are always ways to return to balance. In fact, the consistency and depths at which you've gone with what you may now realize is a perpetual cycle is the perfect storm *and* motivation to end it right here and now!

THE PRACTICE

Now that you realize you're exhausted and most likely *have* been here before at this stage of burnout in some fashion or circumstance in your life, the practice I'm going to share with you is going to assist you with more than just recovery! It's time to get off the burnout train.

The first two steps to end the cycle of exhaustion and burnout are:

1. **Recognizing it and**

2. **Choosing to do something about it.**

The next few steps are easy and stress-free, so it's practically effortless if one's well has run dry. If your energy is completely depleted, and all you have the strength to do is close your eyes and breathe, this is the perfect practice to soothe your body, mind, and soul:

3. **Find somewhere comfortable to sit and put a hand on your heart.**

4. **Hold that position while bringing your attention to the place where your hand is touching your body.**

This step is where the body, mind, and soul integrate and remember they are here to work together. Gentle, physical touch calms the nervous system, brings your soul back into your body, and tells your mind you are grounded and safe.

5. **With your hand remaining on your heart, slowly inhale into the space where your hand rests on your chest. Then just as slowly, exhale softly, breathing air out your nostrils.**

Continue this process as long as you feel it benefits your desire to feel calm at home and safe in your body. We can't move forward or have an awareness of how deeply exhausted and burned out we are until we are fully present and softly, tenderly in our bodies.

6. **Imagine your back leaning against a big, beautiful tree, alive with vibrant life force energy (this is also known as Reiki energy). Allow this tree and its energy to fully support your body as you sink energetically into and merge with the trunk.**

7. **While your eyes are still closed, bring your awareness to the sky above you and see the stream of bright healing light coming down from Source and shining into the top of your head. You can feel the warmth and glow as it slowly pours into you, relaxing, soothing, and healing every cell and muscle on its way down.**

From the top of your head, it soothes and relaxes your scalp.

You feel your eyes and temples relax.

Your cheeks and jaw loosen, and your mouth opens gently.

Your chin drops.

Your neck and throat soften.

Feel your shoulders drop and release.

Your back relaxes.

Your heart expands.

Your torso can feel peace and ease as you breathe into your stomach.

Exhale and feel this healing light continue cascading down the rest of your body past your hips, into your legs, and out your feet into the ground beneath you.

Allow this flow of light source to continue streaming down, cleansing and calming, and healing everything in its path until it feels complete.

All of this cleansing, clearing, and healing energy flows down into the core of the earth, where it is transmuted by the fire and loved by Mother Gaia.

Now, in closing, as you can imagine how a tree receives nourishment from the earth and soil up into its roots, take in one last big beautiful breath of the love energy Mother Gaia has alchemized for you.

Breathe up and into your body all the way to the top of your head.

Allow this flow to rise above you and then come back down, cascading all around you like a loving, refreshing, magical waterfall bringing you renewed energy that seeps into every pore of your body.

Sit for a few moments while the new cleansing energies integrate with your cells and make themselves at home.

This is presence. This is peace. This is grounded. Welcome back!

It didn't happen overnight that you found yourself without your own life force energy. So, it's going to take time and practice to fully restore your resources.

If you truly want to end the burnout cycle, it requires you to commit to a daily practice of self-devotion, making time every day to stay in tune with peace and calm. A cycle is like a habit, and it takes *at least three weeks* to start to undo a pattern. *It takes at least three weeks* to reset default behavior.

This practice is just the beginning, where you recognize you're on a ride that you want off of. My clients, who are caretakers and healers living and not satisfied until they help others improve their lives, come to me for the next step. Once you're aware that you're on a cycle that no longer serves you or those you're here to help, the next step is my work and how I help others: Energy clearing, restoring, and empowering you so you become so familiar with your own needs that choosing self-health is the only default you'll allow. To give and be of service from your highest potential requires you to practice receiving your own healing and staying on top of your own needs. One can only give from an overflowing well. Are you ready to learn how to be an infinite source of energy?

Darlene Sochin, MS, RMT, is a master teacher of the traditional Japanese system of Reiki and a multidimensional intuitive coach guiding lightworkers home to their true potency through workshops, personalized mentoring programs, Reiki certification training, and membership for community and advanced spiritual development opportunities. As the world is changing and the higher light frequencies are pouring onto the planet, lightworkers are waking up all around the world. Often, with just a strong knowing that they are here for something big but not sure where to start, Darlene becomes their trusted facilitator with 20 years of expertise and personal experience in Spiritual and Intuitive Development. With child-like wonder and passionate determination, she lovingly and potently reminds those she works with why they came here and exactly how important their role as a lightworker is for these times in which we are living. Feel loved, held, and empowered by Darlene's desire to help you build a solid foundation from which to serve. You and your daily practice will be this world's opportunity to heal and ascend. Come find your purpose, develop your self-health practice, and shine the great bright light you came to share!

Connect with Darlene:

Website: www.IndigoHealingspdx.com

Linktree: https://linktr.ee/darlene_energy_detective

CHAPTER 18

THE HEALING POWER OF SIBLING RELATIONSHIPS

STRENGTHENING BONDS BY CUTTING CORDS

Dr. Summer Sullivan, Licensed Psychologist, Energy Healer

Sibling relationships possess tremendous power.

Power to solidify a family's connection.

Power to enhance the way we feel about ourselves.

Power to significantly improve the quality of our life.

They can also carry destructive power.

Power to create chaos in the home.

Power to negatively influence the trajectory of one's mental health.

Power to tear families apart.

Something that holds that much power should seriously come with an instruction manual. Imagine being able to cultivate this power to unlock the significant potential of the sibling bond.

MY STORY

Julie's house became a battleground.

"I feel like a failure. No matter what I do, my kids are at each other's throats. Bickering, screaming, fighting. It's like they are committed to making each other miserable. It's absolute chaos at my house, and I can't take one more day of this!"

It was my first time meeting Julie, but before I could even introduce myself, she plopped down on my couch and began sobbing. The size of her tears alone showed me the depths of the pain she was in. I steadied my breath and waited for a break between her cries. "I am so glad you are here with me today. I can see you're in a lot of pain. When you're ready, I would like to hear more about what is happening in your home."

"My children hate each other," said Julie after a long exhale. "We can't even get through a family dinner without a nasty exchange of words between them. Their fights are often physical, and unforgivable resentments are building between them. To make matters worse, my husband and I are constantly fighting."

Julie's story impacted me in many ways. Not only because I felt deep empathy for how much she was hurting, but because I was genuinely concerned about the long-term effects her kids' rivalries could have on their well-being. There are risks embedded in ongoing sibling rivalries that could lead to serious mental health issues, including depression, aggression, low self-esteem, isolation, risk-taking behaviors, and substance use. As Julie's kids neared adolescence, the window of opportunity to transform their strained relationships and heal the family dynamics was closing.

I'm passionate about healing sibling relationships, and I was grateful for the opportunity to help this family. I can't think of a more important role in my life than assisting siblings in developing sacred bonds that can undoubtedly improve the quality and health of their lifespan. Julie's kids deserved to experience the benefits of having a sibling thoroughly, and I was determined to help them initiate happier endings for their whole family and future lineage.

I took copious notes as Julie shared additional details about her family's struggles and detailed the therapeutic interventions they tried with previous therapists. They attempted to implement all the proven steps (e.g., conflict resolution, communication skills, empathy-building) used to mend sibling relationships, but none of them stuck. "No matter what I do to help them, I still feel so powerless. The tools we've learned haven't altered how explosive they are around one another. I never expected it could be this hard to help my kids get along."

As I listened carefully, I wondered if the contention between Julie's kids was **not** a behavioral issue but an **energetic** one. Perhaps the explanation for why they struggled to move past the discord and resentments was due to negative energetic attachments trapping them in an unrelenting cycle. I felt adrenaline surge through my body as it hit me; **where there is chaos, there are cords!** I learned about the influence of energetic cords and the ways they can wreak havoc on the quality of sibling relationships when receiving therapy for my kids. Cords of attachment are energetic structures that form within a relationship to allow for the exchange of emotional energy.

No wonder they are stuck in this repetitive cycle of sibling rivalry. Their energetic attachments keep them in this loop of destructive patterns and wounds. With each additional negative exchange, the cords are growing stronger, making it harder for them to break free.

As I concluded my session with Julie for the day, I jotted down some working theories to guide the work for our next session:

If I can help Julie's kids clear the toxic energy between them, would it be easier for them to let go of the resentments, the frustrations, and the vendettas?

If they were no longer under the influence of negative cords of attachment, would they be free to experience and enjoy a loving sibling bond?

I was eager for our next session so I could test out these hypotheses and apply energetic tools for cutting cords and strengthening bonds. Feeling enthusiastic and inspired, I scribbled at the bottom of the page:

Next session, it's time to cut the cords.

CUTTING CORDS

I learned about the power of cutting cords when my son experienced his first heartbreak. He was four, and my daughter was two.

He loved his sister from the first time he saw her. It was evident in his eyes and his constant desire to be near her. It was as if he had been waiting for her his whole life and many lifetimes before that. He couldn't get enough of her. Seeing this type of love, so organic and innate, was incredible for me as a mother.

Initially, I was anxious about having a second child. I created stories in my head that my son would feel replaced by his new sibling. But it was soon apparent that my anxieties stemmed from my own projections, and a baby sister was just what his heart wanted.

But as the months passed and his fondness for his baby sister grew, she was not reciprocating the affection. I observed my gentle and sweet baby girl forcefully rejecting my son's attempts to be close to her. Her actions suggested she wanted nothing to do with her doting, kind older brother, and my husband and I felt stumped. It was almost like she came into this world with a predetermined opinion of him, and it wasn't a good one! If my son could love his sister so innately, why didn't she feel the same way in return?

Consequently, my son started complaining of constant stomach aches and was increasingly emotional, so I reached out to Dahlia, my trusted energy healer and acupuncturist, for guidance. What I learned that day profoundly shifted the quality of my life and the therapy I provide.

During the session, she confirmed that my son harbored deep sorrow and regret in his stomach even at the young age of four. Some of it was related to the current rejection he felt from his sister, and some of it was trapped emotions he was still processing from their shared past lives.

In her quiet and gentle voice, Dahlia continued, "It is the energetic cords flowing between them that are impacting his physical body. These cords contain imprints from shared past lives where emotional turmoil, anger, and resentment dominated their relationship. Although these cords are invisible to the eye, they are perceptible to our emotions, thoughts, and behaviors."

This instantly awakened a deep knowing within. Through this lens, I realized that my daughter was not consciously rejecting my son but reacting to the intense and uncomfortable energies she sensed between them.

"We need to cut these cords to free them from these entanglements and neutralize the destructive emotions. We can do this together now by visualizing these attachments and focusing our intention on dissolving all energies that are not in their highest and best good to retain. Once we witness this shift, we can activate frequencies of love and acceptance to enhance the balance and harmony of their relationship."

What transpired after that session still feels like a fairy tale. Within hours of Dahlia guiding me through the cord-cutting visualization and energy healing, my daughter sought out my son and crawled into his lap for a hug. Her defenses around him softened, and she instinctively gravitated toward him to receive affection. Over the coming months, I witnessed them grow closer. My son stopped complaining about stomachaches, and we noticed his self-confidence restored. Through their positive exchanges, giggles, and physical touch, I felt like I was watching two old souls reconnect. We now use the practice of cutting cords *as needed* to release typical sibling frustrations and conflicts and to prevent new cords from materializing.

STRENGTHENING BONDS

During my next session with Julie and her children, I shared how energy healing can be a profound modality to transforming sibling rivalry. I explained that the destructive patterns between them were not going to change until we released the energetic cords that were holding them in place. "If you want to release the chaos, we have to cut the cords."

To my surprise, this talk of "invisible energy cords" muddying their relationship made perfect sense to the children. They jumped right into the discussion describing to one another how they envisioned what these nagging cords looked like.

"Okay, so now what? How do we get rid of them?" asked Julie's oldest child.

We then sat together on the floor as I guided them through the sibling cord-cutting visualization, which you can find detailed in "The Practice" section below.

When it was over, I asked them to share their experience.

"The cords between my brother and me looked like spaghetti, so I imagined feeding them to a hungry hippo with angel wings," the littlest one shared as she broke out in laughter. "I think it worked; I don't feel as angry anymore. Can we do it again?"

Julie's eyes welled up with tears, but this time, her tears were complemented with a smile. A spark of hope flickered in her eyes as she bent down lovingly to embrace them both.

This was just the beginning of my work with Julie's family, but it didn't take long for real transformations to materialize. Julie has since reported the vibe in the house has shifted, and she has witnessed the blossoming of a compassionate and loving relationship between their children.

Julie said, as a reminder of what they learned, she hung up the phrase "Where there is chaos, there are cords" on her refrigerator right next to a drawing of an angelic hippo covered in spaghetti.

*Names have been changed to maintain privacy.

THE PRACTICE

The cutting the cords guided visualization practice is an energy healing tool for releasing negative attachments between siblings. This practice also strengthens sibling bonds by harmonizing the energies between them.

When using this tool consistently, children learn to release stress and difficult emotions preventing the build-up of resentments and frustrations. This practice works the same for biological, adopted, and step-siblings.

Benefits of Using This Practice:

- Strengthens feelings of support and togetherness (i.e., the sibling bond)
- Releases frustrations and resentments
- Promotes acceptance and forgiveness
- Decreases sibling rivalry and fosters empathy
- Provides a healthy model for conflict resolution
- Empowers children to learn self-healing techniques

When to Utilize This Cord-Cutting Tool:

- After your children have a fight
- When you sense an increase in irritability between siblings
- When observing a lack of empathy
- To heal a lack of willingness to share and cooperate
- As a family ritual to promote healing and cohesion

THE HOW-TO:

You can tailor this guided visualization depending on the age of your children or specific situation. If your children are old enough, you can walk them through the guided meditation using the script below. If they are too little or not present at the time, you can perform this practice for them.

First, check-in with yourself emotionally. Our emotions and thoughts are constantly emitting frequencies that others can feel. If you are frustrated or fed up, it is probably not the best time to perform this visualization. Remember, children are susceptible and can easily pick up on adult stress. Think about the vibration you want them to achieve through this practice and activate that first within yourself. Engaging in deep, heart-centered breaths should do the trick. Try "Activating Compassion and Calm in Three Minutes or Less" on my resource page at www.DrSummerSullivan.com/resources.

Next, set the stage. Have your children sit comfortably facing one another. Leave a space of approximately five feet between them (close enough that they can sense each other's energies, but not close enough that they can touch). If it's difficult for your kids to sit still, try using a weighted blanket or stuffed animal. The goal is for them to feel relaxed and to be able to attend to what you're saying.

Introduce the idea of energetic cords of attachment. For this practice, we will use the word "cord" to describe the energetic connections that hold negative material (e.g., frustrations, anger, fears, hurt) and "ribbons" that contain positive material (e.g., love, support, laughter). Ask them to imagine what energy cords look like to them. If it's hard for your children to visualize, this is a great time to bring art into the mix. Have them draw themselves and their sibling with cords or connective material flowing between them. Then, they can recall this drawing when participating in the guided meditation.

Choose an intention as the focus for the healing. While the more specific, the better (e.g., to release my anger towards my brother for stealing my game), you can also use this practice for clearing general emotional states (e.g., all this frustration I have towards my sister).

Step One: Read the script aloud to them. (Visit www.DrSummerSullivan. com/resources for a complimentary recording of this guided visualization.)

If you feel comfortable doing so, close your eyes. Place one hand over your heart and one on your stomach. Notice how your chest and belly rise and fall. We're going to sync our breaths, so we're breathing simultaneously. Ready to inhale to the count of 1-2-3, pause for one second, then exhale for the count of 1-2-3-4. Let's do it again: Inhale, 1-2-3, pause for one second, then exhale, 1-2-3-4. Feel your body relax with each breath.

Next, I want you to imagine you have tree roots growing from the bottom of your feet and the bottom of your tailbone. Feel these roots begin to reach down through all the layers of the earth. Feel your body getting heavier and more relaxed as gravity pulls your roots right down into the core of Mother Earth. Imagine there is a crystal there just for you. See your roots wrap around the crystal to create an anchor. Let this anchor be your connection to the loving energies of Mother Earth.

On your next in-breath, imagine breathing up Mother Earth's love through your roots through the bottom of your feet and tailbone. Let the energy of the earth expand throughout your body as you exhale.

Now I would like you to think about something that bothers you about your sibling. It can be a thought, feeling, or memory. Pick the one thing that is bothering you the most right now and imagine that thought, feeling, or memory in the form of a cord.

If not possible, no worries.

See this cord as a physical connection between the two of you. You might see the cord in the shape of a cobweb, a rope, a pipe. There is no right or wrong way to see them; just let your imagination guide you.

What color or material is the cord made from? Does it have a texture? Is it smooth or rough, shiny or dull? What part of your body is the cord attached to? What part of your sibling's body is the cord attached to?

Once you can see these cords in your imagination, try to also sense them in the physical space in front of you. If it's hard for you to see or feel them, it's okay. Just remember, if you can tap into these thoughts, feelings, or memories, then an energetic cord must exist to keep this information alive.

How would you feel if you could release all these bothersome thoughts, feelings, or memories? Would you feel free? At peace? More connected? To achieve these feelings, we need to cut those cords.

There are many ways to cut the cords in your imagination, but the most powerful methods involve you connecting to a spirit guide. A spirit guide can be the Creator of all that is, a spirit animal, an angel, a loved one that has passed away, or even a sword made of the purest white light. Now ask that guide to cut these cords, visualize this being done, and observe what happens. Maybe you see the cords disappearing altogether. Perhaps you see them being cut right down the center. There is not a right way to cut them, as long as you can see or imagine it happening. Next, imagine reaching in and pulling out the roots of the cords from where they are attached to you and where they are attached to your sibling. After collecting those roots, imagine throwing them into a fire pit to be transmuted.

Next, imagine a beautiful rainbow light coming down from above you, wrapping around you, and then around your sibling, creating a figure-eight pattern connecting you in this harmonizing and healing energy. See the ribbons that lovingly tie you expand and grow stronger. Think about the positive emotions you want to feel in your relationship and breathe these emotions into the space as the rainbow light continues to dance around the both of you.

Lastly, thank your spirit guides for helping you heal your relationship. Ask that all lessons your soul wanted to learn through these experiences be part of your awareness to help you grow an even stronger connection with your brother or sister.

To dive deeper into this practice and to learn tips and tricks, visit my resource page at www.DrSummerSullivan.com/resources

Dr. Summer Sullivan was born and raised in Miami, Florida, where she currently provides a unique and transformational blend of psychotherapy and energy healing to children, teens, and adults. As a licensed psychologist and an intuitive energy healer, she is enthusiastic about addressing mental health issues through a holistic lens of mind, body, and spirit. As such, she has been developing innovative ways to integrate energy healing techniques with psychotherapy and dreams of one-day mentoring other psychologists on how to effectively utilize the power of combining both schools of thought.

Through her 16 years as a healer, Dr. Sullivan has studied a vast range of psychological and energetic-based treatment modalities in the pursuit of understanding mental health from all angles. In addition to her doctorate degree in psychology, Dr. Sullivan has received extensive training in energy psychology, emotional freedom technique/tapping, polyvagal theory, family systems theory, ThetaHealing, and healing through Akashic Records. Additionally, she loves exploring past lives to increase the understanding of mental health issues and further enhances the healing potential of her client sessions with her passions for dowsing, sound healing, crystals, and aromatherapy.

Her current passions lie in using energy healing to help families transform conflict and teaching children how to be self-healers.

CHAPTER 19

COMING HOME TO MYSELF

HOW BEFRIENDING MY FRAGMENTS BROUGHT ME WHOLENESS

Steph Furo, Self-Empowerment Guide, Reiki Master

MY STORY

I trudged slowly up to the trailhead, strapped on my snowshoes, and entered the woods. The snow was fresh and soft on this quiet Saturday morning. The trees stood taller than usual, the sky held a crystal-cold blue, and plump snowflakes danced in the air. It was magic, and I was more miserable than ever. I started sobbing as I trekked on.

What the hell is wrong with me? I cried. I came to the woods to face the reality that I didn't have it all together and to find my next step, and it felt like death.

It wasn't long ago that I believed I was in control. I was a stronger and more confident version of myself, my family was doing great, and I had a plan to transition from my corporate job to soul-led work. Check, check, check. I could always count on myself for a good plan and even better management of it

—until I couldn't.

Every plan fell apart. Every relationship was strained. Every duck I lined up neatly in a row quacked "Fuck you" and flew away. If I wasn't going to notice that my pattern of trying to manage and control to perfection was hurting me, the universe was making me see.

I was aware that I could carry a lot of stress and still appear calm on the surface, and this ability was consistently rewarded in the corporate setting with more and more work. I could now see that it wasn't just the weight of the load I carried that hurt me; it was the reason I carried it in the first place: I believed it was all up to me to make things right.

An awareness bomb revealed that I carried this responsibility into every relationship, as well, including with my parents from the time I was a child: *If I just make sure that everything is in order and everyone is happy, we'll all be okay.*

It's a back-breaking job that never ends, and I couldn't live that way anymore—even if I wanted to. I could sense that there wouldn't be much of me left if I kept trying to carry it all myself and carry it perfectly. Most of all, I didn't want to pass this excruciating way of being to my children.

There was no mistaking now that it was all an illusion: *I'm not in control, I never was, and I'd rather be free.*

As I wandered off the trail, floating across the fluffy snow with my sturdy snowshoes, I stopped in my tracks, paralyzed by the beauty around me. I gazed at a sleepy forest covered in a velvety white blanket of snow, completely and utterly untouched. The sun shone boldly through the bare trees, putting a spotlight on the snowflakes that drifted lazily in the air. At that moment, I couldn't imagine anything more beautiful. I filmed it for 20 seconds on my phone, and then I collapsed into the snow crying.

How have I lost myself so completely? How do I go on when I feel like I'm dying? I wasn't going to move until I had an answer. I was already untethered, so where else could I go?

I rolled onto my back into a distinct sense of being held. I was held by the snow but was warm beyond explanation as my tears flowed hotter and faster. I was being held by love, by life, and it whispered in my ear: *Come home, my darling. Come back home to yourself.*

I didn't know what that meant in a rational sense, but I felt it in my bones. My heart understood what my brain couldn't. I have not *known myself* or *honored myself* enough to be authentically me, and I had to uncover my sense of self.

At the same time, my body held an awareness that *the only way out is through, and the way through is to let go.* To let go of who I thought I should be and what life should look like, to let go of trying to manage it all, to allow myself to feel how vulnerable it is to be human.

It's a gift to come undone because breaking down leads to breaking through if you allow it. When something cracks us open, there's a death. But then there's also a rebirth.

As I left the woods that day, I was aware with the knowledge of a thousand lifetimes that I had a responsibility to know and love myself, that only I could do this for me, and that nobody could ever hurt me as much as I can hurt myself. It was time for me to let go of people-pleasing and perfection. It was time to find, gather, and embrace *all* parts of myself, no matter what they looked or felt like. It was time to come home.

The universe is always working on our behalf, and sometimes we get to see how swift it is. It wasn't long before I stumbled into a self-love exercise that resembled another tool I was familiar with, and it was the puzzle piece my psyche needed. (Swan, n.d.) I was being called to come home to myself, and now I knew the way. I went from standing at the threshold, knowing it was all about to change, to entering in.

I re-discovered that while I'm one person, my consciousness exists in many distinct parts or fragments. Some parts of myself and my life have been forgotten. Some I rejected or abandoned long ago, others I hid, and very few I show. Some parts want me to be free, and it's the sole job of other parts whose work it is to keep me safe to lock me in my room. Some parts look like little Steph, some look like the grown-ups in my life when I was young, and some are exaggerated cartoon characters. Though all of them want what's best for me, some of them are wildly misinformed on how to go about it.

And I, being the soul that exists in perfect wholeness and stability beyond these fragments, can find them, gather them, and embrace them. I can find out what they want, how they think they're helping me, educate them on what would be more helpful, and see if we can reach some sort of agreement.

Until I embraced the practice of working with my fragmented parts, I was at war with myself, trying to be one thing: everything to everybody. I couldn't know myself this way because I only existed for others. And as long as I insisted on being perfect, I couldn't see what I couldn't accept about myself, like my tendency to give unsolicited advice or my sometimes-impatient mothering. Once I could see what I was working with, I could work with it.

With time and practice, I've found many parts. For better or worse, they're all part of me, and when I can gather and embrace them, I can calm them. I can give them the love and assurance they've wanted, and I can recover the qualities that they carry. I can teach them that there's a higher consciousness here to play now and that they're safe because I say so. I befriend them, and I feel friendlier inside. I relax into myself, and I relax into my relationships.

The emergence of a sense of self has provided such foundational clarity and confidence for me that it's led me out of toxic situations I wouldn't have recognized before and into soul-aligned decisions that feel better and produce better results in my life.

I'm not in control, but I'm empowered.

I'm not perfect, but I'm home.

THE PRACTICE

I learned the not-so-evident truth in the woods that day that getting stronger is about surrendering and that everything I need is available to me when I loosen my grip. I want to share with you what I've learned along the way and help you touch something that has longed to be seen and welcomed home.

This practice can be done anytime you sense opposing forces in play within yourself. You consciously want something, but you do another. You sense resistance within yourself, like part of you is hitting the gas, and another part is riding the brake. You're confused or frustrated by your actions or inaction.

There are parts to welcome home.

Are you ready?

TURN TOWARD IT

Breathe and feel, reminding your analytical mind that this is deeper work and that you're calling on the wisdom of the body for this one.

Ask yourself what you'll call this part as you call it forward. If you deeply desire to feel healthy and keep eating a box of cookies at night, you'll call forward the part of you who wants to eat cookies at night. If you aim to be an effective leader but notice that you tend to shut people down when they disagree with you, you'll call forward the part of you who shuts people down. If you can't understand why you want to escape from your children despite how much you love them and adore being their parent, you might call forward the part of you that resists or even hates parenting at that moment.

This is self-acceptance at its finest, my friends.

Where's a place you feel stuck right now or frustrated by your actions or inaction?

GET TO KNOW IT

Take a few deep breaths and state your intention: *I consciously choose to become the part of me that* _____.

Allow the sensations of that part to make themselves known in your body and notice what it feels like (heavy, tight, sinking, buzzing, pounding, slimy, sticky, black, etc.). Notice what images or visual impressions you have of this part, as well, and jot down some notes. To amplify this practice, take notes using your non-dominant hand. It will help you stay connected in this abstract place without your ego taking over the process, and it's okay if it ends up looking more like art than language.

With this consciousness activated, ask questions that help you get to know this part. It seems like an enemy, but it's convinced it's keeping you safe, remember? Below are some example questions you can ask, but allow your intuition to lead. See if it feels better to speak of yourself as "me" or in the third person by your name or pronoun.

- What's your job?
- What do you do for me that you're most proud of?
- When did you come into my life?
- Who do you remind me of?
- Is there a name you'd like me to call you by?
- How are you trying to keep me safe?
- What do you want more than anything?
- Are you open to helping differently?
- Are you okay with me talking to the opposite part? (Their permission helps with the integration process, and you can assure them that you won't force them to do anything they don't want to do.)

When you feel complete, state your intention to release that part of you and then call forward its opposite:

- *I consciously choose to release the part of me that_____.*
- *I consciously choose to become the part of me that is opposite to the _____ part.*

Repeat the process here, noting that you're interacting with the *opposite* of the resistance or opposition. Remember to continue taking notes with your non-dominant hand as you observe and experience this part. You may see or hear something when interacting with the first part that informs your questioning here, but this is a good place to start:

- How do you feel about the _____ part?
- What's it like for you to be here?
- What do you want more than anything?
- What are you afraid of?
- What's it like to be seen?

When you feel complete, release this part in the same way.

INTEGRATION

This is the best part! Imagine the two parts sitting side-by-side with you facing them. Your job is to facilitate a healthy co-existence between the three of you, and your power is in your dedication to stay there until you're satisfied with the resolution.

You are not your parts.

You are the ever-present soul breathing life into them all, and you exist in perfect wholeness beyond these splits in your conscious awareness. You're simply helping your body and mind remember that.

Share with the parts what your life is like and what would be most helpful to you. Express your appreciation for everything they've done to try to protect you. Look for the good in each of them that you desire to carry with you.

Decide if you'd like to capture your experience in any other way, and consider a physical activity like journaling, drawing, dancing, or shaking. Involving your body in the process can be very powerful.

Great job, you beautiful badass. May you embody your wholeness and continue coming back home to yourself as you welcome more parts home.

I would love to guide you through this process! Join me here for guided practice and other resources: www.yourempoweredsoul.com/resources

Reference:

Swan, T. (n.d.). Self Love - The E-Course by Teal Swan. https://shop.tealswan.com/pages/self-love-the-ecourse

Steph Furo is a certified holistic life coach and Reiki Master Teacher, and it's her mission to guide others into knowing, loving, and honoring themselves. She believes that we each have our own unique path to navigate but that we share many of the same challenges as we do.

Steph transitioned to this healing and coaching work from a 15-year career in human resources development. She was told that she put the "human" in human resources and found meaning in hiring, onboarding, and developing strong professionals. She saw that so much more life was possible in the workplace, though, and developed a weekly mindfulness and breathwork program when employees started working from home during the pandemic. It evolved into a multi-month course that offered a deeper path to personal and professional development, and it only fueled her fire for this work when it was so eagerly received.

She received a trauma-informed care certification so that she can safely hold a sacred space for healing and expansion, and she draws on the many volunteer experiences that filled her heart over the years. She mentored women transitioning out of prostitution, operated a crisis line for victims of sexual abuse, and facilitated restorative justice circles for men convicted of domestic abuse. When her human resources career took an interesting detour, she spent a year and a half as an HR manager for a non-profit organization on the Thai-Burma border. In addition to hiring and building the processes to support the organization, she learned new languages and developed relationships with the street kids and refugees they served. She reckoned daily with the suffering that exists in the world and the resilience of the human spirit to overcome it.

Connect with Steph:

Website: https://www.yourempoweredsoul.com/

Instagram: https://www.instagram.com/steph_furo/

Facebook: https://www.facebook.com/groups/sacredempowermentgroup

CHAPTER 20

SANCTUARY

CO-CREATING PEACE WITH YOUR HOME

Dr. Christy Robinson, PsyD, MSCP

MY STORY

CUPCAKES AND FUNERALS

As I stood there looking at an empty house, one where I spent a decade living and that would host the last Christmas with my family ever to be had, I couldn't help but wonder how one's entire life can be gone within a blink.

Everything that was my foundation, my life—just vanished, as if it never existed. It seemed like just yesterday that I tore out the carpet with my mother and saw my father walk up to the door to stop by and say hello. I baked cupcakes with my nieces in that kitchen. This home held my hand through a divorce. It watched relationships come and go, but it always made me feel safe and loved. It was a part of me, and I was a part of it.

Now, it was empty. "Come here, Pearl," I called, hearing my voice echo through this once filled, now empty house. The lease was signed, and every single item I owned sold. As I pulled out of the driveway with only what would fit into my car and my faithful Labrador Retriever Pearl, I knew I was leaving everything familiar behind and taking a giant leap into the unknown. Strangely, I wasn't afraid. I had nothing left to lose. All I had in the world was my dog.

I watched my mom slowly die from cancer for over a year while my father was dying the slow death of heartbreak. They were married for 40 years and couldn't stand to live without each other. When my mother was in her final days, my father led the way passing before her. I remember the day she crossed over, watching her arms reaching upward just moments before leaving us. *Is that Dad she's reaching out for?* They died three days apart, and the funerals were within a week of each other.

I could never go into their house again, even to settle the estate; watching my mother's physical death there was too traumatic. I'm still haunted by the things I saw that day. Death is not easy and not negotiable. My mother deserved more than to have my dad's family sitting there talking about sports as my then tiny little mother was being carried out on a stretcher with only a skeleton of an arm dangling out of the body bag. An oversight that would be sketched on my brain for the rest of my life.

Being an only child, I had no one else. As I left, I could barely walk out the door after being infected with Lyme Disease by a mosquito bite earlier that summer. I love baking and always shared the comfort of good food with those special in my life. It was how I showed appreciation. Baking was love to me. I knew I needed change, and I knew I had nothing left to lose. Liz Gilbert said in her book Eat, Pray, Love that "Ruin is a gift. Ruin is the road to transformation." She was right. Sometimes life has to punch you in the gut to take you off auto pilot. I sold everything I owned, leased my house, rented a place I had never seen on an island far away from the mountains, and was going to start a cupcake bakery. I was going to love the whole world through delicious cakes and heal myself along the way.

THE ISLAND

My parents were married at the beach, and we always went there every year together on their anniversary. It was my favorite place on the planet. Even as a small child, I cried when we had to leave, pleading with the ocean to stay. My mom said I would cry out, "Bye-bye, big water." The ocean and me—we'd have a long relationship in life. It would heal me, and I would learn from it. Water has healing, energetic properties, and I needed healing.

So, I was moving to a little island with amazing sunsets. It was just me and Pearl the Labrador now.

I spent several years on that island. It's still the most beautiful place I've ever seen. Each day after work, I raced down to the sound or south end of the island to photograph the sunset. While my photographs were amazing, they did it no justice. The sky looked like it was painted with the most beautiful alchemy of fire and watercolors. The stillness was intangible there. I had a secret spot on the island that none of the tourists knew about. I went there just to be still, just to appreciate that moment and maybe say hello to some frisky dolphins in the sound. They came right up to the dock and popped up to show off their joy. You couldn't help but want to be like them, flapping up and down in the water and playing without a care in the world.

Nothing seemed to matter there except which seashell Pearl picked on our walk on the beach that morning and which catch we'd pick up at the docks to make for dinner that night. Each morning walk, Pearl dug in the sand and selected her shell for the day to take home. She carried it in her mouth for the entire walk. She was proud of that shell collection—each seashell representing a day well spent. Life on the island had an ease about it, and you could feel it in each person you met there. The island embodied what home should feel like. It nurtured us, allowed us to revel in its beauty, energized us with warm sunshine when needed, and other times told us to be still. It knew love. It knew energy. It knew alchemy. I will never forget those lessons.

After the island took care of me for a few years, it gently nudged me to return to life. It whispered, *You have learned your lessons. You know more than you think, and it's time.* So, I returned to the mountains of Virginia and began to seek that balance between where I had been when I drove away that day with Pearl and where I was when on the island. The alchemy was to be found somewhere in the middle.

EXCUSE ME WHILE I GEEK OUT HERE

Why do we crave peace so much? In western medicine, it's starting to become well known that chronic stress is the root cause of many diseases. Ask any doctor what causes most diseases? Genetics, yes, this plays a role, but why do some people with the genetic predisposition to cancer not get cancer while others without genetic predisposition do? Twin studies have shown twins with the same genetics experience different health outcomes.

We all have cancer cells in our bodies, all of the time. They are just our own cells misbehaving for some reason. We have built-in enforcers in our bodies called natural killer cells that are part of our natural immune system. They are lymphocytes that respond quickly to any threat in our bodies, such as viruses, pathogens, and cancer cells. They are even found in the placenta and play a critical role in protecting your unborn child. Additionally, they secrete cytokines that act on other cells in our immune system, like macrophages and dendritic cells, to enhance our overall immune response. These guys are badasses! However, guess what keeps them from doing their job? Ding, Ding, Ding—it's chronic stress.

Emotions that stay trapped in our bodies cause physical disease to manifest. Most autoimmune diseases have no known physical cause other than the body attacking itself for an unknown reason. There is a pathogen, toxin, or stress response repeating in the body, causing illness. Western medicine does not address this underlying pathogen, toxin, or stress. It prescribes a medication for the symptom and dismisses the cause of the illness as unimportant.

Our thoughts have so much to do with everything in our lives, even our medical outcomes. Science has proven that how we think about our medical outcome determines how we heal from diseases, surgeries, and chronic conditions. Why do patients in clinical trials on a placebo drug still show improvement in their condition? Because they believe they're healing. When you believe you're healing, your brain goes to work and instructs your body to do so without the interference of stress hormones. Stress and inflammation, which come from your body's response to physical or emotional stress, are the two roots of all diseases. We just have to get out of our own way!

THE STORY OF A HOME

My journey with Lyme Disease led me to search for healing modalities outside of western medicine. This is when I became aware of energy and started to study a wide range of other perspectives and philosophies. This led me to study under a leading feng shui master. Since losing my parents and battling Lyme, I noticed a pattern. Why had I not completely unpacked my boxes in any of the homes I had for the last seven years? Why had no place ever truly felt like home? Was this geography, or was it me? It's funny how the thing you desire the most in life is quite often the very thing you also fear the most. I desperately wanted a home again after losing mine many years before. I was also absolutely terrified to have this again—because that meant I could lose it. And I couldn't go through that pain again. So, I just never created a home. Sure, I slept there, ate there, and worked there, but it was never home. A house is not a home. A home is created by your intention and energy.

The outer will always reflect the inner. What is going on in your mind will show up in your home. It tells your story. The home that has closets stuffed full of things and a messy bedroom but has a neat and orderly living room tells a story. If this is you, no judgment here? I have struggled with this myself. Just think about it for a minute. We spend so much time in our homes, yet we forget to be mindful and present with them. We forget that they are a part of us and a part of our story.

So back to this home, it tells you that this person is more concerned with the areas of their home that the guests see and less concerned with their own personal private space. The bedroom is sacred and the most important part of the home for self-love. It's where we care for ourselves with relaxation and respite, where we recharge ourselves, and where we connect with our partners. If it is neglected, you likely place more importance on others in life than on yourself. Therefore, the parts of your home seen by others are more worthy of time and energy than those that support you directly.

Your home is your warm cocoon, creative muse, and co-creator in life. It is the foundation for your children to take into the world. They will forever remember how home looked, sounded, felt, smelled, and tasted for the rest of their lives. It will become the compass for their own home later in life. The amazing part is that you can rewrite the story your home tells.

QUIETING THE NOISE OF DISTRACTION TO CULTIVATE PEACE

Distraction can be our friend. It can also be our enemy. And, most of the time, it is a silent one. We are often not aware that it's happening. My distraction was cupcakes. What is yours?

Are you always trying to save or fix someone else? I have a lovely healer friend who seems to always take on a new project to help. As soon as one concludes, the next person arrives right on time. It is natural for healers to want to do this in the world. However, it is also a great distraction from our own healing. Why is it easier to show love and grace to others than it is to ourselves? And, why are we taught as women that others are more worthy of love and attention than we are ourselves?

How often do you just sit with yourself and be? There is no judgment coming from me here. Hell, I did an entire doctoral program this way to deal with being completely alone after losing my family. We all like to avoid pain because it requires that we see some things about ourselves we might not like. But until we are able to tolerate the quiet and feel what is in our hearts and our minds—we cannot experience true peace.

Eventually, we all must face ourselves. We all must love ourselves. Then, we can truly love and heal others. Our fears must be acknowledged, not avoided through distraction. It is the only way. I want you to be free. I want you to release all of the limits you place on yourself.

THE PRACTICE

Introduce Yourself to Your House and Let it Introduce Itself to You

Our homes should be a respite from the world we live in today. When you go out into the world, you cannot always control the type of energy you are exposed to. This is why cultivating a sanctuary home is so important. It will be waiting to nurture, ground, and support you as soon as you walk in the door. Your home is your cocoon, and it can replenish your energy. It can protect you. Your home's energy must always be pure. It must be intentional.

One of my favorite writers, Frances Mayes, has a quote in *Under the Tuscan Sun* that I adore and speaks so eloquently to this concept.

"When you buy a new house, go slowly through the house. Be polite, introduce yourself, so it can introduce itself to you."

~ Frances Mayes

Each room in your home wants to be something. You just have to ask it what it wants to be. This takes time. It takes patience. It takes calm energy. Choose the room in your home you feel most drawn to energetically and intuitively.

Ask yourself these questions:

- What is going on in this room right now, and how does it make me feel in my body?
- Do I avoid this room?
- Does it feel like an afterthought or an intentional space?
- Are there piles of clutter or unfinished projects everywhere?
- Can the energy move through the room freely, or does it feel stuck?
- Is there an area that I want to attract more energy to? Think about an amazing view of nature out of a window, an inviting soaker tub, a great spot where you love being, or a great piece of art you adore.
- How will I use this room?
- What will I do in this room?
- How do I want to feel when I am here?
- Who will I share this room with?
- Most importantly, what is my intention for this room?

Take a little time and just be in your body. You might feel heavy or light. You might feel you can take a deep breath or your breath might be fast and shallow due to the overwhelm of the room. Connect to the room. If you feel anxious or unsettled, that is not good feng shui. If you feel connected, supported, and peaceful, that is good feng shui. Listen to your body and listen to your home. Then, you will know where to start.

Now, I want you to set an intention for this room. If you want to clean it first, you can. Simply mix ten drops of sage essential oil in a spray bottle with water or smudge it with sage. You will feel the energy begin to shift. There are ways to work with the specific elements needed in each space to support your mind and life in feng shui. You will learn to balance the elements in your home and in yourself for powerful intentional change in your life. The connection between your mind and your home can empower you to do this in the most beautiful way, dear one.

Say to yourself, When I am here, I will feel _____.

This room will support me in _____.

Together we will create _____.

I have spoken it, so it shall be.

Then you release the intention to the Universe.

There are many tools available through feng shui to help you work with your intention for a space. Do not get overwhelmed with the process. Work with an experienced feng shui master to dive really deep but start where you feel drawn. For me, it was crystals and plants. I loved working with crystals and choosing them intuitively. I began meditating with them and balancing my chakras with them. Then, I learned how to ground my home with them and how to support certain areas of my life with the properties of each crystal placed strategically in my home. My life changed in the most magical way. I began to manifest through my intentions. You, too, can do this.

If you want to learn more about how to connect your mind and your home for a peaceful life with feng shui, visit my website at www.thefengshuidoc.com

Sign up for The Mind Home Connection and get my guide to the crystals and plants to work with for the top five medical conditions of insomnia, anxiety, guilt, fear, and Grief. You are amazing and will do amazing things.

Until next time,

Christy.

Christy has been studying the mind for 25 years. In 2013, she began to search for healing modalities outside of western medicine. This is when she became aware of energy and started to study a wide range of other perspectives and philosophies. This journey led her to study under a leading feng shui master. Here, she made the connection between the mind and home. During the pandemic, she realized the absolute necessity of creating a home sanctuary as a place of respite from the world.

With her training as a medical psychologist, she was able to connect the universal fears that we all experience in life and how our homes reflect what is going on in our minds. While studying feng shui, she discovered three ancient principles that could empower your mind, your home, and your life.

Christy is a trained medical psychologist with a doctorate in psychology. She also has a master's degree in behavioral neuroscience and completed additional post-doctoral training in clinical psychopharmacology.

She has extensively studied the connection between chronic stress and the development of physical disease. Over the years, she has taken over 48 courses. Her experience in life, neuroscience, and entrepreneurship make her ideally suited to bridge the gap between 5000-year-old learning and modern science in a unique way.

Connect with Dr. Christy:

Website: www.thefengshuidoc.com

Facebook: https://www.facebook.com/TheFengShuiDoc

Free Facebook Group

Feng Shui Mind: https://www.facebook.com/groups/571351207833676

Instagram: https://www.instagram.com/TheFengShuiDoc

CHAPTER 21

BEYOND SURVIVAL MODE

RECHARGE YOUR BATTERY FOR MIND, BODY, SOUL RESTORATION

Katie White, Intuitive Energy Guide, Reiki Master Teacher

MY STORY

I pushed my body to the verge of puking during the workout, leaving as much of the stress and frustration on the mat as I could. Sweat dripped down every inch of my body.

The house was dark and peaceful as the whole house slept. With a startling buzz, the alarm clock went off. I squinted my eyes open to see if it was true. The faint red glow of the numbers on the clock read 3:30 am and lit the room enough to shuffle my feet and put on my workout clothes. Then the noisy thoughts started up.

I'm exhausted. Just start your workout, and you'll feel more ready for the day.

I tried to convince myself.

But the bed is so warm, maybe I'll just crawl back in. No, Katie! You need to get going now to have enough time to get ready and leave before traffic hits.

This is where I pushed my body to the verge of puking during the workout, leaving as much of the stress on the mat as I could.

There, you worked out. Check it off your list. Now go get ready.

I rushed through showering, wrestling with the suffocating nylons, zipped up the fitted skirt, tucked in the restricting blouse, and threw on a sweater. I carried down the three-inch black heels so I didn't wake the baby or husband. I grabbed my lunch from the fridge, heavy computer bag, and purse and headed out the door.

Let's put on some 2000s hip hop and sing really loud to stay awake. I hope there isn't traffic already building or construction. Ugh. Here we go.

The nine hours in the office flew by as I bounced from meeting to meeting, facilitating, questioning, delegating—all day long.

As I sat anxiously in the last meeting of the day, knowing I'd have to haul ass to my car to drive the 90 minutes home and sit in traffic on a conference call, I felt my heart racing, foot bouncing, and my eyes glued to the clock.

I picked up our daughter from daycare. I couldn't even tell you what that was like because I was so caught up in remembering what was talked about on the conference call driving home and all the work I had to do later.

I muddled through unpacking from the day, started getting dinner made, and my husband walked in from work.

"Hi," I said in a somber tone.

"Hey. How was your day?" He kissed my forehead and put his bag down.

"Eh, same crap, different day. You?"

He started going on about his day, and I zoned out.

"Oh, cool," I replied with an eye roll.

We ate dinner and talked about the next day.

"You got Mel in the morning?" I ask.

"Yup, I'll do drop off," he says.

"Okay, and I'll snag her for pick up," I sigh.

He cleaned up the kitchen from dinner while I got Mel ready for bed. I closed the door to her bedroom and sighed a big exhale.

Thank God that is over. I better start working.

I had an inbox full of emails and a long to-do list of actions for work, so I headed downstairs to get my laptop.

Ugh, he didn't fully clean the kitchen, with an eye roll and scuff under my breath. *I better do that now.*

I scrubbed the kitchen counter until it sparkled, wiped down the sink, so it shined, and reorganized the plates in the dishwasher. Because at that time in my life, it wasn't up to my standards.

I plopped on the couch and plowed through the never-ending emails; I noticed the clock.

10:00 p.m. to 3:30 a.m. I counted on my fingers. *Five and a half hours of sleep if I fall asleep right now. More like four hours after I toss and turn all night.*

My heart raced with anxiety that in a few short hours, I'd have to get up and do this all over again.

I lived this lifestyle for a year until one day, I was talking to a coworker:

"Ugh, I'm so tired. I want to quit. I can't keep doing this," I said.

"Yeah, me too. But here I'm 30 years later. Retirement is closer for me," she laughs.

Wait, what?

I simply chuckled back, and we carried on walking to the next meeting.

That day, driving home, the thoughts were swirling.

What did she say? She's thought about leaving, but is still here after 30 years? Is this going to be my life? Am I going to be that person who is here in 25 years saying this to a new college grad? Is this what the dream is? Work your ass off in school, get a good job at a Fortune 100 company, so you can make good money, have a nice house, nice things, a husband, a family, and be miserable every goddamn day of your fuckin' life? This is being successful? This is success?

The inner thoughts went on for weeks.

If this is what life is going to be like, then I'm out. I'll just end this all right now. Fuck this. This isn't a life I want, but there's no way out. I'm stuck here. No, really, is this really life? Is everyone this fuckin' miserable?

Then I started getting sick. Every virus possible attacked my system, trying to get me to slow down. I was miserable, not sleeping, and kept going about the days.

One weekend, we went to visit my best friend and her family. Her house smelled amazing. She told me it was an essential oil that helped support their immune systems.

I froze. *Wait, what, there is something that could help me stop being sick?*

I asked her to tell me more. Just as quickly, we got distracted by the kids, and the next time we started talking, it was about a new topic.

On the drive home, I replayed all the short conversations we attempted to have in between tending to the children. I was so drained from the week, so lost, yet I knew I had to keep doing what I always had, so that was the direction I went. Sunday rolled in, and the anxiety filled my body as I frantically prepped for the new week ahead, and I convinced myself to keep the hamster wheel spinning.

Fast forward another six months; I got myself some essential oils. As I opened the box, I paused to blow my nose because, as you could have guessed, another cootie had invaded my body. I got the diffuser out of the box, set it up, dropped in a few drops, filled it with water, and boom, I now felt I had done something for myself.

This will clear the air of any cooties. This will boost my immune system. This will fix it all.

And while it did help my immune system, it didn't fix my miserable state of mind. So I researched more. That's when I learned other oils could support my emotions.

I'm not even sure what I'm feeling besides being tired or miserable, but maybe if I bathe in these oils, it will fix my life.

Well, once again, I did feel temporary relief. It was in these small pockets of relief that the messages became clearer.

There's no way in hell I can keep doing this. I can't keep fuckin' driving hours on the road, being miserable at home with my family, and I don't even know who I am. What's my purpose? What is the point of living this life? There has to be more. There has to be a place of happiness.

It was this gradual process that led me to know there was no way I'd stay addicted to this work-hustle culture, being the tired new mom, distant wife, and too busy for myself. I forgot who Katie White was. I was losing sight of what made me happy and gave me life. I was so addicted to success and making it.

I was in survival mode.

I wanted a different life. I wanted one with freedom of my time, where I didn't feel so depleted. I wanted to get off the hamster wheel and wake up from this nightmare. Except I had no idea how to start or that it was even possible.

Could I actually leave my job? I work at a Fortune 100 company right out of college. Isn't that the dream job? I make a great salary with benefits. I have paid vacation time and enjoy most of the people I work with. I'm really good at what I do here and sought out for new fancy projects. This is exactly what I went to college for, so isn't this the life I signed up for? If I leave, what will people think? What was the point of going to college? Was it all a waste of time? What will I do? If I get a new job somewhere else, would it be the same thing? Is the grass greener on the other side?

From the outside, my life was picture perfect.

During the last five years of my corporate career, I found myself in a deep depression but smiling through it all. I acquired new allergies to foods and environmental factors. I was the skinniest of my life and had a toned body after having a baby, but I felt so insecure in a bathing suit. I was secretly miserable in my marriage, playing along like it was all okay. Motherhood was numbing, and I went through the motions to make sure she stayed alive. I looked at myself in the mirror and didn't even know who was looking back.

Just before my ten-year work anniversary, I quit.

"I'm giving my notice. My last day will be December 31, 2018," I said to my boss.

So what was the catalyst that brought me to say those brave words?

In the brief moments of peace and solitude by myself, I knew I needed to make a change. I knew I couldn't change others, but I could change myself. It had to start with me. No one would do it for me.

If I stayed on the hamster wheel and did nothing, I can say with confidence that you wouldn't be reading this chapter. I'm not even sure I'd be here.

Coming from a technology background, I wanted to restore myself. Like you would a broken computer, you'd choose a restore point and revert back to that last good version.

As I explored coaching and healing to support me through these incredible life changes, I learned that I actually did not want to restore to an old version of myself. There wasn't a time in my life that I wished I could go back to. This was about me moving forward into a place of unknown and newness. Then one day, it clicked.

I wanted to restore my soul.

I have found restoration in making myself a priority, saying what was on my heart and mind in a safe space, and moving the years of pushed-down emotions out. Through life coaching, energy healing, and having sacred containers held for me, I proved to myself that it's possible to heal. When I started to show up for myself, I learned I could make a difference in my life and allow that to ripple outward because I am a light.

If you're reading this, then you have proved to yourself that you care about your wellbeing. I'm so honored to share this practice with you. You can make this change. You can step into your power and take back control of your life. You get to connect within your soul. You get to tap into your unlimited potential because you are a light, too.

I'm special, but so are you, beautiful soul.

THE PRACTICE

Spirit so kindly shared this vision with me, and it's the inspiration behind this chapter.

Imagine yourself, your body, as a rechargeable battery. Your entire being runs off the juice inside the battery.

The battery loses power as the day goes on, depending on what situations, people, environments, thoughts, emotions, and physical strain occur during your day. Certain activities cause the battery to deplete faster, and there are other activities that boost it back up.

So what's the formula for recharging the battery?

Self-Devotion Practice + Quality Sleep = Fully Charged Battery.

On most days, sleep alone is not enough to fully recharge the battery. Even if you gave your body the perfect amount of sleep, it wouldn't be fully charged the next morning. Therefore, without a self-devotion practice, you will continue waking up feeling depleted and drained.

Here's an example of the impact a self-devotion practice has on your life:

Picture this; you're at work where your boss dismissed your comment. That made you feel unheard, stupid, and crappy. The rest of your day goes on. Maybe even snapping at your spouse or child that evening because they brushed off your feelings. You go to bed. The next morning, you're still carrying the low vibration emotions in your body. Rinse and repeat.

For a moment, imagine that you carved out time before bed for yourself to tune into your body and do what your soul desires. You've released the day and began the recharging of the battery; therefore, you'll sleep better waking up fully charged! You're proving to yourself that you have respect for how you feel—physically, emotionally, and spiritually.

As you practice self-devotion, you'll quickly recognize the emotion at work, take a moment for yourself, and shift your energy. Now snapping at your spouse or child may be avoided; you wake up feeling refreshed and come back to work the next day without the heavy emotion.

Creating a self-devotion practice that activates restoration while you're still awake can be simple and take as little as five minutes. I'm going to show you how to open up space for yourself now.

1. Create or find a quiet space in your home that is filled with things you're drawn to, a space where you're excited and feel safe being alone.

Imagine walking into this space. It's a comfortable temperature, dark, with a soft glow from a salt lamp and fairy lights, tranquil music playing, and you sit in a chair, feeling safely held with a fuzzy blanket and fluffy pillows, taking a deep breath in smelling the grounding essential oils diffusing and feel calm as you sip warm soothing tea.

2. Look at your day; where is there a minimum of five to ten minutes that you can sit in this inviting space?

It may be on a lunch break, before you go to bed, or right when you get home. It may be getting up ten minutes earlier in the morning, but it doesn't have to. I promise you have this time while you're awake. It also doesn't need to be the same time every day, but build it daily, get excited to be in this space, make it a priority, and name it something fun!

3. Get snuggled into the space and close your eyes. Take three deep breaths, feeling your belly expand on the inhale and contract on the exhale. Now, ask your body any question, like what is the back pain saying or what do you need at this moment?

This is where you get to tap into your intuition and before you freak out thinking you don't have one—yes, you do. It's always with you, always has been, always will be. Sometimes she needs to be dusted off. You've heard the phrase "Gut feeling?" That's intuition. You may feel a tingling or warmness in your belly or heart, hear a small inner voice, or know the truth. These are all ways your intuition is speaking to you. Allow your body to talk, then thank your body for communicating to you.

4. Next, ask your soul what it wants right now. Trusting the first instinct, then go do that thing!

The message may be to continue sitting still, breathwork, journaling, gratitude, tapping, sound healing, oracle cards, dancing, exercise, getting outside, reading, calling a friend, a bath, etc. The possibilities are endless! Whatever comes up, trust that first thing and go do it. If what comes up isn't physically possible, then imagine it in your mind like a movie or journal a story, engaging your five senses and embracing the experience.

5. Reflect on how you feel, check in with your body and soul again, and repeat as many times as needed.

This is the foundation of being able to show up for yourself with love and self-devotion and break the cycle of survival mode. You just tended to your needs in five minutes. Check out the resource page for a guided meditation that walks you through this practice.

When you show up and respect yourself deeply, this is where the healing occurs. This is where I have found investing in programs deepens the relationship with myself because it shows my soul that I deeply desire to be the best version of myself and gives me space to explore, be accountable, and empowered while offering mindset shifts and deeper healing.

Sweet friend, keep going, see the challenge through. You can overcome survival mode, and I promise there is a light inside of you—a light so bright that this world needs you. You can create a deep self-devotion practice. You'll see the impactful and effective results of how you feel and experience life. It keeps you motivated to show up and do it again and again. This is what builds the belief that it's possible to heal. It's this belief that the battery is recharged and restores your mind, body, and soul.

Katie White is an intuitive energy guide, Reiki Master Teacher, and owner of Pure Sparkle. In 2016, she felt the nudge to shift her life and discover the light within her. She made the bold decision to leave her corporate job and trust her intuition. Through her healing, Pure Sparkle was born. She believes every woman deserves to feel connected with her most powerful, intuitive inner self. So many women overwork themselves by putting the needs of everyone else before theirs, barely surviving. Katie's been there before, feeling depleted and having no energy left. That's why she has devoted her life to teaching women how to break that cycle. She is an overall illuminator, which means being in her energy is going to fully light you up from the inside out, and you will feel your most radiate self just by being in her presence.

While her work is fun and lights her soul on fire, she also enjoys outdoor adventures with her family, running the wooded trails, soaking in the ocean waves or mountain top views, dancing to 2000 hits, meaningful conversations with friends, and investing in herself.

Connect with Katie:

Website: https://puresparklellc.com/

Resources: https://puresparklellc.com/resources

Instagram: https://www.instagram.com/thekatieewhite/

Facebook: https://www.facebook.com/katiewhite1113/

CHAPTER 22

CHAOS TO GRACE

RECOVERING FROM TRAGEDY IS POSSIBLE

Katie Steinle, Energetic Specialist, International Human Design
Analyst, Qigong/Reiki Master Teacher

MY STORY

The abyss. That's where I've been for the last five years. I've been to Heaven, Hell, and every place in between. This is what it feels like to love someone with mental illness.

For me, that was my son, Parker. Watching him suffer and not be able to help him like a mother is wired to do left me feeling lost and devastated. Navigating an illness that has such little understanding and support, losing him, trying to make sense of it all, and then keeping myself from dying of a broken heart—it was all just too much to bear. It's a completely overwhelming and destabilizing feeling of living in the unknown every minute of every day.

As humans, we don't like to live in the unknown. It's our mind's worst nightmare not being able to tell if you'll be safe and secure in the next hour. I spent years not knowing if I would be woken up in the middle of the night by my son saying, "Mom, I need to go to the hospital," or wondering if Parker was going to make it to his next birthday. He made it to 18.

My body was in constant fight or flight mode. The crescendo of scrambling so hard, pouring every ounce of your life force into saving your child, was excruciating. I tried desperately to get ahead of the unknown every minute of every day for years, only to fail and lose him after all.

You'd think that would be the end of the story. But it marked the beginning of a new level of the abyss. This chapter felt like someone placed a massive rock on me and dropped me into the deepest depths of the ocean. Down, down, down, I sunk until I reached the bottom. I can't move. I can't breathe. All I could do was become familiar with that space and that feeling because I was going to stay there a very long time. Through years of deep energy work and learning a completely new way to communicate with my son, I have managed to rise above the tragedy—offering healing and hope to others.

I've been surrounded by mental illness my entire life. My grandfather committed suicide after battling diabetes for years which left my mom understandably depressed. My sister was diagnosed with schizoaffective disorder. My dad was a World War II veteran that saw far too much and kept to himself. My husband has ADD. I think if we all dig deep enough, we'll find mental illness in every family and ourselves to a certain degree. My beautiful son was touched by a little aspect of all of these things, which made it extremely challenging to narrow down a diagnosis and a game plan. Parker was in and out of the hospital 20 times in the last few years of his life. He'd be in the hospital for weeks at a time, sometimes having doctor after doctor examining him, each one throwing around a different diagnosis only to have the next doctor rule that out. The doctors would tell me, "Mental illness is somewhat of a guessing game." It's so unique to the individual, and they have a limited number of medications, so it's like throwing paint on a wall and seeing which one sticks, if any.

As the pressures of high school and life grew, so did Parker's anxiety, mood swings, and eventually depression while he watched his aspirations and dreams slowly slip away. By this time, I, too, had anxiety and was completely overwhelmed and depressed. You feel so incredibly alone because mental illness is something no one wants to talk about or admit. The hospitals and programs seem to just spit you out once they've deemed you're no longer in crisis mode—off you go, best of luck, onto the next. We tried everything. Ultimately we lost Parker because the only thing he felt would help him get a handle on his extreme anxiety was Xanax. Since the doctors wouldn't prescribe it to a teenager, he found someone who gave him a pill. Unknowingly, it also contained a lethal amount of Fentanyl. I tucked him into bed one night, and when I went to wake him the next morning, he was dead.

The Qigong community I belonged to organized an energetic support event a few days after Parker's death. For an hour, they did specific Qigong exercises focusing on sending me love and connection. I remember talking on the phone to a friend who was helping plan the celebration of life service and looking at the clock, thinking, *I should really get off and spend this time focusing on receiving the energy that was coming my way* as the minutes ticked on. About a half-hour in, I felt the energy shift in the room. Minutes later, I started to see something materializing in front of me, almost like how light comes off a candle flame.

It was there, just briefly, almost fading in and out. It hit me: *Could it be possible my son was able to use all the extra energy being sent my way to come through and communicate with me?*

I jumped off the phone and glanced at the clock, realizing I now only had 15 minutes left, and there was a chance I could connect with my son! I ran up to his room, yanking a picture of him off the wall on my way. Clutching his picture against my heart, I sat on his bed sobbing and praying. Having practiced Qigong for years, my energy system was open enough for me to feel Parker's presence along with angels comforting me with the understanding that surpasses words and peace that surpasses understanding.

It slowly faded out, and there I was back in my heartbreak, wanting them desperately to come back. But it was the beginning of me realizing Parker could continue to communicate with me regardless of space and time.

I've done an incredible amount of soul searching and healing in the last few years. I was always fascinated by people and energy and was in the process of obtaining a certification in Human Design when all this happened. Human Design decodes a blueprint of your genetics and unique energetic expression. It maps out your life, including your strengths and the lessons you're here to learn. What a synchronicity that I was studying a modality that helped me make some sense of why things unfold the way they do. It became clear that my mission moving forward was to learn to connect with Parker's energy in a new way so that we could work together to help people discover their life's meaning, get back in touch with their dreams, and the power that lies in embodying their uniqueness. Parker was not only showing me this with constant signs and communication but was telling me, just as I guided him through his earthly life, that he was now here to guide me. If I could learn to trust, surrender, and accept, nothing short of miracles could happen. This was a lot to take in, and I'm still a work in progress.

I discovered Quantum Biofeedback which I found tremendously helpful in shifting my all-consuming grief. Even though my higher self understood the love that binds us lasts forever, the physical part of me was still suffering a nervous breakdown. Every day when I woke up, it hit me like a punch in the gut: *No, this isn't some horrible dream. My darkest nightmare has happened.*

I replayed the events of Parker's struggles and death in excruciating detail and lay frozen in agonizing pain and sorrow. If I couldn't even lift my head, how was I supposed to lift my body and get out of bed? It was too much, so I stayed horizontal. Family and friends worried, telling me, "You have to get up, get moving. Choose life." All I wanted to do was die and be with my son. I searched the cosmos, desperately trying to find my baby and make sure he was safe. I found on days I couldn't get out of bed that if I could listen to the perfected hertz frequencies the biofeedback system uses to harmonize and balance stress, I could start to calm whatever emotions were flooding me, just enough so I could sit up.

Just put one foot in front of the other, Mom, I'd hear Parker say. *Take one step at a time. Keep moving forward.* So I did.

I started doing healing sessions for friends while I was in my Human Design and Qigong Instructor certification programs. I remember when Parker died thinking: *I'm damaged goods. There's no way I'll ever be able to continue with my passions.* Interestingly enough, people continued reaching out to me for healing sessions. I know this was orchestrated from above. This was my way of finding grace and meaning despite the tragedy. There were days I wondered if I could pull it together and focus on something besides my all-consuming grief. I noticed that as I began to put my attention on helping someone else, it allowed me to take the focus off my pain. It gave me energy. I could hold space for whatever someone was going through because I realized all the years of trauma I went through gave me an incredible level of empathy. As I heal others, I heal myself. This was a way for Parker and I to continue to connect and work together. In some sessions, clients would actually feel or see Parker standing over my shoulder!

Being around Parker and so many others who struggle to fit into society's standards made me realize most of the people labeled as having a mental illness are actually incredibly intelligent, sensitive, and creative souls. They have such a high level of awareness of universal energy that the filter which allows us to process sensory input is almost fully open, allowing them to take in every sensory perception at once, which can be incredibly overwhelming and ungrounding. When you're sensitive, your energy field is so open you find yourself taking in other people's thoughts and emotions, not even consciously aware you're doing so. You take them in as your own, which can overwhelm your nervous system, easily leading to anxiety, self-judgment, and distortion of reality. The gift of being so open is usually a high level of creativity, but since everything is energy and creative insight usually comes in bursts if you don't have a regular creative outlet, this can easily turn into overload. You're driven to look for ways to check out and numb all the input. You end up at a doctor's office, and all they know is to throw medications at you to numb all the feelings.

It's challenging to lead with the heart, isn't it? It's a vulnerable place to be swimming in all those emotions. I read one time that the body can only hold an intense emotion for 20 minutes. Oh, how many times I've been curled up in a ball sobbing hysterically, only to find my body gives out after a certain time, even if out of exhaustion. When emotions get overwhelming, check in with your environment through your senses. What can you see, hear, smell, and taste? This will help ground you.

I've found nature to be the best place to retreat to when the outside world proves too much. Put your feet on the earth, and connect with a power greater than you. It heals and recharges you so you can deal with everything coming at you. Check your breathing. I can't tell you how many times I would literally catch myself forgetting to breathe when I was in crisis mode. Look down and find your feet. This will help you get out of your head and into your body. Tell yourself you're safe at this moment, even if you're in the emergency room. Don't go into victim mode. Trust me, I get it; some days, you can't help but look up at the sky and ask God: "Why are you doing all this to me?" That's where you have to do a reframe: It's not happening to you; it's happening for you. I roll my eyes at that sometimes, but it's true. Even going through what doctors would tell me is the greatest pain a human can suffer, losing a child, I can now see the 30,000-foot view of how many lives Parker and I are touching, and it puts things into perspective and allows me to live from a state of grace. I practice acceptance and forgiveness of even what seems to be unacceptable. Trust you are here for a reason and purpose—even if that is to model for others what living in instability and pain looks like. Everything is unfolding the way it is for a reason you might not even be aware of yet.

I've learned some things having navigated the valley of the shadow of death. Honor yourself first. A lot of our problems stem from us putting other people's standards before ourselves. We all need solo time to just be. "Rest when you need to rest" was the best advice I got for succumbing to immense grief. Sit in the sun and let it dry out the watery sadness. We hold emotions in our muscle's fascia, so yin yoga and Epsom salt baths are extremely helpful in balancing an overtaxed nervous system. A nurse told me that when your nervous system short circuits, it can take several years to rebalance. So give yourself space and grace. Be your best friend; tell yourself every day how good you're doing. When caring for others, it's important to recognize that sometimes you can do everything in your power to shift things, but you ultimately need to surrender to a higher power and realize you can't control someone else's karma. But you can absolutely hold space, love, and prayer for what they're going through. Parker taught me that life is about contrast; don't be afraid to have deep experiences. That's how you know you're truly alive. Realize the difference between trying to control versus caring from a place of love and trust.

Where thoughts go, energy flows. Start rewiring your brain, so you think differently. You can be in victim mode or self-empowerment mode. No one would blame me if I laid down and died from a broken heart after all I've been through. Parker guided me to see how his death empowered me to live from a higher level of perspective, not so much for myself but for others who need a hand to pull them out of the bottom of the well I once lived in. One of the ways you bring yourself through challenging times is to acknowledge that we don't always have control; you don't have to hold on so tight to life. This isn't about letting go or giving up; it's more about having enough detachment so you can think clearly. That is when you can tap into your power and know you're never alone. Don't compare your journey with anyone else's. We're all here to be exactly who we are, no matter how messy that might look. Meet yourself each day where you are at.

Try to think of life in terms of order and chaos; chaos leads to order which leads to chaos. Our lives are always at some point within this cycle of beauty and pain. When you learn to be in the space of what is, you'll trust there is some order or greater knowledge to gleam, no matter how out of control the situation seems. I'd like to share with you a tool that helped me embody this. This will help you structure your emotional waves—the highs and lows of life. Quiet your mind and open your heart so you can let inspiration flow through you without attachment to your thoughts. When you show up just as you are, there is no rejection or abandonment. Self-love means your cup is full from within. Love and accept yourself for who you are, and it will set you free.

THE PRACTICE

BALANCING CONTROL WITH TRUST MEDITATION

1. Find a calm, quiet space and sit comfortably. Start by taking a few nice, deep, letting-go breaths. Close your eyes and turn your focus inward, opening up your heart space. Raise your hands, so they're facing each other.

2. Call into your right hand any feelings of control, betrayal, and concern. In your left hand, hold all the ways we seek to trust ourselves, something greater than ourselves, to receive trust and share trust.

3. Holding control in the right hand and trust in the left, breathe in all the ways you try to control life. Breathe out all the ways you can trust. Breathe in trust, breathe out control. Become aware of the energy between your hands as you bring forward any memories of control or any unprocessed energy. As you call forth old patterns of needing to control to feel safe, meet them with trust. Breathe in trust, exhale trust.

4. Allow control to become your teacher. Where have you felt betrayed when things didn't work out the way you wanted? Allow

the awareness of trust to expand. As you feel the energy of control and trust balancing between your hands, start to move them into a vertical position with your left hand on top facing your right hand on the bottom. Feel your ability to trust yourself and those around you to trust themselves. Breathe in the power of receiving trust and exhale sharing trust, allowing a wave of trust to expand throughout your entire field. Receive the greater connection of trust, forgiveness, and acceptance within your heart.

For an audio version of this meditation and deeper insight into living a self empowered life visit

https://katiesteinle.com/mentalhealthresources

Katie Steinle, Energetic Specialist, International Human Design Analyst, Qigong/Reiki Master Teacher, and founder of Discover Your Design, uses Human Design to unlock your energetic blueprint allowing you to realign with your true essence and tap into your greatest potential. Get clear on your greatest strengths, know where your energy is being hijacked, and unlock your unconscious mind so you can start co-creating your best life. With 20 years of energetic mastery experience, she combines Human Design, Quantum Biofeedback, and energy work to calibrate your life force back into resonance with your purpose. Katie will assist you in discovering meaning in your life. She teaches powerful new ways to stay resilient and adaptable in these ever-changing times while maintaining a state of creativity and flow. Katie cherishes time connecting with family and friends, nature, and the cosmos. With Parker as her spirit guide, they work together helping people rediscover meaning in their lives and love in their hearts.

Connect with Katie:

Website: www.katiesteinle.com

Facebook: https://www.facebook.com/groups/discoveryourhumandesign

Instagram: www.instagram.com/discoveryourhumandesign/

YouTube: https://www.youtube.com/c/DiscoverYourDesign

Linked In: https://www.linkedin.com/in/katie-steinle-a19aa24/

CHAPTER 23

BODYTALK

FROM BATTLEGROUND TO SACRED TEMPLE

Marcela Chaves M.S, LMHC

MY STORY

I was freezing, shaking cold, naked and afraid. I should have known that something was wrong with me being fully naked for the first time at 19 in front of the plastic surgeon and not my boyfriend.

Please God, let this bowl of beans feed my cells the nutrients I haven't been giving them.

That was my prayer the day before the surgery. I had been hiding my eating disorder for years. It was like I was asking my cells to cram before the big exam. I think that was the first time I talked to my body.

I know I have not been good to you.
And it's not fair to ask you to make up for the damage I've caused.
But please, please, please take these beans and feed all my cells and help me through this surgery.

Every delicious bite was like sending soldiers to war.

A war I had been in with my body for as long as I could remember.

I couldn't remember a time when I didn't try to cover up my body. I was a 13-year-old wrapped up in a towel on a hot summer day so nobody could see me. I strategically left the towel, jumped in, and calculated how many eyes were watching to get out and cover myself back up.

Up until I moved away from home, I was ashamed of being so curvy, of having a big ass, a big mouth, and wide hips. Every day I spent an hour rubbing giant blocks of ice on my thighs and butt in the shower, as if somehow, I could freeze my ass into a smaller, cuter little ass. Looking back, I see the madness of not accepting the beautiful curves God gave me.

I took diet pills and laxatives, purged, followed endless diets, and had reduction massages where they literally beat the shit out of you, left bruises, and then wrapped you up in plastic and stuck you under heating lamps. Nobody knew. They just smiled and told me how pretty I looked when I lost weight. It made me so angry to want that. Because I knew the price I was paying to receive those empty words—they didn't know I figured out how to make myself throw up so I could eat with my family. They also didn't know about all the coffee I drank or the cigarettes I smoked.

I wouldn't let my boyfriend see me naked. I felt so ashamed of my body. I was good at hiding in plain sight.

I thought getting a boob job was the solution. I had no idea the invisible force I fought was trauma embedded in my body from being molested at the age of three.

They later told me I woke up screaming from the surgery. They sedated me again. Maybe this was my body crying at the latest assault?

A week later, as I stared at my naked body in the mirror, my joy for my bigger breasts didn't last long. One incision wasn't healing properly.

Fuck.

My father was against the surgery. As a cardiovascular surgeon, he believed surgery should be left for life-saving purposes. When he was a young intern, he saw a priest go in for a nose job and never wake up from the anesthesia. Was he punished for his vanity? I don't believe we have a God that punishes us for our vanity. If anything, God is always ready to love us back into alignment once we're done torturing ourselves.

I put so much pressure on my parents that they caved. And now I had to wake them up at 3 a.m.: "Mom, Dad, my incision is leaking!"

The next two years were an absolute nightmare.

The doctors didn't know why I wasn't healing. The hole kept getting bigger. Did I mention I was starting school away from home, in another city, by myself?

My life as a brand-new college student consisted of going to the doctor, going to class, and secretly changing the pads in my bra because I was leaking, and they couldn't explain it. I couldn't let anyone touch me because the pain was sometimes unbearable.

Then one day, I could see the implant through the hole in my breast. It was like I was staring into a black hole.

Doctor: "Honey, we have to take it out, let the breast heal, and then put it back in."

Me: "What do you mean take it out? I'm going to have one breast with an implant and one without?"

Doctor: "Yes. I'm so sorry. It's only for six months."

Me: "Six months?!"

And just when I thought I couldn't feel worse about myself and the situation:

Doctor: "We're going to get you fitted for a prosthetic breast at the League for Women's Cancer."

Why is this happening?

Like the priest, am I being punished?

I don't think I was being punished. At least not by God. I brought this on myself. Years of hurting myself finally caught up.

I made a vow. I got on my knees: *Please, God, forgive me. I promise I will never hurt my body ever again.*

This ended my eating disorder and started my journey to healing my relationship with my body.

I went in for surgery number two and woke up screaming again.

Broken.

That's all I could see when I looked in the mirror and saw my naked body—the scars. I felt mutilated.

I eventually broke up with my boyfriend. I didn't tell him what I was going through. I didn't want anyone's pity. The only people that knew were my parents and my roommate.

I wish I could go back and tell my 20-year-old self that she was worthy of love and support. That she was beautiful, and she wasn't broken. That she didn't have to go through this alone. I should've given my boyfriend a chance to support me through all this. But the idea of being seen during my most vulnerable time was unbearable. I guess I didn't feel worthy of being loved when I saw myself as broken. I thought love was reserved for the perfect.

This went on for a total of five surgeries.

I remember wanting to be able to hug people again.

While I had the prosthetic breasts from the Cancer League, they looked real from afar, but if you hugged me, they would slide out of place. It was as if I stuffed my bra with two balloons filled with sand. They weren't soft like real breasts, and they would shift easily. One boob was off on vacation in Bali while the other one was getting groceries. Now I get to hug people every day, and the boobies stay in place. Maybe this is one of the reasons why I love to dance so much now. I've given myself permission to be close to those I choose. I get to feel another's body next to mine to the sound of music. The language of the body is pleasure and peace or disease and discomfort. And allowing myself to have fun and dance is a part of what makes me happy and alive.

I felt like I was hiding my body and in isolation my whole life.

The earliest memories I have of my body screaming out was when I was nine. The person who molested me was visiting. At the time, I had no conscious memories of the abuse. But my body remembered. I remember getting in my pool. He was outside watching me from a distance. And as I emerged from the water, I came out covered in hives. It was like I was having an allergic reaction to the cold. This had never happened before. Now looking back, I can't help but feel enormous compassion towards the little girl in me and the wisdom of my body screaming out.

Our bodies are communicating with us. The question is: Are we listening?

In my life I've had many teachers, my body being one of the most important teachers. But there were two women whose life and death shook me to the core of my being. Today I'm going to tell you about one of them.

Sylvia was your typical alpha-fem—hard-working, go-getter who believed if she didn't do it, it wouldn't get done. She was the one at work to always get the job done; she was the one running around taking care of her two beautiful kids, helping her parents, taking care of her home—you know exactly what I'm talking about. She's the woman society has decided gets the badge for being Super-Woman, the one who leaves herself last but takes great care of everyone else. One morning at age 50, she didn't wake up. The same woman who thought if she didn't get the job done, everyone would fall apart? Well, she died in her sleep, and everyone moved on. Someone else will be walking her kids down the aisle; someone else will take her daughter shopping for her prom dress; someone else will hold her son's hand when his heart breaks for the first time. I wonder how many times her body tried to tell her to stop. I wonder how many opportunities did she override because someone else needed her, and in her mind, it was urgent and couldn't wait.

In 2019 I was diagnosed with basal cell carcinoma. It was caught early, and I can proudly say I went from cancer to cancer survivor in about a month. But this made me sit up and pay attention. I wasn't going to waste time and energy asking God: "Why me," but instead, what I needed to learn from this and do differently for my body. Clearly, my body was talking again, and I was listening.

I hired an amazing coach, someone I trusted. And it was the most money I had ever invested in myself at the time. But I knew I was worth it. My health and my body were worth it. He taught me the basic things my body needed to keep healing. It took my relationship with my body to another level, but I also remember being mad at myself.

Me: "I'm paying you thousands of dollars, and I'm not doing some of the basic things you are asking me to do. Why would I do that to myself?"

Armando: "Maybe this has to do with self-love?"

It was like someone had dropped a bomb on me, and it kept exploding in slow motion.

Self-love?

Hmm. Was I not loving myself?

I realized I'd come a long way from hurting myself, but I didn't realize I wasn't loving myself.

And this triggered the next part of my journey.

THE PRACTICE

The question that changed my life:

1. How can I love myself more deeply?

I tried not to be mad at myself when I wasn't doing the things my coach asked of me, but instead would try and get curious and ask myself: How can I love myself more deeply?

At first, I didn't think I was getting any answers. But then I could see my body talking to me. I saw my body come alive when I would dance bachata; I could feel how happy I was every time I would put my feet in the grass, every time I was in nature; when I was snuggled up with my son; when I ate healthy foods; when I would go to the beach at night. Pleasure the power of pleasure. My body was letting me know what was good for me and what wasn't.

It was through asking this question that the "goddess hour" was born. This ritual is pretty much a non-negotiable. I take a shower or a bath at night, with the lights off and just the light of a single candle. This is my favorite ritual of the day. I can look at my naked body with love; I mean, we all look good naked when lit by candlelight. At first, I listened to my favorite soft music, but then I discovered it was my favorite time to talk to God. First, I borrowed God's love for me. I call it God's hug. I take my towel at the end of the shower and hug it while the hot water pours down my back. I feel held. I pretend it's God hugging me, reminding me I am loved—telling myself that I am loved. I make everything about this time a ritual of honoring my body, loving my body, listening to my body, admiring my wet soapy skin in the candlelight, and admiring my curves. Treating myself as a goddess every time I apply my essential oils. My body comes alive. It feels good to be the object of someone else's affection and adoration. But being able to love myself like this every day is a powerful practice for me. My love for this sacred temple grows every day.

Of all the jobs we take on as women, mom, wife, stay-at-home mom, employee, CEO, PTO, room mom, daughter, and sister, there is nothing more important than taking care of this sacred vessel.

It's through this sacred vessel that we can tuck our loved ones in at night, hold their hand when we pick them up from school, wipe the tears away when they are sad, hold them when they wake us up in the middle of the night with fever, play with them, laugh, kiss, dance, climb mountains, make love, explore new lands, feel the breeze of the ocean.

I get to really appreciate this gorgeous vessel that I'm in and all the magic it provides. And all I have to do is listen to my body and pay attention to what it's asking of me. Eating became a healing experience and another opportunity to nurture my body. It was like I was creating a relationship based on love and trust.

The more you honor your body like a temple, the easier it becomes to:

- get that mole looked at
- schedule the appointment with the doctor
- get your physical
- schedule the thermography
- go for that ten-minute walk
- eat healthy, unprocessed foods that taste delicious
- drink enough water

We are so easily distracted by all the noise around us. I promise you it's incredibly easy to override what your body is trying to tell you when you're plowing through your to-do list or binge-watching Netflix. Silence is necessary for our healing and for us to hear what our body is whispering.

Give yourself moments throughout the day when you can just tune in to your body and ask: How can I love you more deeply? Your body will answer. Just start with one minute and check-in: How can I love you more today?

I know your family needs you. Your clients, your kids, the dog, everyone needs you.

And sometimes it feels impossible to choose.

But I'm here to remind you that your body needs you to choose you every time.

When our hierarchy is clear, it helps guide us during the storms.

Making good decisions when we are not feeling well is not easy. Our frontal lobe, which is responsible for making good decisions, is impaired.

I know it all feels really important at the moment. But it can wait. Your body, your health, won't.

A few years ago, a client hired me to help her decide whether or not to have bariatric surgery.

In her soul, she felt the bigness of the decision she was going to make. And wanted to be sure.

We had less than a month to make this decision.

The most important thing I can tell you from our work was that she learned not to make any decisions around her body from a place of anger. Was she getting this surgery from a place of love? Or was she angry at her body?

As she did the work and got clear on her why, she realized it was coming from a place of anger.

She canceled the surgery.

And she listened to her body and the things that made her feel alive. She started training for marathons again.

That moment—knowing that someone I cared for was able to make a decision for her body from a place of love made everything I went through worth it.

As healers, it's easy for us to see others through the eyes of love; this work is about being able to do this for ourselves.

Once we stop the battle with ourselves and start the journey to healing that relationship with our bodies, we go from battleground to sacred temple to glorious playground. Our bodies are powerful temples of pleasure and joy and will always guide us to living our best lives if we are willing to listen. I hope you let this one question guide you and your body on what I consider the greatest adventure. I can't wait to hear what your body is whispering.

As for me, I came out of hiding, ended the war, and embraced this beautiful body as a sacred temple. I've danced bachata in front of 400 people, learned how to play the guitar and serenaded my grandmother for her 90th birthday, playfully posed while a gorgeous model took pictures of me on a yacht while I was in a bathing suit, went on my first health retreat this year, rode ATVs, hiked the most beautiful mountains, discovered magnificent caves, went shooting for the first time and hit the bullseye. I've taken my son to swim with the dolphins and snorkeling in a man-made coral reef, to just name a few of our adventures. And I'm just getting started.

I listened to my body, and fun is my medicine.

Marcela Chaves MS, LMHC, is an expert clinician, master healer, and spiritual teacher who has been empowering women and men for over two decades to create the life of their dreams! She is a powerful hybrid of experience, science, and spirituality. She can help you do this because she did it for herself first. Now she teaches her clients her system how to integrate success and well-being with ease and joy! She lights up when she can partner up with her clients and support them on their journey of creating a life that they love.

One of her passions is supporting and empowering spiritual entrepreneurs and healers to uplevel their physical codes to match their spiritual ascension. Marcela discovered in her own journey that as she evolved spiritually, her body required higher quality care. She describes it as if you were given a Maserati engine; you need to give it the higher quality fuel. Nothing brings her more joy than empowering other healers to live an abundant life of greater health and wealth, all while having more fun with their families!

This groundbreaking support, combined with her clinical experience of 22 years, will allow healers to truly step into their full power while experiencing radiant health and creating a practice they love.

Marcela has been interviewed as a guest expert on Parenting for IHelpmoms.com supporting thousands of women and men throughout the country and internationally. She has the most amazing son, and together they love doing life with their family and friends. Her soul is fed by snuggling up on the couch with her loved ones, being in nature with her feet in the grass, the beach at night, great food, and dancing bachata every chance she gets!

Connect with Marcela:

Website: www.marcelachaves.com

CHAPTER 24

BODY PSYCHOLOGY

LISTEN DEEPER TO YOUR BODY TO REDUCE PAIN

Krissi Williford, MS, CPT

MY STORY

When I was 12 years old, I lost my best friend to cancer. It was shocking, to say the least. I didn't understand what was happening and struggled to heal for over a decade. I ran from it. Only after my nervous breakdown did I really begin that healing process. It was still another ten-plus years before I decided to tune in and be open to the opportunity available to me in my healing. This was that moment in the meeting place where I decided not to give up on myself.

I know what it feels like to be in chronic pain and struggle with mental health. I've lived through depression, anxiety, grief, shame, abandonment, anger, disordered eating, ADHD, and probably more emotions related to mental health than I'm aware of. What I've learned has allowed me to help people in a way that is missing in most mainstream health and fitness practices.

Working in health and fitness is my purpose, but I got here through the physical and emotional pain I endured for many years. I remember the exact turning point. I was in the middle of my workout when I looked around the gym and saw men and women doing different exercises, adding weights to their bars, pushing through with sweat dripping down their faces. Not me. I was on the floor, doing physical therapy.

I was supposed to be a fitness coach, yet it felt like a door was being slammed in my face. I had chronic pain, and my pain wasn't allowing me to do what the others were doing. It limited my movement, performance, and coaching abilities. I questioned myself, my worth, and my career choice. I felt jealous, confused, defeated even, and I judged myself for it all.

Even though I was ready to give up, it was at this moment that I met myself, my true self, the one who'd push forward despite all the things working against her. She was the one who remembered that our body is resilient and will heal and recover itself if we support it properly. The one who'd get the answers for her own pain and then share it with the world to influence people to eliminate their pain for supreme results.

This is also where I meet a lot of people in my work—in this meeting place. They've tried everything, but their body still hurts, and they have no answers for why or what to do about it. I feel I do my best work here because even though it's a place of pain and many negative emotions, it's also a place of hope and opportunity, which is what I provide for my clients.

My path to this meeting place is one that took place over many years. It wasn't one thing that put me there but rather a culmination of events.

I was overweight as a child, and when my friend passed, it catapulted me into sports and fitness. It was how I coped and distracted myself from the reality I didn't want to experience. The gym was an outlet for the anger, grief, abandonment, depression, and anxiety I was feeling. For ten years, I held it all in and tried to pound it out of my body in the gym. So much so that when I was 23 years old, I suffered a nervous breakdown. My body was in flight or fight and under chronic stress for so many years that it couldn't take any more. All it took was one more triggering event.

My nervous system was at its limit from the stress I unknowingly put on it. The weight of emotional stress was too much to bear. And the negative effects of chronic dieting for weight loss and over-exercising limited my capacity to handle much more.

Soon after, it was time to graduate college. I had no idea what I'd do, but I needed to finish, and exercise science was the easiest route. Although I enjoyed it, I hadn't yet developed the passion that I have for it today. As it happened, I was a basketball referee too.

I started refereeing right out of high school when I was 18. I told myself I did it to stay close to the game. I had a level of peace there that I couldn't find anywhere else. When I learned it could be a full career, I pursued it. I loved it; I felt a deep desire to be successful on the court, and as I worked toward that goal, the wear and tear on my body continued. So did my running from the reality I needed to face. Eventually, I ended up in chronic pain.

Most would tell you my pain came from being an athlete and that it's normal. But when no one could help me eliminate my pain, I began questioning everything including my career path(s). I was refereeing but also working in the gym as a personal trainer—two industries that required good health and physical ability.

I tried so many things to help myself. I trained with a running coach who was also a physical therapist. I saw a chiropractor and massage therapists and tried Reiki and energy healing and others. I tried different exercise and therapy programs. I did all the things. Yet, I still hurt every day. It was hard to move and do things like stand, walk, exercise, and simply get out of bed. I had chronic tension and pain in my body, and it challenged my mental wellness. The voice in my head was constant *I'm never going to get out of pain. I can't coach or referee, so what am I going to do? This isn't fair. I'm stuck and can't even help myself. What did I do to deserve this?*

At the end of my rope and the bottom of the barrel, I was ready to give up. But I didn't. Because that moment in the gym was when I made the decision that would change my entire path in life and career, it was the moment I decided to fight, not only for myself but for all of you. I would fight in a way I had no strategy for. I had no direction, support, or Google search to tell me which way to go. I remembered that the body is resilient; it can and will heal. I knew willingness was all I needed, which is why today I tell my clients to "Show up and be willing. I'll take care of the rest."

Something you may not know about chronic pain is when your body hurts all the time, you feel bad. And when you feel bad, it weighs on your mental health. You tell yourself things like, *I'm not good enough. I don't deserve to get better. My pain is my punishment. I'll never get better or stop hurting.* When mental health isn't good, you have no energy and no will to keep going. You feel defeated because movement helps your state of mental health, but when your body hurts, you don't want to move. When you don't want to move, it congests your state of mental health. And mainstream fitness and physical therapy aren't teaching what you need to know to get out of that state of pain.

I help men and women tune into their body so they can finally move without pain. It's health and fitness coaching, but the work we do together goes far deeper than a workout. Because your body is talking to you, trying to help you heal, feel better, and generate awareness so you can get unstuck. It's body psychology. And there's a place for it in your holistic mental health strategy.

If you ever think about what your body does, it's amazing. The systems and processes by which your machine operates are nothing short of a miracle. Most people don't know much about how their body works. They live life never considering how many things come into play to allow us to simply take one step or pick up a glass.

Maybe you've heard of your nervous system, digestive, visual, vestibular, muscular, or skeletal systems. There are a couple of body systems that aren't talked about so much in health and fitness. These are the ones I want to bring to your attention because they will help all the others function better and improve your mental health.

Your body is an electric system. How it communicates with itself, you and the environment is energetic. You may or may not be able to feel the energy moving through your body or from the outside world. But have you ever felt bad and gone outside for a few minutes only to come back in feeling better? Or what about when you go to the beach and come home feeling refreshed? That's the energy exchange. You exchange your negative energy for the positive energy of the earth. It's why you feel better after being there. And it's a useful tool for helping both your physical pain and your mental health.

You also have a limbic system. This is your emotional system. And it's the one I'll speak most about here because it's the one that's talked about the least in health. The limbic system involves memory and emotional state and connects the conscious with the unconscious functions of your body. This system plays an important role in how your body feels related to emotions.

So, let's focus on how you can begin to interpret what your emotional and physical pain states are giving you to consider. The body is very literal in its communication to you. There's an interpretation for everything. I'll give you the basics, but if you're having pain in your body that you don't fully understand, you can contact me for more insight at krissi@xcitefitnessal.com. Think about what your body parts do because it will usually give a good foundation of the insight you need.

Your mouth is used to speak, talk, and communicate. Issues here indicate that you're not speaking what you want to or not telling your truth.

Legs, hips, knees, ankles, and feet move your body. You can't walk, run, sit, or stand without them. Issues here indicate you're unhappy with the direction of your life. Or maybe there's a situation you don't want to walk through.

Your low back is part of your core stability system, great for carrying loads. Low back pain indicates that you feel like you're carrying extra loads. This could be additional stress you're putting on yourself or taking responsibility for something that isn't yours.

The shoulders are an expressive part. They're attached to our hands and arms that we use to carry things. Pain in the shoulders indicates bearing or carrying burdens or responsibilities that aren't yours.

Headaches are usually about tension or control, representing situations causing additional tension or stress. These could include emotional upsets, hurt feelings, inner pressure, and unpleasant situations.

Addiction or alcoholism is used to escape or get away from situations, life, and reality. Trying to avoid feelings and the inability to cope with them. It also fills a void you may have that may come from disapproval, rejection, or despair from self or others.

Being overweight represents the need for protection. This could be caused by trauma or any form of abuse. The extra weight protects the body. It also represents a need to be fulfilled in love and life. Stuffing yourself with food represents stuffing your feelings which is a way to protect yourself from feeling them.

Inflammation represents rage or anger. The inflammatory response is a defense mechanism. It's part of your immune system which signals inflammation to fight bacteria and pathogens. Both rage and anger stimulate fight or flight and put you in a position of defense.

General pain is trying to get your attention. It can also indicate feelings of guilt, anger, frustration, or that something is imbalanced.

Constipation and elimination problems have to do with holding on to or trying to get rid of emotions. In constipation, you're holding on to your emotional stress, and in excessive elimination, your body is trying to rid itself of what is stored.

Another way to look at this is what is your symptom causing? For example, if you're experiencing irritation, it usually represents something irritating you. UTI and skin rash are both examples of physical symptoms representing irritation.

Your body will talk to you and try to help you go in the direction that you need to go. When you don't listen and take action, it tries harder to get your attention. The harder it tries, the more pain, discomfort, sickness, or disease you'll experience. Your body will keep trying until you get it.

Emotions are energy, and they get stored in your body. Many times we aren't taught in childhood how to deal with our emotions. It's important to feel and express your emotions because this helps you process them out of your body, so they don't get stuck. Not having this skill leads to long-term emotional suppression, which causes sickness, disease, and pain. Once you begin to tune into your body, explore what it's giving you, and receive the growth that's there for you, you'll begin to feel better.

The beautiful part of all of this is that everything that happens to us during our life is for our highest good. Although it doesn't feel that way when we're going through it, it'll show up for you on the other side of it.

When I look back, I can see everything that happened for me, including losing my best friend, positioned me to do this work. Without that experience, I wouldn't have played basketball or got into fitness. Playing basketball was my friend's dream, but she couldn't, so I did it for her. Refereeing wasn't only a connection to the game; it was a connection to my friend. When I retired from refereeing, it was something I had to grieve. I grieved for her and, if I'm honest, for myself too. What made it easier was that I could see the path I was meant to be on, and I was willing to receive what was being given to me.

Chronic pain showed up in my body because I wasn't doing what I was supposed to be doing with my life. I had sacroiliac joint (SI) injuries because I was in the wrong place. I had a systemic candida overgrowth from deep resentments. I felt depressed because things were out of my control. I had migraine headaches from long periods of stress and anxiety from feeling boxed in and helpless. My body was screaming at me, trying to help.

Because I've learned to interpret what my body is saying, I can see this in hindsight. Now, when I have pain in my body or something doesn't feel right, I tune in because I know my body is trying to get my attention to tell me something and help. It's easier to walk through what's going on now because I can make the adjustments. You can too.

Evaluate your current body. How does it feel? What pain do you have, where do you have tension, and what's not working well in your body? Remember, we're being literal here. What does that system, part, organ, or area do or represent? Think about what's going on in your life, past or present. What connections can you make with what's coming up for you and your current state with your body?

Leave nothing unturned because it's all connected. The things you think are insignificant may just hold the insight you need. Once you put these things together, you can begin to address those issues and make adjustments to improve your mental health and physical body.

THE PRACTICE

Something I use with clients who are overwhelmed emotionally and hurting physically is a sensory warmup to stimulate their nervous system and communicate safety. I'll share it with you here so you can incorporate it into your daily movement strategy. I'm giving you a simple version, but I'll walk you through the whole series on a video recording with a download of all the exercises at https://www.krissiwilliford.fitness

Remember the energy exchange I mentioned before? You also have an energy exchange with your own touch and the touch of others. For this, we'll utilize you so you can take full responsibility for incorporating this into your daily movement.

You'll do each of the following movements ten times unless otherwise noted.

Here's how it goes:

- Stand with your feet under your hips or sit if it hurts to stand.
- Using your fingertips, tap the bone around your eyes (under the eye, side, and eyebrow).
- With open hands, wash your face as if you're using a bath cloth.
- Make claws with your fingers and run your fingertips over your scalp, whatever you can reach.
- Massage your ears top to bottom.
- Massage the base of your skull where it meets your neck at your hairline.
- Use open hands to rub the opposite shoulder in front; do both sides.
- Use open hands to rub shoulder to fingertips on the opposite arm.
- Turn your arm over and rub with open hands, fingertips to shoulder.
- Use open hands to rub your ribs on the opposite side.
- Use fists to rub on the back of your hips at the top of your pelvis.
- With open hands, rub down the front of your legs, around to the back, then up to your hip on the back of your legs.
- Take three big, deep breaths; inhale through your nose and exhale through your mouth.

I'll leave you with this. Your body and your mental health are connected. Your body and mind are both resilient. You can heal, recover, and rediscover yourself. Being in chronic pain is no way to live. But it's your responsibility to tune in, receive the message, and move yourself toward the vision of your life that you hold in your mind.

Krissi Williford is a corrective exercise expert and neuromuscular specialist. She's coached fitness and health for more than a decade. She has a BA from The University of Alabama, an MS from Western Kentucky University, and holds various health and fitness certifications.

She is the founder and owner of Xcite Fitness, located in Birmingham, Alabama, where she helps men and women eliminate their pain, tone their body, and get stronger so they can love the way they look and feel.

Krissi believes that health and fitness strategies should be individual to the person, and she does not support a cookie-cutter approach. The methods she uses to get the best results are on the cutting edge of what she believes will become mainstream fitness in the future. She gets excited to share her perspective and to shift the thinking of her clients into something that will support long-lasting results.

Krissi lives in Birmingham with her daughter, Kelley Grace, who is the namesake of her childhood friend. In her free time, she enjoys traveling to new places, watching the sunset, sitting on the beach or the side of a mountain, training in the gym, creative arts, sports, and experiencing the joy of childhood with her daughter.

Connect with Krissi:

Website: https://www.xcitefitnessal.com

Facebook: https://www.facebook.com/krissiwilliford

Free Facebook Group: https://www.facebook.com/groups/xcite.fitness

Instagram: https://www.instagram.com/krissiwilliford

Tiktok: https://www.tiktok.com/@krissiwilliford

Youtube: https://www.youtube.com/channel/UClcXY91G4Y3o_Nqq0OsCafg

CHAPTER 25

GET BETTER IN BED

L.O.V.E. YOURSELF TO SLEEP WITH FOUNDATIONAL HABITS

Kelly Myerson, MA, OTR

MY STORY

Clutching my phone, I slid down the wall of the bathroom. Through tears, I attempted to text my husband, but my tears distorted my vision. Attempting to gather myself, I pressed the button to call him.

Pick up, pick up, pick up!

"Hey, Babe, I'm at work. . ."

"I can't do this anymore!" I blurted out, wailing. "I give up!"

"What happened?" He responded, growing concerned.

"It's been two weeks since we locked down, and I'm so overwhelmed! I can't work, be a mom, a teacher, and keep the house clean—I just can't do it all!" I held my head in my hands, sobbing—tears falling and my chest heaving.

"Babe, you don't have to do it all." He spoke with deep compassion. "We're in this together. We're blessed. I'm still working, and we're going to figure this out."

I took a deep breath, knowing my husband was right. What was I doing? Why was I, in the middle of a pandemic, flexing back into old patterns of perfectionism?

Because those grooves are deep, girlfriend, I heard my inner voice rolling her eyes at me.

I was immediately more annoyed at her presence than upset about my current state. Her attitude was enough to spark my defiance, and I took a deep breath before speaking. I wasn't okay, but I was willing to move in the direction of okay.

"I'll be okay," I spoke softly. My sobbing settled. "Can we talk when you get home? I need help figuring this all out."

Hanging up, I took a moment to breathe and get back in my body. I spent two weeks creating the perfect office and the perfect school room. I sent pictures of the setup to my mom and sister—so proud of what I created.

Not pictured were the hours of work blending into family time and extra cups of coffee for motivation. I paused to calculate how many hours of actual sleep I had in the past week.

Not enough, Kel, not enough.

I shook my head, coming back to the present moment and my son. He was sitting with me, sweet and patient.

"Buddy, Mommy is feeling really overwhelmed." I reached over to pull him into a hug.

"It's okay, Mama." His sweet little voice was reassuring and soft. His eyes were full of unconditional love and hope.

"Let's go outside to play." I held his little hand in mine and squeezed it, reassuring him I was okay; we would be okay.

Maybe you're a working mom, like me, and working from home while schooling your child (and attempting to avoid all feelings of doom and gloom) was mission impossible.

It was during those first few weeks I realized just how big my network was. I missed my family and friends. I missed my work friends. I missed my quiet commute time. I missed the clear separation between work and home. I felt lost, unsure of where we were heading, and keenly aware that the beautifully color-coded schedule couldn't hide the unsustainable nature of my work-life imbalance.

In the evening, the door opened softly, and I heard the jingle of keys landing on a table. My husband came around the corner and walked to the sink to wash his hands. He dried them on a paper towel and tossed it into the garbage can. Moving towards me, he extended his arms for a hug.

"Are you okay?" He looked deep into my eyes, searching for the truth.

I set my shoulders back and nodded my head.

"I will be, but the demands of work and school are too much. It's not sustainable."

"What can I do?"

I looked in his eyes and smiled, "You're already doing it."

It takes courage to announce you're falling apart or failing. It's something I avoided most of my life. It took a pandemic for me to realize all the ways in which I denied my own needs and well-being to satisfy the expectations of others.

Two weeks into lockdown, I crumbled because I had built my routine on a foundation of sand. My husband and I cleared the path and decided to rebuild from the ground up.

Steve and I have always been driven. We've supported one another through each of our dreams and aspirations. But this marked the first time we spoke the intention aloud to prioritize our well-being.

We agreed to wait to begin any task—for home or work—unless our individual and family wellness needs were met. We learned to pour from an overflowing cup.

That's where we got it right. We put on the freaking oxygen masks! Our oxygen became rest, nutritious food, time together as a family, time spent in nature, and most importantly, great sleep!

The quality of my sleep has always been a barometer of my mental health status. My mental health status has always been reflected in the quality of my sleep. They are two sides of the same coin. Sleep is foundational and sacred self-care and self-love.

Imagine yourself holding and rocking a baby gently to sleep. Envision your surroundings; the colors, the lighting, the space between things, the bedding, and the decor. How does it make you feel? Calm? Serene? Loved? Restful?

Cultivating a routine and habits within a sacred sleep environment is the path by which you can love yourself to sleep.

As a new parent, I fostered great sleep for my son by creating both a lovely soothing nursery and routines to support ease in falling and staying asleep. What if we could apply this approach to ourselves?

With the environment set, the next phase is cultivating habits, which become routines, and finally, gorgeous rituals. As a science nerd, I've done research on how habits are created. The studies show they take longer to plant themselves than you think! My experience has proven new habits dig in deeper when they're chosen by us and infused with joy and pleasure.

THE PRACTICE

Many individuals who struggle with sleep procrastination, myself included, become reinforced by the activities we choose instead of going to sleep. How do you procrastinate sleep? Do you mindlessly scroll social media? Do you binge shows on Netflix? Or do you push yourself to finish all the items on your to-do list? That last one is something I often hear from overwhelmed working moms.

I've stopped giving myself the scraps of energy left at the end of the day. Let's all agree here and now to no longer operate from overwhelm. Loving ourselves first is a key component of our mental health. Now, I realize that's a loaded statement, and it oversimplifies a big obstacle for many of us.

Let's help you learn to love yourself to sleep and improve your health and well-being in bed! My first tip is to consider your sleep routine as the time you sleep plus the time preceding *and* following the actual hours you're asleep. Most adults require around 7-9 hours of quality sleep, so you'll need to figure out how much time you'd like to build into your routine.

Additionally, your wind-down and wind-up routines don't have to be completely independent of the other people you live with or your family.

In fact, building in family rest time has made it easier for all of us to get the sleep we need.

My golden hours of rest start officially at 8:00 p.m. and last until about 8:00 a.m. I get about eight hours of sleep, so the remaining four hours are all about building my well-being. To be fully transparent, 7:30–8:00 a.m. falls during my commute, but even my commute time is self-care time. I love to listen to inspiring podcasts and Audible books or rock out to music that makes me feel good.

My unofficial downtime starts closer to 6:00 p.m. on most days. Dinner as a family became a bright side to the pandemic and continues to be one way we enjoy each other's company and rest together. If I can swing it, I'll begin chilling out closer to 4:30 or 5:00 p.m. What has surprised me the most is setting the intention to rest more and focus on my well-being, meaning when I work, I'm extremely productive.

Cultivating a routine to help your body and mind be ready for sleep is crucial.

I love an acronym, so I've created one just for you. It's L.O.V.E. Feel free to sing the song in your head as you're reading.

L is for lulling and loving yourself to sleep. O stands for owning your routine. V is for vitality, as in how are you building yours? Finally, E stands for environment. Keep these components in mind as I take you through creating a routine to L.O.V.E. yourself to sleep. Grab a journal and a pen to jot down your thoughts as we go through each component.

L: LULL AND LOVE YOURSELF TO SLEEP

Winding down at the end of the day is one of my favorite self-care routines. As I was pulling together all the components of my rituals, I realized how much the bookends of my day reflect one another. Here are my steps beginning around 8:00 p.m. and how I slowly begin the next day.

1. **Turn off technology.** I have a "do not disturb" set up for my phone, smartwatch, and computer. I plug my phone in for the night and leave it until after my morning routine the next day. I have an iPhone, so my list of favorite people can get through to me in an emergency.

2. **Take a shower.** A hot shower at night has become the perfect way for me to soothe myself and prepare for sleep. I've found the length of time doesn't matter. I love to add calming music, and I always use my favorite bath products. You can check out some of them on my resource page, https://www.beingwellwithkelly.com/hmhresources. Getting into my pajamas a couple of hours before bed, all clean and relaxed, feels decadent.

3. **Prep my bedroom and set out clothes for the next day.** Ninety percent of the time, I get up and make my bed. Turning down my bed at the end of the day feels like a gift I wrapped for myself. Even as committed as I am to sleeping, mornings are not the time I do my best thinking. By setting out my clothes for the next day, I can enjoy an easier morning.

4. **Love on my munchkin during his sleep routine.** On a typical day, I'm ready for bed *before* I help my kiddo with his routine. Even if he has trouble falling asleep, I can remain present with him because my essential sleep routine is complete.

5. **Journal or mind-dump items on my mind.** My nervous system is typically calm by this point. However, as a self-proclaimed busy brain, a quiet body often invites my mind to become active. I have a bedside journal, which can be used to dump out items I'm repeating in my head, such as my grocery list, ideas, concerns, to-do lists, etc. I write it all out in no particular order and plan to come back to it the next day. Sometimes, I like to list out those things for which I am grateful. I'm a huge fan of AquaNotes, which are waterproof note pads you can write on when wet. So sometimes, I make my lists or journal while in the shower.

6. **Get into bed.** The scene is set, and my body and mind are at peace. I slip into bed, and as I nestle in, I feel deeply grateful. Taking a moment to breathe deep, I rest a hand on my heart and the other on my stomach. I send myself healing love. Then I close my eyes and allow sleepiness to wash over me. If I need a little more time, I visualize the next day in my mind's eye step by step until I drift off.

7. **Sleep.** Sleep, glorious sleep! Whether I get the perfect eight hours or wake frequently, I focus on the sleep opportunity. Sleep opportunity is the amount of time you've allotted for falling and staying asleep.

When I wake up in the middle of the night, I allow myself to shift to the practice of resting completely. It's a mindset shift. If you need help making that shift, reach out for guidance. You can find my contact info on the resource page, https://www.beingwellwithkelly.com/hmhresources.

8. **Wake up in a state of gratitude.** Before my eyes open, I take a deep breath and repeat in my mind, *Thank you for another day to live, laugh, love, and play.* As my feet hit the floor, I say, "Left foot, thank right foot—you."

9. **Enjoy my morning routine.** My routine includes treating all my senses with coffee, essential oils, music, and meditation. It gets to be my focus because I prepped for my day last night.

10. **Make my bed and get dressed.** Getting ready for my day is super simple on purpose. I've peeled away all the unnecessary pieces and chosen those I love.

11. **Turn on technology.** I'm now available for work and communication. I'll check email and log onto social media.

O: OWN YOUR ROUTINE

I've given you a clear picture of what my sleep routine includes. Now it's your chance to cultivate the routine which works best for you. Owning my routine means I've informed others about my availability. My family knows what to expect from me in the evening. Honestly, I feel more connected to them by focusing on myself first.

V: FOSTER YOUR VITALITY

Vitality is everything! Nourish yourself throughout your day. Don't hold back on filling your days with joy. In fact, make a joy list. Then put those items in your calendar *before* all your appointments and commitments. My shortlist includes writing poetry, drinking coffee outside, and listening to 80s jams.

E: ENVISION YOUR ENVIRONMENT

Close your eyes and envision the scene around you while you're holding a baby in a nursery. Tune into your heart and breathing. How do you feel? How does your body feel? Now envision yourself in the coziest bed in which you've ever slept. Bring in all your senses.

For me, revamping our bedrooms was the first step in creating great sleep for my family. You can read more about how to do this in my chapter, *"Sacred Sleep: Cultivate the Best Sleep of Your Life,"* in *The Ultimate Guide to Healing, Volume 4.* Find it here: https://www.beingwellwithkelly.com/books.

I used to believe sleep was an obstacle to completing my to-do list. It turns out, through great sleep, I'm a healthier version of myself *and* capable of accomplishing more! Everything feels possible, and it just keeps getting better. Resting has become a superpower, the way by which I'm more effective and efficient.

You get to put yourself first. You get to cultivate the habits and routines which support your mental, physical and spiritual well-being. I'm so excited for you to get better *in* bed. Rest well and good luck creating your own foundational habits to L.O.V.E yourself to sleep.

Please reach out and let me know how your journey with sleep is progressing. I love to nerd out with folks on their experiences! Share your success stories with me at kelly@beingwellwithkelly.com Be sure to visit the resource page for this chapter for more inspiration and tips at https://www.beingwellwithkelly.com/hmhresources

Kelly is an author, podcaster, and sleep specialist who will cultivate space for you to emerge from stress and overwhelm to lead and savor the life of your dreams. As an occupational therapist, Kelly has over 20 years of experience specializing in sensory integration techniques. Her background in occupational therapy provides a unique perspective on development and the human condition. She values personal power and inspires all of us to build our capacity to surpass our potential by living in alignment with our true selves.

With a Master's degree in strategic communication and leadership, she brings data-driven techniques leading to lasting change. Over the past 15 years, she has experience teaching topics including self-care, leadership development, outcome measurement, sensory processing related to anxiety, and sleep. Kelly is a holistic entrepreneur bringing a wealth of experience and fun science to the table, whether speaking to engaging guests on *The Mystic Nerd Squad Podcast* or supporting women in revitalizing their lives.

You can check out her other five chapters in the Amazon Best-selling books, *"Sacred Sleep: Cultivating the Best Sleep of Your Life"* in *The Ultimate Guide to Self-Healing, Volume 4, "Courageous Self-care: Putting Myself First to Serve Others"* in *Find Your Voice Save Your Life Volume 2, "Radical Self-care for Caregivers: Nourishing Yourself Through Grief and Loss"* in *Sacred Death, Sacred Rest: Be at Your Best by Doing Less* in *Sacred Medicine,* and *"Harmonize Your Divine Masculine and Feminine Energy: Get Shit Done and Feel Good Doing It"* in the recently released *Wealth Codes: Sacred Strategies for Abundance.* All available at https://beingwellwithkelly.com/books/

For additional resources related to Kelly's healing journey and to connect with her, please visit https://www.beingwellwithkelly.com

CLOSING CHAPTER

Thank you so much for joining this movement toward holistic mental health! Your commitment to these practices will absolutely shift you into a higher state of empowerment, and empowerment provides momentum for the deepest healing to occur with greater ease!

By now, you've started developing your own roadmap for your unique journey of healing and expansion. With practice, the formula you've created will become automatic. You are reprogramming your subconscious mind and energy field to embody a more confident, unwavering, liberated version of yourself.

When we reprogram our subconscious minds, we have a strong foundation from which to do anything. Your subconscious mind believes you're the person you're trying on for size, and you'll notice shifts in your outer world because of this. Trust the process.

Especially if you've been experiencing symptoms for much of your life, ideal results are not going to show up overnight. This is intentional: Too much change at once is very hard on our nervous system, and we don't want to break the human!

It's much more loving to be gentle with ourselves and trust that each step we are taking is leading us to the highest version of ourselves. Speak to yourself as you would speak to a young child or animal who is struggling— with compassion, patience, and faith in their resilience.

If you desire support during this process, I strongly recommend reaching out to the authors in this book. Each one of us is here to receive your reflections and bravery to share where you are. You will be welcomed with open arms by every single person in this collaboration.

I'm so proud of the group of authors that came together for this volume. They are all beautifully heart-centered, knowledgeable, and service-based humans eager to share their medicine with the world. Just because they're authors doesn't mean they're celebrities who aren't open to conversation, so start one by sending a quick hello!

I can't wait to hear all you've received from these pages and the changes unfolding in your life. I'm celebrating you for picking up this book and choosing to devote to yourself, which has a ripple effect on your loved ones, colleagues, and the world at large! Your decision to pick up this book was truly one of service to everyone around you.

Sending you so much love on your journey,

Laura Mazzotta

EMERGE
HEALING & WELLNESS

MORE ABOUT LAURA MAZZOTTA

Just by reading this book, you're acknowledging your deep desire to change your life! Whether it's conscious or subconscious, something greater than you brought you to these pages.

It could be your frustration with a particular area of your life or yourself, or just a burning desire and knowing that you want more, are meant for more, and you're curious to explore.

That's the voice of your soul, nudging you into your next stage of change. Listen up, my friend! Kicking the can down the road is only going to delay the infinite joy you get to experience! Trust me: Been there, done that!

WHY I'M COMPELLED TO DO THIS WORK

I was a successful therapist in New York for almost 20 years. I adored my job and clients and had a waiting list for five years! Why would I leave? I made an amazing name for myself and was guiding people through some of their darkest times.

However, I leaned back because of the signals from the Universe, the consistent knocks on my door I couldn't fully understand. I would listen to some, but not deeply enough. I kept taking time off to attend to my parents as they both received cancer diagnoses. I cut back my hours significantly to have more time with my three kids. I spent a month in hospice with my father before he passed.

But I was still preoccupied. I was preoccupied with my business and how it was thriving. And then I realized it had become my identity, my primary source of pride and self-security. Despite the close relationships with my family and the joy I felt in my life, I was hiding a deep sense of unworthiness behind my success as a therapist.

The Universe wanted more of me, but I wasn't sure yet.

Then, in August 2016, I became seriously ill with sepsis—dangerously ill.

After being dizzy and weak for over a year, along with the loss of cognitive functioning, my neurologist informed me I would continue to deteriorate. For the first time in my people-pleasing, rule-following life, I disagreed.

I just didn't see that as my future. I knew it wasn't true. I didn't know why or how I knew, but I confidently knew. This was my intuition speaking, and it was loud. I started meditating, working with energy healers, and meeting with naturopaths and functional medicine doctors.

And I got better, little by little. The progress I have made on my journey of self-healing is leagues beyond where I was told I would be. The beautiful thing is that all of us have this ability within us! We are infinite beings, infused with universal love and a consciousness that can transcend anything that manifests in this human life.

I've tried several modalities over the past six years and have narrowed down the most potent spiritual technology for efficient healing:

1. The Akashic Records: When I enter this space, there is no dis-ease or discomfort. When I close it, I am immensely energized. This is where I download specific healing protocols for myself and my clients.

2. Reiki: The most gentle, unconditionally loving space to be held and soothed. Healing extends to past lives and your ancestry.

3. Tapping/EFT: Shift that energy, baby! This is where we move around the stuck and stagnant energy to create space for more possibility and vitality. Check out my free EFT Playlist: https://bit.ly/3Ae0OKp

4. Meditation: Cultivating an intimate relationship with your Higher Self.

5. Mindset/Coherence: Bringing the mind online with the heart, spirit, and body, so they can work in integrated alignment. Making decisions from your heart, body, and soul versus your ego.

6. Bodywork: From soft tissue work to stretching, dancing, exercise, Tai Chi, or Qi Gong, embracing the physical body as one of our most powerful healing tools is critical for permanently internalizing healing practices. This includes the breath!

7. Inner Child Work: Opening your field to the wonder, play, and deep-seated wounds that desire to come forward for empowerment.

The power of spiritual and energetic healing is limitless. We're only beginning to scratch the surface of what's available to us through infinite intelligence. That's why this is such an exciting journey! Regardless of the old stories we need to work through (and you don't need to work through them all), becoming wholly informed about who you are at your deepest core is an exhilarating journey!

Although I have successfully helped and supported countless therapy clients, energetic and spiritual healing offers a depth of transformation not fully accessible through therapeutic tools. Full healing is only possible when you attend to all of the critical layers: physical, emotional, mental, energetic, and spiritual.

I'm so blessed to guide others on their unique path to deepening their healing in the most potent, efficient, and effective way, so they can experience how long-lasting healing can be. The Akashic Records is 100%

the space to do that. It's also the safest space to conduct healing work as you are lovingly held by angels, loved ones, guides, and ascended masters.

And guess what? You'll just continue to expand from there. When you work with the Creator of all things, you get to create all things. You get to feel into the level of power you hold to create change, personally, professionally, and collectively.

Where would you like to start your journey? I'll meet you exactly where you are and guide you step-by-step from there. I can't wait for you to truly meet yourself, eyes widened, in awe of the magic that's been waiting there all along.

For those of you who have tried traditional therapy or felt an aversion to it for some reason, this is for you: Akashic healing unlocks in one session what you would accomplish in years of traditional therapy. Gain optimal self-awareness and realize the highest form of yourself by messaging me to schedule your free connection call! You can contact me through my website at https://www.theakashictherapist.com/contact

Together we will craft your customized plan for reaching the highest level of vitality, wellness, freedom, intimacy, and abundance! The primary areas I help people with are:

- Confidence/Empowerment
- Self-Awareness, Acceptance, and Appreciation
- Deep Self-Love
- Intimacy with Yourself and Your Relationships
- Momentum
- Clarity and Decisiveness
- Fulfilling Your Soul's Purpose
- Intuitive Expansion
- Freedom and Joy
- Spiritual Business Growth
- Knowing and Claiming Who the Fuck You Are!

I can't wait to connect with you further! The more people that interact with this high-vibe energy, the more we learn about the infinite: It expresses itself differently through every human.

Let's change what mental health care looks and feels like together!

With so much love,

Laura Mazzotta

EMERGE
HEALING & WELLNESS

WHAT PEOPLE ARE SAYING

"I have worked with Laura Mazzotta since I was a teenager, and I truly don't know where I would be without her. She is brilliant, compassionate, and has the deepest desire to truly help you from the inside out. She is so informed on multiple different topics and has a wealth of knowledge unlike any other. I love that Laura is willing to call me out when I need it but in the most loving way possible. I have seen her in both her traditional and spiritual practices, and I truly saw the shift in how potent her energy has become. She was phenomenal as a traditional therapist, but as a spiritual practitioner, she is able to dive even deeper and truly heal the core issues. Her healing is long-lasting and continues even without conscious awareness. I continue to become a kinder, stronger, wiser person every single day because of her. I can't recommend Laura enough."

~ Cassidy B.

"There is so much to say about this awesome lady. Not only is she the kindest, most understanding person I have met, but she has the most beautiful energy and wisdom about her. Even just talking to her releases tension within my energy. Our session was amazing! She is a powerhouse full of information and is HIGHLY intuitive. She brings through SO much information and really guides you in a way where it is easy to understand. She makes sure to answer all questions/concerns you have and give you more than enough throughout your session to help you relax into a blissful mind state. 20/10 recommend!"

~ Haylee L.

"Wow! Laura Knapp Mazzotta! That was wild! In all my years of personal growth and development, I have never expressed in words what came out today. I am blown away by the session. I definitely need to re-watch and let it keep sinking in. Love OMG with a passion."

~ Anonymous

"I'm so so grateful for your guidance and support in my healing journey. . . all the things you helped guide me towards. . .to honor this time as sacred, that slowing down and being still is healing, the deeper healing that needed to take place outside my physical symptoms, that I am completely supported by my loved ones, angels and guides which brings me so much peace, to continue to have faith, that healing is not linear, that I need to feel joy and have fun along the way. . .that I will be okay, and there's a more incredible joyous life ahead; I know that because of YOU, I will continue to move forward. You are a gift, Laura. Working with you in the space of the Akashic Records saved me. I am so incredibly grateful for you."

~ Donna

"You are so compassionate and loving! I truly feel like you're living in the 5D and helping the ones called to you to get there too. What I mean is. . .I feel like you're vibrating at a high frequency like monks do, and I want to come and hang out with those kinds of vibes, lol."

~ Anonymous

"Over the years, I have worked with psychics, mediums, spiritual healers, and card readers, and I will say, all of them paled in comparison to the Akashic Records reading from Laura. I appreciated the preparation she required of me prior to our session, which helped me focus in on the questions that were a priority which allowed the session to be ultra-efficient and clarifying. She was very sweet, supportive, and patient with me going through this unfamiliar process. And the best part is that every single thing that she brought forward from the Akashic Records was incredibly accurate! I also appreciate all the tools and homework that were suggested by the records to assist in my energetic recovery to help steer me back on track to my true purpose in life. Thank you, Laura!"

- Julie B.

"Thank you! I really mean it—you bring my magic forward! I feel like I've been able to let go of so much crap I was forcing myself to do and lean into what's really ME, and it's made all the difference in the world—in countless situations!"

- Anonymous

"Laura Knapp Mazzotta. So, this was probably the most profound hypnosis/meditation I've ever experienced so far in my life. I am not even sure what to do with all of this other than be so fucking grateful I'm now aware and can find my center again. My reason. God's reason. Thank you for holding space for me as I shared. Laura Knapp Mazzotta, wow. Just wow. I can't even keep track of how much being in your world has touched and influenced my life. . .I love you."

- Darlene S.

DEEP, IMMERSIVE GRATITUDE

To the Universe/God/Source/my Higher Self for the infinite wisdom, blessings, unconditional love, and momentum. I am deeply grateful to serve as a messenger of your intention.

To my body for alerting me to the areas I needed to heal, for my highest good and the highest good of all. Thank you for your unconditional forgiveness as I pushed through repeatedly without hearing your cries. I honor and revere the deep wisdom you hold for my optimal wellness and vitality.

To my husband, who is my best friend, rock, and constant cheerleader, being in the place I am today would not exist without you. The late-night conversations, soothing of my fears, reminders of my beauty, kicks in the ass to live and speak my truth, and ridiculously tasty meals have all led to this. This is as much my accomplishment as it is yours. We are the strongest, bravest, most unwavering team, and I thank God every day for the magic of our relationship. Thank you for seeing me the most clearly, having the utmost faith in me, making me deep-belly laugh every single day, and serving our family at the highest version of yourself. You are my hero, and I love you with every ounce of my being.

To my children, whose patience while I'm working from home is deeply appreciated. Thank you for the beautiful lessons you reflect to me on the daily. Thank you for your palpable love and cuddles. Thank you for helping me notice when I'm not myself. Thank you for teaching me the extent to which my love can expand. Thank you for showing me the magic of individuality and personal purpose: Each of you are such powerful, unique, and impactful beings with huge hearts and your own path. My love for you expands with each passing day. Thank you for choosing me to be your mom. It's truly the deepest honor.

To my mother, who has always encouraged me to follow my biggest dreams and cheered me on every step of the way, you embody the grandest joy, and I am so grateful for the laughter and play you invite into my life.

To my dog, Zuri, who always gets my butt up and moving for walks, and never ceases to make me smile, laugh, and infuse me with the deepest love and comfort.

To my stellar team, Daisy Farrell and Cassidy Bell, thank you endlessly for supporting and believing so deeply in this mission and in me! I could not have orchestrated this magic without you, and we are fully in this together. Congratulations to you both for bringing this deep gesture of service to life!

To my clients who have bravely shared their stories and reflected on areas for my own growth and growth for the mental health system at large, your individuality is what contributes to a larger change in this field. Thank you for being you.

To my first therapist, at age seven, who held such compassionate space for me that I pursued my dream of becoming a therapist myself. Thank you for initiating this gateway into self-understanding.

To our book designer, Dino Marino, thank you for your expertise in bringing this beauty to life.

To our family, friends, mentors, and book launch team members, thank you for your encouragement, feedback, and support, from idea creation to full-on publishing. We are so grateful to have you by our side to celebrate this gorgeous collaboration!

To Laura Di Franco and Brave Healer Productions, thank you for your fiery energy, clarity, confidence, enthusiasm, and heart of service. Following your intuition on that morning you had a wild idea has served thousands and thousands of humans worldwide. You are an absolute force, and I'm deeply grateful to be partnering with you on this epic project.

THE PRIMARY WAY TO DIVE DEEPER AND SUSTAIN THIS WORK:

VITALITY

If you are ready to drastically enhance your vitality so you can experience a life of freedom, exhilaration, intimacy, passion, and expansion, VITALITY is for you!

This is a comprehensive 7-month program for sustaining your highest state of vitality at any layer (physical, emotional, mental, energetic, and spiritual). With 20 years as a therapist, six years as an energy healer, and my own extensive experience with functional and holistic medicine, I will guide your personalized healing journey to a path of wellness, clarity, confidence, and empowered momentum.

This program is for you if:

- You're ready to take control of your own healing.
- You're ready to make sovereign decisions without apology.
- You're ready to serve as the most solid, unwavering foundation for yourself, loved ones, and/or clients.
- You're ready for consistency in your health, wealth, relationships, and emotional swings.
- Intellectually, you know you're worthy, but you can't seem to get there on the feeling level.
- You've experienced chronic mental health or physical health symptoms that don't interfere with your ability to function but put a huge damper on the enjoyment of your life.

Because of the level of impact this program has, you need to devote yourself to your personalized protocol so you can maximize results. There are meetings and practices in place to ensure your momentum is backed to fully follow through and maintain this.

Choosing your vitality as your top priority is the #1 way to sustain your wellness, relationships, intimacy (self and other), mission, and income. You need to take this seriously for longstanding change.

I am going to be doing all these practices with you. This program comes from my own desire to embody them at a deeper layer as well. There's always room to grow as humans—this healing journey has been profoundly effective and impactful, and I want to extend it even further by sharing it with you!

Also, as it goes with any program with Laura Mazzotta, this is going to be a blast. I will never host a call, live, or module without deep belly laughs. This process gets to feel fun and light, and natural. That's what I'm here to guide you toward, and I promise I can do that for you.

The personal foundation you build in VITALITY secures who you are, communicates to the universe that you deeply value your wellness above anything else, and roots it all in the unwavering love, expansion, and stability of your soul.

You're human. No matter what, things are going to come up. Anchor yourself in your vitality, and you can accomplish everything you desire. In fact, you will find a natural flow that feels easeful and perfectly aligned.

To read all the details, you may visit:

https://www.theakashictherapist.com/vitality

Laura also offers a landmark spiritual and energetic Trauma-Informed Care Certification for spiritual entrepreneurs looking to scale their business while opening tons of space for freedom, intimacy, vitality, and connection! This program is the first of its kind and will leave you with an unwavering foundation for your own trauma cues, as well as holding the most solid space for loved ones and clients. The material in this experience is unparalleled and has absolutely blown clients away with its depth, applicability, and mastery of trauma cues. Email Laura for more information at emergehealingandwellness@gmail.com

OTHER BOOKS WITH LAURA MAZZOTTA

The Ultimate Guide to Self-Healing, Volume 1
Chapter 11
Tapping
Easing Difficult Emotions

Sacred Medicine
Chapter 9
Chanting in The Akashic Records
Accessing Potent Healing at a Cellular Level

The Ancestors Within, Volume 3
Chapter 23
Ancestral Relationships
Deepening Intimacy to Enrich Understanding

Wealth Codes
Chapter 22
Ancestral Mapping of Wealth Consciousness
Craft Your Unique Wealth Identity Using Potent Data from Your Lineage

Purchase signed copies here: https://www.theakashictherapist.com/store

I Believe. . .

You are a master alchemist with the ability to shift your reality at any moment. The more moments you choose your growth and expansion, the more you will become the desired version of yourself.

Following your desire is the guidepost to your soul's purpose. Place your shame aside of doing things differently, create your own set of rules, and define happiness in your own unique way.

There are infinite possibilities at any moment. All you must do is tap into your creativity and ask how you can make things easier. There is always an easier way.

Once you begin this journey, there's no regression. You can't screw up so badly that you've ruined your progress because mistakes don't exist: Each move you make is exactly aligned to the lessons required by your soul. Remain open, and you will forever be in motion toward actualizing your highest self.

I love you.

I believe in you.

I will hold space for your highest good until you can hold space for your own.

Love,

EMERGE
HEALING & WELLNESS

Laura

Made in the USA
Monee, IL
07 October 2022